MAPPING POLICY PREFERENCES

MAPPING POLICY PREFERENCES

Estimates for Parties, Electors, and Governments
1945–1998

IAN BUDGE, HANS-DIETER KLINGEMANN,
ANDREA VOLKENS, JUDITH BARA,
ERIC TANENBAUM

with

RICHARD C. FORDING, DEREK J. HEARL,
HEE MIN KIM, MICHAEL D. McDONALD
SILVIA M.MENDES

OXFORD
UNIVERSITY PRESS

OXFORD

UNIVERSITY PRESS

Great Clarendon Street, Oxford OX2 6DP

Oxford University Press is a department of the University of Oxford.
It furthers the University's objective of excellence in research, scholarship,
and education by publishing worldwide in

Oxford New York

Athens Auckland Bangkok Bogotá Buenos Aires Cape Town
Chennai Dar es Salaam Delhi Florence Hong Kong Istanbul Karachi
Kolkata Kuala Lumpur Madrid Melbourne Mexico City Mumbai Nairobi
Paris São Paulo Shanghai Singapore Taipei Tokyo Toronto Warsaw
and associated companies in Berlin Ibadan

Oxford is a registered trade mark of Oxford University Press
in the UK and certain other countries

Published in the United States
by Oxford University Press Inc., New York

British Library Cataloguing in Publication Data
Data available

Library of Congress Cataloging in Publication Data
Data available

ISBN 0–19–924400–6

1 3 5 7 9 10 8 6 4 2

Printed in Great Britain by
J. W. Arrowsmith Ltd.,
Bristol

This book is dedicated
to our co-members of the Manifesto Research Group 1979–1998

David Robertson

Colin Rallings	Martin Slater
William P. Irvine	Takashi Inoguchi
Peter Mair	Kaare Strom
Michael Laver	Jorn Liepart
Sydney Elliott	Pieter Tops
Torbjorn Bergman	Karl Dittrich
Richard I. Hofferbert	Hans E. Keman
Margareta Holmstedt	Tove Lise Schou
Franz Horner	Francois Petry
Alfio Mastropaolo	Paul Pennings

PREFACE

This book uniquely empowers its readers by placing the data it describes directly in their hands, encoded on the CD Rom sold with it. The estimates of party and electoral preferences and of government policy and votes, which it provides from 1945–1998 for 25 democracies, constitute the richest source of evidence for comparative policy analysis now available.

In preparing and documenting such an extensive and diverse data-set the authors and their associates have relied on the help of many people. We must thank our publishers OUP for their willingness to go along with and improve upon our original ideas about electronic publishing. In particular we should acknowledge the constructive role of our editor and editorial assistant, Dominic Byatt, and Amanda Watkins, together with our technical adviser, John Campbell.

Our special thanks go to Julie Lord. Without her expertise, patience and good humour in dealing with our many drafts and amendments in her preparation of our manuscript, this work would never have been accomplished. We are truly indebted to her professional skills. Similarly we would like to thank Hilary Hobson for her inestimable advice and technical prowess in producing the format of our text.

Others who have provided invaluable support include Carole Ward, whose help in preparing numerical assistance has been much valued. We are also very grateful for the advice provided by the staff of the EUROLAB at the Zentralarchiv of the University of Cologne, notably Ekkehart Mochmann, Ingvill Oedegaard and Bruno Hopp, in terms of documentary storage and computerization of coding procedures.

The preparation of statistical and documentary materials for this volume has been made possible only by the virtue of the unstinting long-term support of the Wissenschaftszentrum (Social Science Research Centre), Berlin. Data transcription has been facilitated by a Nuffield Foundation award.

We should also like to extend our thanks to the European Consortium for Political Research and all financial supporters of this project since its inception in 1979, without whose generosity the publication would not have been possible. We would like to acknowledge financial assistance provided by the Bank of Sweden's Tercentenary Fund, the British Social Science Research Council (E/00/23/0020/1), the European Social Fund and the Stiftung Volkswagenwerk which supported the project as a whole. In addition, we would like to record our thanks to the following foundations for their support of individual researchers involved in this project—The Nuffield Foundation, the British Academy, the Social Sciences and Humanities Research Council of Canada, the US National Endowment for the Humanities, the Danish Social Science Research Council, the Stiftungs-und-Forderungsgesellschaft of the University of Salzburg and the Japanese Ministry of Education.

CONTENTS

Introduction

CONTENT ANALYSIS AND POLITICAL TEXTS

Ian Budge and Judith Bara

About the Book

This book is innovative both in content and form. In content because it presents the richest data on the policies and preferences of key political actors available today. In form, because the estimates appear on a CD-ROM sold in the book, whose printed section provides the supporting information and instructions necessary to use the data intelligently. By buying the book therefore users acquire both documentation and usable data at a stroke, without having to engage in long correspondence with archives or other data-holders.

So convenient is this format that it will probably become the normal mode of distribution for social data within a few years. At the moment, however, this book leads the way in putting a major data set directly in the hands of consumers, cutting out middlemen and intermediaries.

About the Data

The data themselves should be of considerable interest. Centring on the policy priorities publicly endorsed by political parties in their election programmes; and extending to the preferences of electorates and governments, they cover areas at the heart of rational choice theory, and indeed of political economy, policy analysis and comparative politics. They are also extended in time-covering most or all of the post-war period for the countries included here—and comparative in character—placing 24 OECD countries and Israel within a uniform coding framework. Pooling the estimates is therefore easy, though of course they also lend themselves to comparable time series analyses of individual cases.

Uses of the Data

The kinds of questions that can be put to this type of evidence are practically unlimited, answering points that have been the concern of party analysts and government specialists—not to speak of students of national politics—for many years. Is there a decline of the Left or of the Right? Is it the end of ideology? How have issues changed over the post-war period? How close are the members of ideological party families across national boundaries? How close is the New

Left or the New Right—or New Labour—to the old versions of these doctrines? Are parties getting closer and more consensual or more conflictual and further apart? Which party in each national system gets more of what it wants than others? How do parties relate to each other within coalitions? How do they form coalitions in the first place? How well do they reflect or respond to public opinion? Do the manifestos slow shifts in fundamental values over the years, acting as a kind of litmus whereby we can judge general societal change over the post-war period? What are the policies of parties in specialized areas of economics such as labour market policy? And how far do they relate to what governments actually do?

THE UNIQUENESS OF THE MANIFESTO RESEARCH GROUP (MRG) ESTIMATES

Most of these questions have already been asked—and answered at least in part. New ones will undoubtedly be posed once the data spread through the social science and policy analysis communities. This is because the estimates are very rich and differentiated. Most alternative indicators of party policy are formed by one (Castles and Mair 1984: Huber and Inglehart 1994) or a limited number (Laver and Hunt 1992) of static variables, relating to an imprecise time point and possibly also to party behaviour rather than just preferences. In contrast the Manifesto Data consist of many policy variables (at least 57 basic ones) with several leading indicators based on combinations of these, and a potentiality for constructing many more in line with the interests and needs of the investigator. This versatility, together with the extended time period which they cover, allow social and political change to be studied either broadly or minutely—permitting the use both of the telescope and microscope.

Because of their uniquely extended coverage, the estimates presented here are the best ones—usually the only ones—available to validate other estimates of policy preferences. This is particularly true for the computerized textual analyses being developed at the present time. Computers can easily count words in an electronic text. But how do we know that these are really telling us what we want to know about policy? An easy way is to compare the estimates these generate with the previously validated ones from the Manifesto data. For more detail on this see Chapter 7 below.

THE TEXTUAL BASIS OF THE DATA

The basis on which the policy estimates have been collected and formed is textual. Policy has been characterized quantitatively by examining parties' and governments' own statements of policy, in the shape of election programmes (manifestos) and declarations in the Parliamentary debate before a vote of confidence or investiture, as the case may be (for 10 countries with coalition governments). It seems better to base estimates of policy on what actors themselves have said, rather than on other people's judgements of what their policy is, whether these are academic specialists (Castles and Mair 1984: Laver and Hunt 1992: Huber and Inglehart 1995) or electors (Gabel and Huber 2000). Electoral impressions of party policy may well be important and influence the vote. But they are a different thing from the statement of policy made by the party itself: indeed the nature of the relationship between the two is an interesting empirical question in its own right which can be investigated with our data.

Electors' own preferences are estimated here by assuming that they vote for the party whose policy is closest to them (Chapter 8). They cannot therefore be related empirically to the party policy stands we report, since in the end they derive from these. They are useful however in giving an indication of what electoral preferences are and how they have changed over time. They are also useful for 'centring' survey-based indices of public opinion within the party policy space so that they can be related to where the parties stand (Budge 2001).

TEXTUAL EVIDENCE AND THE DEMOCRATIC POLICY PROCESS

Ultimately therefore all the policy estimates in this book derive from particularly authoritative documents issued by parties and governments. Such documents have been neglected as bases for systematic political analyses up to this point. More readily quantified sources, above all surveys but also expenditures and budgets, have been at the centre of attention. Yet public opinion and financial outcomes really lie at the fringes of the policy-making process. Democratic decisions, as well as public reactions to them and debates about them, party formulations of priorities and preferences, bureaucratic reports on their implementation and judicial interpretations, are all reported in texts and documents. Indeed democratic decisions would hardly have the status they do if they were not so reported (legislation for example). Democracy is about communication and the way we communicate is principally through the written word. (Even when spoken, on radio and TV, it is usually from a script).

Texts therefore are the major source of evidence we have for how democracy functions. Historians of course have always recognized this. With limited exceptions however they have generally used single documents to interpret particular situations. Thus their analysis may inform us why party governments under the French Third Republic became weak, or how British Labour reformed itself in the late 1980s and early 1990s. Their approach however does not allow them to raise more general questions such as how parties generally function in democracy or how they organize themselves to carry on government.

For that we need more general textual evidence, covering hundreds or even thousands of specific documents. The only way to make this evidence manageable is to collect and organize it in statistical form. The particular way this has been done with party manifestos and government declarations is described in the chapters below—basically it is by counting the sentences of manifestos and declarations into one out of a set of 54 original policy categories. In the rest of this Introduction we give a general history of the 'content analysis' of political texts, as a background to our own methodology and procedures, which are covered in detail in the rest of the book.

CONTENT ANALYSIS: HISTORICAL BACKGROUND

Content Analysis is a method developed for the analysis of documents in the early 1930s in the United States. It was conceived at least at first as a tool for communications research. But even at this early stage, a political component appeared.

Indeed, the very first large scale study based on content analysis, which was carried out in 1930, examined the proportion of space in American newspapers taken up by reports on foreign policy in an effort to discern which subject editors regarded as important (Madge 1953). In 1933 another study, initiated by Hornell Hart as part of a symposium on 'Recent Social Trends in the United States', examined patterns in American literary publications—books and periodicals—in terms of the proportions of space devoted to a variety of subjects. In these studies newspaper coverage was literally measured by a ruler applied to the paper itself and results were reported in 'column inches' (Berelson 1971).

Four years later Harold Lasswell adapted the method to undertake a study of psychoanalytical interviews on the basis of the systematic application of classification categories (See, *inter alia*, Lasswell and Kaplan 1952; Lasswell and Leites 1965). He went on to utilize this classification scheme to analyze a broader range of topics. Ironically it was the threat of war in 1939 which led to a breakthrough in the development of content analytic techniques, Lasswell, at the behest of the US government, took on responsibility for the 'World Attention Survey' which investigated the content of foreign newspapers. It was assumed that the German and British papers would carry considerable amounts of material on US policy, but this was found not to be the case. More importantly, the analysis showed how the papers could presage considerable shifts in policy and strategy. For example, several months before the signing of the Molotov-Ribbentropp Pact, Lasswell's method revealed a tailing off in negative references to the Soviet Union in German papers—and likewise, a diminution in negative references towards Germany in Pravda. Indeed, in the German case, fewer and fewer references of any kind relating to the Soviet Union were evident (Berelson 1971).

Thus content analysis became a significant intelligence weapon. Elaborate coding categories were developed and standardized, indices were established and coders were monitored to ensure that their results were comparable. Simpler methods continued to be applied elsewhere, as when Lazarsfeld and Berelson

(1944) estimated the amount of publicity given to rival candidates in the 1940 Presidential Election.

In the half century following World War 2, the use of content analysis to further the study of various types of social behaviour increased. Many disciplines, notably in the area of cultural studies, devised their own approaches, often used in conjunction with other research tools such as discourse analysis and ethnomethodology. Content analyses have proved to be useful in both qualitative and quantitative analyses and can be considered as a bridge between the two. Again, Lasswell and his associates pioneered many of these developments, applying the technique to political rhetoric as for example in Leites' study, *House Without Windows* in the 1950s, or to analysis of the evolution of social values over time (Namenwirth and Lasswell 1970). Interestingly in the context of this book, the last study coded a selection of US party platforms from the mid-nineteenth and twentieth centuries into eight value categories noting changes in their relative salience between parties and over · time. Temporal differences were most marked, bringing Democrats and Republicans closer to each other in the later period.

In the case of political science, significant developments took place from the late 1940s, mainly in the US (Pool 1951; Berelson 1952; Lasswell, Lerner and Pool 1952; Ranney 1962; North, Holsti, Zaninovitch and Zinnes 1963; Chafee and Hochheimer 1985). Apart from developments in International Relations stemming from Lasswell's pioneering work they were mainly developed for the analysis of elections and voting behaviour—not unnaturally since this was the main area in which quantitative analyses of politics flourished at that time. Attention was still primarily devoted to media coverage and impact, as the major external influence on voting which could be covered by survey evidence only imperfectly. Again, there was a problem of electoral perceptions of the media being potentially distorted indicators of what they were actually saying (c.f. our observations on perceptions of party stands above).

FOCUSSING ON PARTY DOCUMENTS

In retrospect, it is amazing how quickly content analysis techniques developed and how rapidly they spread to the study of other 'objectively given' documents like platforms and manifestos. In part this was because the coding techniques applied to interview protocols, particularly to answers to 'open questions', were readily transferable to texts. Studies of the media intensified both in terms of number and depth (Iyengar 1993; Namenwirth and Brewer 1966; Namenwirth 1969; Namenwirth 1970; Namenwirth and Lasswell 1970; Miller 1977) However, attention began to turn also to party election programmes.

One reason for these being the first formal documents studied was clearly their prominence in the election campaign. (Even when not widely read they were adapted and launched with great publicity and picked up by the media).

Besides this directly 'political' reason however they were also of interest to political philosophers as a practical application of concepts like justice and fairness, and a working out of more abstract political theories in a real life context. It is no coincidence that the first comprehensive analysis of manifestos was undertaken by a theorist, David Robertson, under the supervision of Brian Barry whose influential *Political Argument* (1965) was itself a close qualitative analysis of the textual handling of political concepts.

Another stimulus to the study of manifestos was however given by the emergence of rational choice theories of party competition, most obviously Downs' *Economic Theory of Democracy* (1957). Barry himself (1975) had written a well known review of both the theory itself and problems with it. The theory gave a central place to party policy positions and party movements along a basically 'Left-Right' policy continuum.

Many attempts were made to operationalize and 'test' the 'Economic Theory' in the 1960s and 1970s. Since survey data was increasingly available and quantitative political scientists were trained in its use, party positioning and indeed party space itself tended to be represented in terms of electors' own perceptions of them. (For a critical review see Budge and Farlie 1978). Such studies had severe technical shortcomings, however. It became clear that electoral perceptions were not the same thing as actual party positions. Moreover a potential tautology was involved in basing estimates of party position on electoral data since the main point of the 'Economic Theory' was to relate party movement to the preferences of electors.

The party policy position for elections was most clearly and authoritatively stated in the only document parties themselves ever issued—the manifesto, platform or election programme. Realizing this, Robertson started research in 1968 on the British party manifesto back to 1922—a study he carried up to 1974 and eventually published in 1976. The codings were designed to test the modified Downsian hypothesis that parties move to the policy extremes when they think they will definitely win or lose the election (in neither case do extra votes count): but move to the policy centre when they think the outcome unclear, and every vote-increment may help.

SALIENCY CODING OF MANIFESTOS

Robertson's work is of central interest in this context because it was the basis from which the data set contained here was constructed and from which our coding practices developed. Robertson himself was co-director of the Manifesto Research Group (MRG), which was formed in 1979 with the present authors at the core, to analyze documents in 19 democracies comparatively and within a common framework (Budge, Robertson and Hearl (eds.) 1987). The central idea behind Robertson's original coding, and the MRG-schemes, based on intensive reading of the texts themselves, was that parties argued with each other by emphasizing different policy priorities rather than by directly confronting each other on the same issues.

This is quite a surprising discovery, given the common idea that political leaders have yahboo responses—everything one side urges must be flatly repulsed by the other (c.f. Table 3.5 below). But it is confirmed by all word by word or sentence by sentence examinations of the election texts that have been carried out up to now. Very few of these directly negate words/phrases/sentences on the other side. Mostly, ideas about what to do on each issue are shared (cut taxes, extend welfare, etc.). What differs is the degree to which taxes or welfare are mentioned by the different documents.

A rationale for this is given in Table 3.3 below, and discussed in full in the supporting text. Briefly, this is that the authors of manifestos see no point in going counter to majority opinion on each issue. They therefore endorse the majority point of view but stress those issues on which they are more trusted to carry it out—tax-cutting for Conservatives and market Liberals, welfare extension for Socialists. Election programmes therefore try to promote a party's 'proprietary' issues and priorities and downgrade other issues and priorities.

Of course, one can still use these varying emphases to create indices of support for Left versus Right or for any number of other political causes (Chapter 1). But they are based on the differential emphases given to issues by parties rather than direct confrontation on each issue (Chapter 2). The manifesto is composed and written as a whole and the overall balance of subjects carefully considered. Thus it is naive to think that the party position can be estimated in isolation for each area. It is overall priorities that matter rather than particular stances taken in isolation—particularly as such stances are generally shared between the parties.

This particular feature of political rhetoric had already been highlighted by Stokes (1966). He however thought that the centrality of 'valence' (one-position) issues like corruption—who could be for it?—undermined Downsian representations of parties moving along a Left-Right continuum. In his view these could not accommodate the most important feature of party competition, which was the tendency for one party to take an unassailable position on the central issues. Robertson's concentration on differential emphases to create policy spaces (c.f. also Budge and Farlie, 1977: 421–48) cleverly got round this, while still respecting the 'valence' nature of political rhetoric (Riker 1993: 81–126).

OTHER ANALYSES OF PARTY DOCUMENTS

Robertson's concentration on relative emphases to differentiate parties had already been foreshadowed in another national context by Borg's (1966) analysis of Finnish election programmes. More holistic studies (Thomas 1975; Ginsberg 1976; Harmel, Janda and Tan 1995) have tended to go directly from a reading of (portions of) documents to the creation of overall indices of party position similar to the Left-Right scales in Chapter 1, without going through a more detailed coding operation first. This has generally limited the uses of these analyses to the specific purposes pursued by the investigators. A more detailed coding scheme (c.f. Chapters 4 and 5), particularly where sentences or words are the units of analysis, has more flexibility. The extent to which the MRG scheme has lent itself to recombinations and other uses is reviewed in Chapter 2.

Party documents other than the manifesto have less frequently been analyzed, possibly because the latter is so uniquely authoritative as a statement of the party position (Chapter 3). Rose's 1964 analysis of resolutions to the British Labour and Conservative conferences concurred with analyses of the manifestos in finding much agreement when they dealt with the same subject, but also a great deal of talking past each other on different issues (Rose 1964 and 1969).

Rose also, however, took up the analysis of manifestos from a more immediate point of view—identifying pledges for action made by British parties which subsequently entered government. Only specific commitments to act ('we will cut unemployment') were considered thus excluding vaguer general statements like 'an economy based on more jobs'. The interest in identifying such pledges lay in seeing whether the party in government subsequently passed appropriate legislation or took specific action to fulfil them (Rose 1974).

Pledge studies were thus heavily focussed on the semi-normative question of the party mandate and whether it was actually carried out in democracy. Parallel analyses were carried out in the United States (Page 1978; Pomper 1980), and compared for Britain and Canada by Rallings (1987).

A general conclusion of these earlier studies was that pledge fulfilment was respectably high—round about 75% in most cases. However, the pledges that actually got carried out were the more specific ones, like making a given increase in pension payments. Parties tended to keep away from 'big' pledges in the central areas of policy and when they made them had a more spotty record of fulfilment—a tendency confirmed by Royed (1996) for British and American administrations of the 1980s. Studies of pledge—fulfilment elsewhere, however, (Greece, Kalegeropoulou 1989; Netherlands, Thomson 1999) have found specific pledges being made (and fulfilled) on quite important matters of policy.

RELATING MANIFESTO CONTENT TO GOVERNMENT BEHAVIOUR

What pledge studies have done is focus attention on the extent to which programmatic statements can be used to predict and evaluate government behaviour. Democracy is a system which brings government action into line with popular preferences through party competition and voting choice in elections

(Saward 1998). In this process manifestos and platforms play a central part, giving voters an indication of what parties would do if elected and thus offering them a basis for informed policy choice. The essential democratic requirements for an electoral mandate policy are that there is some difference between parties so that electors *can* make a choice: and that once elected the party will do more or less what it promised to do when in government.

Studies of pledge implementation are obviously centrally concerned with these questions. But other characterizations of manifesto content, such as the estimates in this book, can also be related to government actions. If they indicate anything at all, relative emphases measure party priorities for government. Given a way of measuring government priorities the extent to which programmatic policies do get carried through can be estimated, just as with the more specific pledges.

Two such studies have been carried through on the basis of the estimates given here. The first used government expenditures in different areas as the measure of government action (Klingemann, Hofferbert, Budge, *et al.* 1994). Programmatic emphases proved to predict expenditure trends very well, for eight out of ten countries over the post-war period.

The countries for which the programmatic-output match was not so good were Belgium and Netherlands (up to 1990). This raises the question of whether coalition governments with their blurred party accountability and necessity for policy compromises are not in general less able to fulfil the electoral mandate than single-party governments. A further study based on our estimates (Laver and Budge (eds.) 1992) related programmatic emphases to those contained in the declaration of government policy or coalition agreement. It found that many parties were as likely to see their policy reflected in the declaration if they were outside as within government. This raised the question of why they entered coalitions at all, and led to a general test and assessment of standard 'policy closeness' theories of coalition formation. The parties most likely to get their policies accepted in government were first of all those in countries with some alternation between electoral alliances (above all, in Scandinavia) and centrist parties occupying a semi-permanent position inside coalitions. All the data from these studies is included in this book and are thus accessible for readers who want to do replications.

It would, of course, be more satisfactory to relate programmatic priorities directly to the central actions taken by governments, i.e. to legislation and administration. Creating indicators for these would be a vast task. Early indications that a close match between emphases and outputs might be expected come from the one country where an index has been created (Stimson, McKuen and Erikson 1995). Platform emphases coded into a Left-Right scale had a high correlation with Presidential liberalism (r=.81) (McDonald, Budge and Hofferbert 1999).

COMPUTERIZED ANALYSES OF POLITICAL TEXTS

Political texts are increasingly scanned into electronic form and there is in principle no reason why all should not be scanned—manifestos and legislation alike. This could immensely simplify the task of relating party priorities in election programmes to legislative and administrative actions which is all recorded in documents. All that one requires is a computer procedure capable of summarizing the texts in relevant statistical form.

This is, of course, a big requirement, even though programmes for counting key words have been around for thirty years (Stone *et al.* 1966). Their prime purpose, however, has mostly been to provide in-depth analyses of individual texts, rather than to create comparable distributions across large numbers of documents, as is done here.

Much experimental work is currently under way to develop trustworthy computer procedures which will code units of text—possibly natural sentences—into categories and indices like those produced manually for this book. The basis in most cases is a 'dictionary' of key words identified either *a priori* (e.g. from the MRG coding instructions) or inductively from the text, or both. The balance of words in a sentence then determines which category it is put into (Chapter 7).

With a computer procedure the reliability of the estimates is not the problem it is with manual coding (Chapters 5 and˙ 6). A given procedure applied to the same text will always produce the same results. The major problem is validity— are the computer estimates giving us the information we want without distorting errors?

Of course validity is also a problem with manual codes. Estimates which have been widely used for a long time however have clearly been found to work well for the various purposes to which they have been put. In the case of the data presented here the estimates have produced plausible results in a variety of research contexts (Chapter 2). Their extended time-coverage also enables 'maps' of policy movement to be compared with the historical record to see if anomalies can be detected (Chapter 1). Different measures of party policy positions can also be compared with them to see if there is agreement (Chapter 6).

The different formal criteria of validity are discussed below. One difficulty is that the Manifesto policy estimates are by far the best available. Thus it is a bit hard to validate them against other measures—even though, when compared, they do well (Chapter 6). Having been more exposed than any other estimates to multiple checks, and having surpassed them, these estimates have acquired a uniquely authoritative standing. This makes them central to the developing field of computer processing in two ways:

a) suggesting words and codes for dictionaries which might then be applied to coding words or sentences in the texts

b) forming an authoritative standard for validating the final computerized estimates. The basic problem with the latter is knowing whether they really characterize the relevant policy positions of parties—relevant at any rate to political representations and theories. Their ability to match the MRG representations, which have already been shown to be relevant, is an important check on this.

The Manifesto estimates allow direct comparisons to be made with computerized ones since they both rest on the same general counting procedures based on saliency assumptions (see above and Chapter 3). All current computerized approaches count the frequency with which certain key words like taxes are used by one party relative to the other(s). Such words are taken as one-positional—(cutting) taxes, (expanding) social services, just like most of the MRG categories (supporting) peace, (strengthening) democracy. On this basis they are used to assign textual units to policy positions. This allows comparisons of the two sets of estimates to focus on measurement similarities and differences stemming from reliance on words rather than sentence-meaning.

Once validated, computerized procedures can be applied more widely and flexibly to political texts than the hand-coded ones presented here. But to be acceptable they must first match their results. One reason for publishing the MRG estimates at this point is to ensure they can play their part in this exciting new development by sorting out promising computerized coding procedures from dud ones.

CONTENT ANALYSIS: OPERATIONALIZING FORMAL APPROACHES WITH MANIFESTO DATA

In the preceding sections we have discussed the evolution of content analysis without focussing precisely on what it is and what it entails. The first major political scientist to write systematically and comprehensively about the technique was Bernard Berelson, who produced a methodological paper in 1952. This still forms the basis of much of the methodological debate to the present day. Berelson defined content analysis as a 'research technique for the objective, systematic and quantitative description of the manifest content of communication' (Berelson 1954: 481).

This has been adapted by Weber (1990: 9), who believes that content analysis is

'a research method that uses a set of procedures to make valid inferences from text. These inferences are about the sender(s) of the message itself or the audience of the message. The rules of this inferential process vary with the theoretical and substantive interests of the investigator.'

There is a significant shift here from a definition which emphases the public, shared nature of the approach ('objective . . . description of the manifest content') to a subjective conception, in which the results of the analysis reflect not only textual content but also the 'interests of the investigator'. Not only coding categories but also rules for assigning textual units to them are shaped by theory i.e. the conception one has of the communication process under investigation (see also Stone *et al.* 1966: 6–13 on 'inferences').

This point clearly has implications for the study of election programmes, as of other political texts. We have to have some idea of how they are written and used and what purposes they serve in the election campaign before we can devise relevant categories and rules of coding (Budge, Robertson and Hearl (eds.) 1987: 24–5). This is why the theoretical basis of our categories (Saliency Theory) is assessed in Chapter 3.

The fact that some sort of theoretical framework has to be adopted in order to devise categories and rules in the first place, does not make the investigators blind slaves of the initial theory nor does it render their results incapable of contradicting it or refining it. A misapplied or wrong-headed theory is unlikely to support relevant codes and procedures. The ability of the analysis to 'work' for the purposes for which it was intended is thus an implicit check on the theory on which it is based—one which our data pass (Chapter 1 and 2). More explicit checks can also be built into coding procedures themselves, as with the experimental bipolarities in some of the MRG categories (Chapters 3 and 4). The codings themselves and the associated 'saliency' ideas about party competition (that parties do not confront each other head on over specific issues but instead emphasize 'their' issues and de-emphasize others) survive the in-built checks well.

As Weber notes above, inferences are made about the senders of the election message and about the audience which receives it. Election programmes have the advantage of being the only comprehensive document or declaration which the party as such makes. Usually the procedure for adopting it is written into the party constitution, so it is very clear what the document itself is. However, factionalized or internally divided a party, it has as a legal entity adopted the programme at a particular point in time, after a more or less elaborate consultation process. These are clear attributions which other indicators of party policy positions lack, being mostly based on other people's (experts' or electors') *perceptions* of what the policy is, which is a very different thing. Whereas the Manifesto data clearly constitute preferences or intentions of the party, and thus qualify as explanations or trackers of subsequent party behaviour (in government for example), perceptions and judgements about policy stands are often based on that behaviour itself so it is unclear how they can serve as explanations of it without tautology (Budge 2000).

Electors of course are the prime audience to which election programmes are addressed—even if these often aspire to impact on them through shaping media discussion rather than directly. Studies of mass communication have often stressed that we cannot simply assume audiences receive the message as intended. Indeed, we noted above that electoral perceptions of party policy should be taken as a dependent variable which may or may not coincide with party attempts to define their own position (c.f. Gabel and Huber 2000). In this sense, manifestos may tell you more about how party strategists think about electors than what electors themselves think.

Given an additional assumption, itself subject to empirical checks, that electors vote for the party closest to them on policy grounds, one can, however, make theoretically-grounded inferences as to what the electoral policy-position is. The procedure for inferring the policy-position of the median elector from the distribution of votes and positions of parties, is discussed in Chapter 8. The actual estimates obtained from this procedure for the Left-Right scale, and attitudes to Market Reliance, Economic Planning, Welfare and Peace, are reported in the CD-ROM.

Electoral preferences inferred from party-positions cannot of course be used to explain party movement as would be desirable from a Downsian perspective (Downs 1957). However, they may give guidance about where to locate measures independently derived (from public opinion polls, for example) in the space. Measures of public opinion liberalism (Stimson, McKuen and Erikson 1995) have been developed for the US and will probably be constructed for other countries with poll series in the next few years. Median voter estimates therefore, besides being of general descriptive interest, may indirectly aid the development of Downsian representations of electoral preferences and party movement, within the same space. They may also feed in to econometric and other models of government outputs as measures of public preferences to be compared with those of parties and governments.

RELIABILITY AND VALIDITY

In line with general specifications for content analysis our coding procedures thus provide a systematic and quantitative description of the content of manifestos which can be used as the basis of inferences about senders (parties) and receivers (electors) of the messages contained within them. Both content description and inferences are theoretically grounded. This fact gives rise to two measurement concerns: are the procedures derived from the theory reliable, in the sense of giving the same results every time they are applied? And are they valid, in the sense of actually telling us what we think they tell us about content and senders? This second concern broadens out from a concern with measurements as such to questions about whether the underlying theory is itself correct (Weber 1990: 18).

Reliability is the simpler and more basic question. Computers will always apply the same procedures to the same text in the same way. This is not always true of the human coders who have produced the Manifesto data however, even when the same person has independently recoded the same text. More variation might be expected from different people coding different texts in different languages (inter-coder reliability).

National series within the total data-set have been subjected to standard stability and inter-coder reliability tests (Budge and Farlie 1977: 422–3; Budge, Robertson and Hearl (eds.) 1987: 23–4 and passim). However, given the complications of working in different languages, more emphasis has been put on strong central supervision and checks on the coding process, facilitated in the 1990's by electronic links (Chapter 4 below). For example, from the mid 1980s the actual copy of the original coded text, with every (quasi) sentence annotated with its coding category, has been preserved centrally. In this way every individual coding decision can be referenced.

In particular, accuracy has been stressed (Weber 1990: 17). Standard pre-coded texts have been circulated to coders with extensive supporting documentation (some of this is reproduced in Appendices 1 and 2). The coded texts have been used both for training and also as a check on the degree to which coders have assimilated instructions—a blank text is coded and sent back to the supervisor, who compares it with the central standard. If unsatisfactory the coder is retrained until (s)he reaches the required standard.

Emphasis has also been placed on the overall stability of the coding procedures as well as on individual codings. In this context Chapter 5 is highly relevant, comparing data coded for the period 1945–83, to the mid-eighties, with the complete data set at the end of the 1990s (1945–98). The comparability of a range of results obtained from analyzing the two sets independently offers reassurance about the similarity of procedures during these two major phases of collection.

Their reliability forms some guarantee that we have developed reasonable procedures. The wider question concerns their validity—are they really telling us what we think they are or what we want to know? Weber (1990: 18–21) distinguishes five types of validity:

a) face validity—the correspondence, as judged by the investigators, between theoretical concepts and measures. We can say generally that the Manifesto data seem to discriminate between parties in the way anticipated by Saliency Theory, with different parties selectively emphasizing topics according to their own general ideology

b) construct-validity—does the coding correlate with other measures of the same construct (convergent) and not correlate too highly with measures of other concepts (divergent)? The difficulty with assessing convergent validity in the context of party policy stands is that the manifesto-based estimates form the best measures, for the reasons given above. However, there are high correlations between various types of estimates as noted in a number of investigations (c.f. Gabel and Huber 1999: Chapter 6 below). On divergence, measures of government policy, coded into similar categories as manifestos, show sometimes strong divergences from individual party policy (Laver and Budge, (eds.) 1992, passim).

c) hypothesis validity—do relationships among variables mirror anticipated theoretical relationships? One can say in general that our data have been used with plausible results in a variety of theoretical contexts—party competition, (Budge, Robertson and Hearl (eds.) 1987), coalition formation, (Laver and Budge (eds,) 1992), output analysis (Klingemann, Hofferbert, Budge *et al.* 1994), also by investigators outside the original group (Baron 1991; Schofield 1993; Adams 1998). Many hypotheses, particularly on coalition formation, have been rejected on the basis of the data. But the rejection seemed reasonable. In general where there were strong theoretical reasons to expect a particular pattern of results, the estimates have produced them.

d) predictive validity—the extent to which forecasts about events external to the study correspond to actual events. Here perhaps the strongest evidence is given in Chapter 1, where the Left-Right movements of parties tracked across the post-war period in 25 countries are shown to correspond to the historical record, sometimes with great precision. Major turning points of post-war party politics are reflected in the party movements. Party emphases on policy also tend to anticipate shifts in government expenditures or policies, though the extent to which this is a causal relationship is controverted (Hofferbert, Budge and McDonald 1992; McDonald, Budge, Hofferbert 1999).

e) semantic validity—when persons familiar with the languages and texts examine lists of units placed in the same category and agree they belong together. Clearly the acceptance of the codes by a wide variety of investigators and coders in many different countries conforms to this requirement, particularly as they extend over so many different languages and party systems.

PLAN OF DISCUSSION

This Introduction has related our procedures to the general development and concerns of content analysis. The following chapters flesh out this discussion by covering the points we have raised in detail. We go from the uses and applications of the estimates (Chapters 1 and 2) to the theory underlying them (Chapter 3) and then on to the actual procedures applied (Chapter 4) and examinations of their reliability (Chapter 5) and validity (Chapter 6). The role of the Manifesto estimates as a standard for evaluating computerized analyses is then considered with examples (Chapter 7) and in Chapter 8 we show how to make inferences from party preferences to those of governments and electorates. Chapter 9 makes suggestions for starting the analysis with the data which follow on disk. One useful suggestion is to start with graphical displays, which give an immediate overview of party policy positions and movement over time, of the sort now considered and presented in Chapter 1.

The Appendices and the text files included on the CD-ROM provide necessary background information—which parties issued the documents any way? (Appendix I) and detailed protocols for coding (Appendix II, augmented by material in the CD-ROM). The nature of the variables included in the data-sets is detailed (Appendix III) and a list of parties for which data was unavailable to the MRG researchers is given (Appendix IV). The average positions of parties along four major policy stands constructed from the variables within the data-sets follow (Appendix V). Finally, we provide a list of cases which form the basis of the Government Declarations data-set (Appendix VI) together with a description of the variables included (CD-ROM).

Part I
Policy Spaces, Preferences, and Texts

1

Finally! Comparative Over-Time Mapping of Party Policy Movement

Ian Budge and Hans-Dieter Klingemann

INTRODUCTION

The crowning achievement of the Manifesto Research Project has been to measure party policy change in a variety of countries over an extended time period along the Left-Right dimension. Being able to do so is important because of the centrality of this dimension in political discussion and analysis, confirmed by its spontaneous, near-universal emergence in our previous analyses of election programmes (Budge, Robertson and Hearl (eds.) 1987). It is probably the single most important indicator of party policy, and a pointer to underlying ideology which meshes with membership of a generic 'family' and other distinguishing party characteristics.

This is not to say that the Manifesto estimates do not cover other aspects of policy. We have also created summary indicators of support for Planning, Market Reliance, Welfare and Peace, (Appendix V) scores for which are given along with Left-Right ones in the CD-ROM. There are also, of course, the 54 standard categories into which sentences were originally coded, each of which traces some aspect of party policy in detail over the post-war period.

All these indicators can be represented graphically just like Left-Right movements (Budge 1999). As it is impossible to present everything in print we concentrate on the latter here, leaving it to readers themselves to create comparable graphs they are interested in for any series from the CD-ROM (also for governments and electorates, if they wish to focus on policy change there).

The Left-Right graphs are substantively important, first of all from a descriptive point of view. They give a precise measure of where a party stands ideologically over an extended period of time (Figure 2.1 below for mean measures of party position on the Left-Right scale). More informatively, they show how it has varied its Left-Right positions at each election. Figures 1.1–1.25 trace such movements and are well able to answer questions like whether there is ideological convergence or divergence over time. This in turn enables us to confront more apocalyptic assertions of the 'End of (Left-wing) Ideology' (Bell 1962) or the 'End of History' (Fukuyama 1991). To anticipate, what seem to emerge in most cases are 'trendless fluctuations'—though this is not to deny that movements in the short-term are not driven by strategic motives (Budge 1994).

This being so, the spatial representations of this Chapter are very suitable for checking on models of party competition in the Downsian tradition. Indeed, as noted in the Introduction, it was a concern to operationalize such models and their variants which drove early work on this project. Just looking at Figure 1.1, for example (the US) indicates how questions about party competition can be tackled directly on the basis of that picture alone.

Given that the graphs measure party closeness and distance on central matters of policy, they are also highly suitable for generating predictions about coalition-formation, either on the basis of the most common proximity models, or from more sophisticated ideas like the 'power of the median' (Laver and Budge 1992). The degree to which coalition partners get policy-payoffs can also be checked by comparing their policy positions in the preceding election with the government's position (not mapped here but available in the CD-ROM). Other output measures such as government liberalism can also be related to varying party positions (McDonald, Budge and Hofferbert 1999). Wider questions such as the impact of policy position on class mobilization can also be raised (Evans, Heath and Payne 1999).

Chapter 2 reviews many applications of the Left-Right maps and other Manifesto estimates in detail. From this it is clear that there are few aspects of democratic politics not illuminated by these data.

The Left-Right graphs also have an important methodological bearing. This is particularly important in the context of this publication, dedicated as it is to presenting and evaluating the manifesto estimates for a wider public. Most chapters are therefore concerned in one way or another with the question of how reliable and valid they are and how well they function to operationalize relevant theories. As the previous discussion of their substantive implications illustrate, the Left-Right 'maps' are directly relevant to Downsian type theories of party competition and to many models of coalition formation. Seeing is believing, so we do not rely simply on assertions or citations to prove this point but present the maps for readers' own inspection and evaluation.

No matter how well the maps function as representations of theoretical models, we must also be concerned with how well they mesh with the real world. Weber (1990: 18) describes this as predictive validity, which is the extent to which forecasts about events external to the study correspond to actual events. In the case of Left-Right movements we are more concerned with postdiction—checking how far significant historical changes in the parties or party systems correspond to significant changes in party policy position. Does the famous renunciation of Marxism by the German Social Democrats in 1959 correspond with a rightward movement in the subsequent election programme? Do Clinton's and Blair's well-documented lurches to the Right in the 1990s match with the paths traced in our representations?

More generally, one can also seek to validate the representations in terms of a general fit between what we already know about party positions (their ideological families, for example) and the general locations of corresponding national parties in the Figures. We expect the maps to distinguish clearly in general between the spatial locations of these parties whatever temporary manoeuvring they may engage in, since we know on other evidence that they *are* different (von Beyme 1985: 29–136). Only if general differences hold can we take temporary moves to right or left as substantive findings rather than methodological errors.

The ability of the Left-Right maps to meet these validity criteria constitute a holistic check for the whole data-set, because the scales are affected directly or indirectly by policy changes in all the policy areas covered by the coding frame. Holistic checks of our estimates are the most appropriate ones because of the open-ended and expanding nature of the data, with new elections and countries constantly being added to it. It is a tough check because there is a real independence between the 'internal' and 'technical' procedures for coding programmes and the public historical record of the post-war period. Our conclusion is that the estimates survive the test with enhanced credibility, but readers can judge this for themselves on the basis of the evidence below.

CREATING THE LEFT-RIGHT SCALE

First though, we must briefly describe how the scoring system was created and why it seems plausible both on theoretical and empirical grounds. The scale is made up by adding percentage references to the categories grouped as Left and Right, respectively in Table 1.1, and subtracting the sum of the Left percentages from the sum of the Right percentages.

In the Figures presented in this Chapter, therefore, negative scores represent Left positions and positive scores represent Right positions (sometime this has been reversed as in Budge and Hofferbert 1990; Klingemann, Hofferbert and Budge 1994). At the extreme (never in practice attained) a party devoting its entire programme to Left-wing issues would score −100: similarly a totally Right-wing programme would score +100. In practice parties fall in between, but one potential difference between countries is indeed the range of scores needed to accommodate party movements in the figures below. The scale generally opposes emphases on peaceful internationalism, welfare and government intervention on the Left, to emphases on strong defence, free enterprise and traditional morality on the Right. A first question about its construction is why issues were grouped in this way. There is after all no logical or inherent reason why support for peace should be associated with government interventionism though the latter might well be designed to secure greater welfare. On the other side, the three concerns of the Right could in theory vary quite independently of each other.

The fact remains however that ideologies and parties do put them together. A first guide to grouping the categories is therefore found in Marxist writings, which do put together emphases on intervention and welfare together with workers having nothing to gain from capitalist wars. Rightist ideologies are harder to pin down but the grouping of defence, enterprise and morality is certainly familiar from the writings and speeches of exponents like Reagan and Thatcher. The association of these themes in actual party documents is well attested by earlier investigations of election programmes (c.f. Budge, Robertson and Hearl (eds.) 1987).

Table 1.1 Scoring a Left-Right scale on the basis of the manifesto estimates

Right emphases: sum of %s for		Left emphases: sum of %s for
Military: positive		Decolonization
Freedom, human rights		Military: negative
Constitutionalism: positive		Peace
Effective authority		Internationalism: positive
Free enterprise		Democracy
Economic incentives		Regulate capitalism
Protectionism: negative	minus	Economic planning
Economic orthodoxy		Protectionism: positive
Social Services limitation		Controlled economy
National way of life: positive		Nationalization
Traditional morality: positive		Social Services: expansion
Law and order		Education: expansion
Social harmony		Labour groups: positive

Having grouped these categories together on theoretical grounds their 'fit' with each other was investigated through factor analysis on the then existing MRG data up to broadly 1983 (Laver and Budge 1992). All the categories differentiated on *a priori* grounds as Left-Right did indeed turn out to fit on one dimension. This dimension, scored in the percentage terms outlined above, was then input to further factor analyses to see, inductively, if further variables loaded on to it across all countries. One or two did, whose inclusion could also be justified on *a priori* grounds. They were accordingly added into the scales.

Factor analysis introduces an element of induction (what categories actually co-vary consistently?) into the creation of the Left-Right scale. This was used to check out pre-conceived ideas rather than to suggest construction for several reasons. First, factor analytic results reflect the data as they are but give no guarantee that if they change the same results will be obtained—even though in the case of our estimates actual results do not seem to vary much over time (Chapters 5 and 6 below). Secondly, because factor analysis does so well reflect tendencies over the whole of the data to which it is applied, it makes parties, which on the face of it have little to do with each other, interdependent in terms of ideological positioning. To take an extreme example, the Left-Right location of the Italian Christian Democrats in 1992 could be affected by what the Finnish Communists were saying in 1948. We avoid this by using simple percentage scores without weighting, which give the same position for an individual party regardless of what the others do.

Their dependency on the data at a particular time-point and interdependency of positioning seem weaknesses of other Left-Right scales based directly on factor-analysis (Budge and Robertson 1987; Bartolini and Mair 1990). Gabel and Huber's (2000) attempt to construct a Left-Right scale drawing on contributions from all categories in the coding frame does have the advantage, however, of maximizing the information available from our coding.

There is a sense however in which the Left-Right scale used here also draws on holistic information over all the categories. Twenty-six go directly into the measurement, with 13 Left items being added and subtracted from the sum of 13 Right items. Thus a party that makes 200 total statements with 100 (or 50%) of them about Left items and 40 (or 20%) about Right items receives a score of −30 (i.e., 20–50). This subtractive measure is consistent with saliency theory. Of all the statements the party made, on balance, 30 more units were devoted to Left matters than to Right matters. Imagine that at the next election this party says exactly the same things it had said last time but adds 200 new statements about an issue that is not of concern to the Left-Right scale (e.g., favourable statements about protecting the environment). Now the party is making 400 total statements, and relative to that total they are making only half as many Left statements (25%) and half as many Right statements (10%) as they did for the first election. The party's Left-Right position is recorded as moving from −30 to −15. That is, the party is scored as considerably less left-leaning at the second election compared to the first. It has moving toward the center by virtue of devoting attention to policy matters that are not within the categories relevant to the Left-Right scale.

Measuring positions in this way means that all variables, whether typed as explicitly Left-Right or not, feed into the measure. In this sense the graphs shown below summarize tendencies over the whole of the documents, not just one bit of them. This means that checks on their validity reflect on the standing of the estimates as a whole. Thus, the checks on 'predictive validity' reported in this chapter join the other holistic checks on the validity of the data set reported below—which in combination render the Manifesto estimates the most thoroughly scrutinized and checked of any policy-indicators currently available.

Allowing the Left-Right measure to reflect tendencies in the whole document seems substantively reasonable. The election programme is not made up of a series of discrete statements on different areas of policy which are then stuck together without overall editing. On the contrary document is carefully considered by a revising committee or even by an individual: each part is checked in relation to the others and the balance of the whole finely calibrated The easy way to change positions without offending previous supporters is to make the same assertions about Left-Right issues while saying more or less about other matters, and thus throwing them up by relief or diverting attention elsewhere. Political rhetoric is a more subtle matter of nuances and relative emphases than is allowed by analysts who feel that if parties do not make blunt assertions or counter-assertions they are not taking up a position at all.

Part of the proof must, as always, be in terms of the useful and accurate measurements the left-right measure produces. In the rest of this Chapter we examine and comment upon maps of Left-Right movement for various groupings of post-war democracies, starting with the largely English-speaking ones in the Section below.

POLICY CHANGE IN OVERSEAS DEMOCRACIES WITH CONSTITUENCY-BASED LARGELY PLURALITY VOTING

We group countries in terms of their electoral systems and voting rules, as these should have some influence over party policy competition. Such rules also correlate broadly with cultural divisions, since countries with plurality voting rules are largely English-speaking.

The obvious country to start with is the United States, in terms of its cultural dominance and political importance. There has up to now been some question as to whether American parties *can* be placed along a Left-Right dimension comparable to that dividing Socialists and Conservatives in Europe (e.g. Ware 1996: 25–6), having so often been taken as pragmatic and non-ideological in nature. Figure 1.1 shows that as far as platforms go they can.

Indeed the US parties are more clearly distinguished from each other than many Socialist and Conservative parties are in Europe. They maintain a clear distance between themselves and they do not leapfrog.

This is not to say that policy-positions do not move and change. Those sceptical about the validity of a Left-Right representation in the American context may be happier when they note how the policy-changes graphed here mesh convincingly with crucial turns in post-war political history. Thus Eisenhower's relatively hard line position of 1952 (Korea, Corruption and Communism) moderated a great deal after 4 years of centrist administration in 1956, a trend continued under Nixon in 1960, 1968 and 1972. In between, the Goldwater candidacy of 1964 produced a sharp turn to the Right. Under Reagan and Bush the party turned, and substantially stayed, to the Right.

Meanwhile the Democrats with their Fair Deal and Great Society stayed firmly in a moderately leftward positions with the exception of Humphrey's lunge towards the centre in 1968. The party drifted Rightwards in the 1980s but it was left to Clinton in 1992 to make a decisive shift, downplaying government intervention and stressing social solidarity and family values.

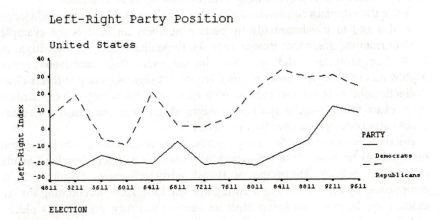

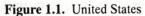

Figure 1.1. United States

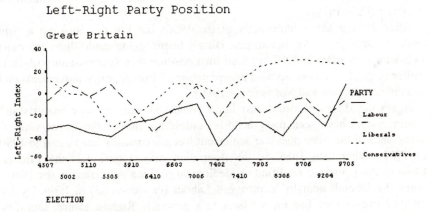

Figure 1.2. Great Britain

There are few or no anomalies in these time series in terms of what we know from the public record. They also correlate convincingly with Stimson et al's (1995) index of Presidential Liberalism (r=.81, c.f. McDonald et al, 1999) more direct evidence of predictive validity than we have for other countries.

While the estimates summarized in Figure 1.1 tie in with previous knowledge they also add to it substantially by putting numbers on it. It is for example evident from the graph that Reagan took the Republicans much further Right in 1984 than Goldwater did in 1964—indeed even Dole remained further Rightwards in 1996. Because of this Clinton's change of policy still left clear distinctions between the two parties. With more exact knowledge we can write a more exact history—quite apart from being able to test out theoretical ideas about party convergence over the time series

Britain is in many ways the country whose party politics have been influenced most directly by those of the US—more even than those of neighbouring Canada (Figure 1.5 below). The graph of British party movement (Figure 1.2) is complicated by the presence of a third party, the Liberals. Concentrating for the moment on the two main competitors we can see that they are correctly placed and clearly distinguished—never leapfrogging nor overlapping. Labour remains generally on the Left in substantially the same range of positions up to the 1997 General Election, when under Blair's leadership they crossed the centre line for the first time in their political history.

The Conservatives made a similar strategic move Leftwards in the early 1950s, with their acceptance of the Welfare State and most Labour nationalizations. This was followed by a steady drift Rightwards, interrupted only by the crisis election of February 1974. Mrs. Thatcher gave this tendency a notable push in 1979.

After drifting about uncertainly in the 1950s the Liberals took up a firm centrist stance from the mid-sixties. Blair's leapfrogging made them the most Left-wing contender in 1997 but their own position then is consistent with their earlier ones. (For a more detailed interpretation of British policy movements and strategies see Evans and Norris (eds.) 1999).

Again the British record seems fairly consistent with the way analysts and commentators have seen party histories unfolding, though the Conservatives' acceptance of the basic post-war settlement has more usually been dated to 1950 or 1951, rather than 1955. In the Australian case (Figure 1.3) the Liberal-Country Party alliance modified its ideological position only later, in the 1960s, when the Liberals actually leapfrogged Labour (or vice-versa) in 1966. By the 1970s however they had moved back to a generally Rightist stance, this time more closely co-ordinated with their partner's programme.

It is indeed a moot point whether Liberals and Country should be represented separately in Figure 1.3. Having been permanent government and election partners for the whole post-war period, the Country Party programme often reads like the rural and country section of the Liberal programme. If averaged,

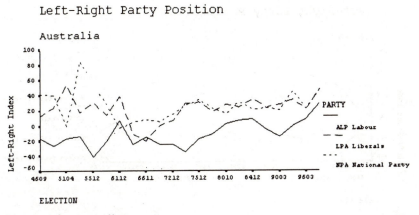

Figure 1.3. Australia

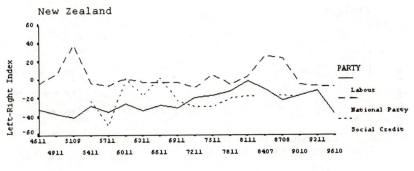

Figure 1.4. New Zealand

Left-Right Party Position

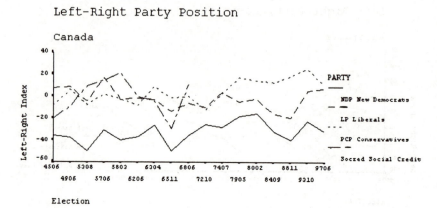

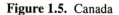

Election

Figure 1.5. Canada

Left-Right Party Position

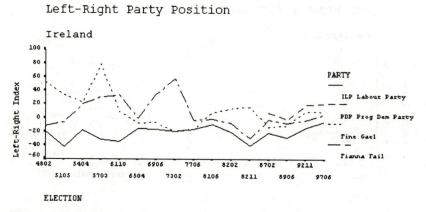

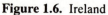

ELECTION

Figure 1.6. Ireland

their joint policy path would be steadier and the overlap with Labour in 1966 would not take place.

Even with the parties shown separately they are well distinguished from Labour and clearly on the right side of the Figure in both senses of the word! Even without Country's almost totally Right-wing programme of 1954–55, the alliance is generally more Rightist than either British Conservatives or US Republicans. Labour keeps generally to the Left until the 1980s. Its leapfrog in 1961 happened in the aftermath of the Leftist Evatt's removal as leader and pressure from breakaway Catholic members of the party.

New Zealand Labour (Figure 1.4) kept a more consistent policy position to the Left, before moving to the centre in the 1970s and 1980s. This prefigured but far from mirrored the party's extremely orthodox and restrictive stance in government of the late 1980s. Indeed its actual taking of power was accompanied by a move Left so far as the programme was concerned. This could cast doubt on the accuracy of our estimate were it not that many commentators also saw government actions as inconsistent with their mandate (Gibbons 2000).

National's stance was fairly centrist until Muldoon began to shift it to the Right in 1981. Both parties' Rightward shift at that point looks like a reaction to the economic crisis of the 1970s—more severe and long-lasting in New Zealand than anywhere else. The change in election system to PR by 1996 seems to have produced a push to the Left. Social Credit's role as a distinct third party in the system seems to have deprived it of a stable position on this dimension as it fluctuated from centre to left in search of protest votes.

In Canada (Figure 1.5) the third party is on the contrary the most distinctive. This is because the NDP is the only socialist party in the system. It is clearly located to the Left and never leapfrogs with any other party, though there is a clear convergence between its own and the Liberal party's position in the late 1970s and early 1980s.

The two major parties in the traditional Canadian set-up, Conservative and Liberals, leapfrog and overlap quite extensively before 1974 but thereafter move clearly apart. The main parties together with Social Credit are indeed practically indistinguishable in the fifties and sixties, an era dominated by the populist John Diefenbaker as leader of the Conservatives. His blend of Canadian nationalism, combined with a willingness to intervene whenever he thought national integrity was threatened, undermined traditional Conservative-Liberal differences. So it seems correctly captured by the ideological confusion of these years.

Ireland (Figure 1.6) displays something of the same pattern, also deriving from a situation where the most ideologically distinct party, Labour, is the third one in the system. Fianna Fail, the dominant party of most of the post-war years, covers a range of diverse tendencies with a strain of populism which might have placed it between the other parties. Labour's only possibility of gaining power however was to form an electoral alliance and coalition government with a common programme, as they did in 1972 and in 1977. The rapprochement was made possible by the leftwards movement of Fine Gael, which paid electoral dividends but thoroughly muddled up ideological positions. Since the seventies Fine Gael has reverted on the whole to a position right of Fianna Fail but very close. The secession of the free market Progressive Democrats from Fianna Fail has aided in its transition to a middle position. The Irish parties are coming closer in the 1990s however, partly as a result of forming government coalitions with each other.

Japan—hardly an English-speaking democracy—is included here (Figure 1.7) because its unique electoral system lines it up with constituency based plurality voting systems such as most of the preceding countries have. The most distinctive party ideologically is the ruling Liberal Democratic Party, with a clear and consistent centrist position. The socialist JSP also has a well-defined position to the Left, most of the time.

Its approximation to an LDP position in 1990 could well be attributed to the weakening of the dominant party during this period, which actually took the JSP into the leading role in a coalition government.

The Japan Communist Party also has a clearly distinctive profile until the collapse of the Soviet Union in the late 1980s, after which it shadows and leapfrogs the LDP. The Komeito (Clean Government Party) remains distinct from the LDP, though it leapfrogs and overlaps the other small opposition parties on the Left. This seems natural since the only prospect of forming an alternative government to the LDP was to seek points of agreement among the smaller parties. These power relationships seem well mirrored in the picture our estimates give us for the later post-war period in Japan.

POLICY CHANGE IN CONTINENTIAL SYSTEMS WITHOUT PR OR WITH HEAVILY MODIFIED PR

Figure 1.8 traces the movements of parties over the Fourth and Fifth French Republics. Not only did the regimes differ—from Parliamentary to semi-Presidential (sometimes more Presidential than others), but the parties also changed in terms of splitting and amalgamating and changing names. It was only in the 1970s that the current four-party system came into being with the parties distinguished by their membership of ideological tendencies (two on the Left, two on the Right).

A further element of confusion is introduced by the difficulty in many cases in distinguishing between an election programme as such and a preceding booklet or book (often among the 1970s best-sellers) on which it may base itself. We do not unfortunately have most of the actual election programmes for the neo-Liberal UDF, the second party of the Right, apart from 1993 and 1997.

Despite this ideological positions are reasonably clear if we discount the impact on the Left of the successive crises of the Fourth Republic and the change of regime. These show up particularly for the Communists, with an

Left-Right Party Position

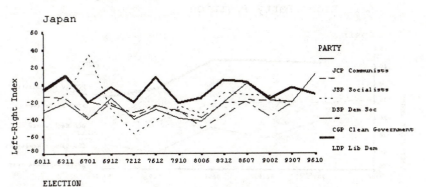

Figure 1.7. Japan

Left-Right Party Position

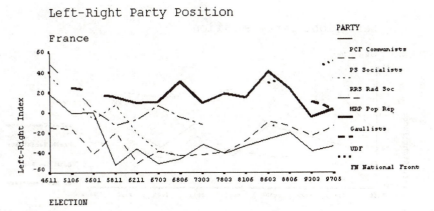

Figure 1.8. France

Left-Right Party Position

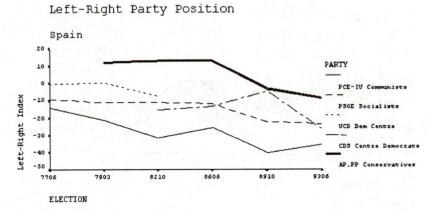

Figure 1.9. Spain

Left-Right Party Position

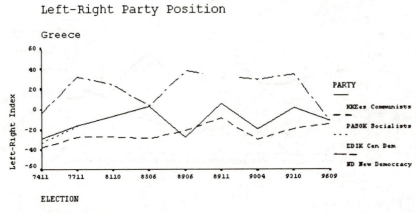

Figure 1.10. Greece

initial Rightist position followed by Leftist stances which did not prevent them being outflanked by the Socialists in 1962 and 1973.

Kitschelt (1994: 139) finds it implausible and invalidating that this could be shown as happening by our estimates, but does not cite any counter evidence to support the criticism. Only if one legislated that Socialists could never appear on the left of Communists anywhere at any time, could we take these displacements as relevant to the question of validation. Provided that party families generally take up the positions expected of them, such as a mean Communist position to the Left of Socialists, (c.f. Figure 2.1) we can surely accept occasional leapfrogging as substantive information and ask why this occurred, rather than leaping to the conclusion that the estimates must be wrong.

In point of fact the French Socialists of the 1970s were pushing a radical reform programme on a somewhat reluctant Communist Party, which led to the acceptance of a 'Common Project of the Left' in 1972. In these circumstances a considerable convergence was to be expected and who was slightly further to the left hardly matters.

After the 1970s the Socialists and Communists take up their expected positions, still mirroring each others' movements, however, as is only natural given their explicit or implicit election pacts. In fact the two main parties of Left and Right each stick close together on their respective sides because French elections are essentially a contest between Left and Right as a whole, not between individual parties. The Gaullists are very distinctive throughout, but this is partly because we are not able to see the UDF leapfrogging them as would no doubt appear if we had their missing programmes.

So far as its democratic regime goes, Spain (Figure 1.9) had relatively plain sailing after the mid 1970s. This is reflected in the emergence of an increasingly moderate Conservative Party (Partido Popular) competing with moderate Socialists (PSE). These two became the major rivals for power after the collapse of the Democratic Centre (UCD) in 1983. Its effective successors, the CDS, have not managed to anchor themselves in a stable centrist position. The United Left with the Communists keeps itself firmly to the Left with no leapfrogging. Indeed none of the Spanish parties overlap others, with the exception of the CDS.

Spain in fact is convincingly represented by our estimates. At first sight Greece (Figure 1.10) is not. Here the Left is occupied by the Socialists (PASOK). The Communists are in the middle, except for 1989. At two points they converge with the (conservative) New Democracy Party. However, this is less implausible than it seems because they actually formed a government together with NDP (to impeach the PASOK leader) at the end of the 1980s.

The reality underlying this is that PASOK and New Democracy are the main contenders for power in Greece. The latter guided the country through the transition to democracy from 1974 onwards. In 1981 however PASOK stormed to power with a radical reforming programme which promised to push the

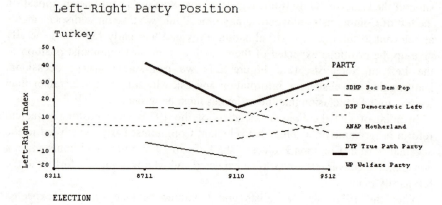

Figure 1.11. Turkey

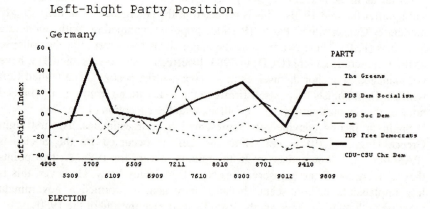

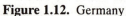

Figure 1.12. Germany

country into the 20th century—more truly radical than anything the Communists, rooted in the Civil War, had to offer. During the 1980s PASOK built up a dominating position which could only be broken by an alliance of the other parties. So we again have an Irish situation in which ideological opposites are brought together in pursuit of power, in a conservative-communist government. The alliance gave PASOK a continued opportunity to position itself to the Left of the Communists. Figure 1.10 therefore makes sense in terms of the relationships between the Greek parties—certainly not often paralleled elsewhere.

Turkey also presents a particular case—the only one where the Army continues to intervene in the semi-democracy (Figure 1.11), which indeed was only restored in 1983.

The Army however is unusual in working to uphold a secular modernizing Republic against threats from Islamic traditionalists or Kurdish secessionists. It will tolerate political parties and political competition provided they do not transgress State values. Indeed it has been instrumental in setting up or encouraging 'reliable' parties, of which the Motherland and True path parties are represented in the graph.

Less tolerated are secular parties of the Left supporting civil liberties and related reforms in the State structure, represented by the short-lived SDHP or the Democratic Left. On the margin of tolerance is the moderate Islamic Welfare Party, which even formed a coalition government in the 1990s but was then proscribed. Its Right wing traditionalist position shows up in the graph, as does the lay (but neo-liberal) position of the Army-sponsored parties.

POLICY CHANGE IN CONTINENTAL PR SYSTEMS WITH ELECTORAL ALLIANCES

This group of countries consists of ones where PR helps create a multi-party system, but where this is focused to some extent by the parties' tendency to line up against each other in two opposing groups (usually of Left and Right) which form clear-cut alternatives for government. This should have some influence over the clarity of the policies which we graph below.

In Germany (Figure 1.12) the ruling coalition parties usually announce their intention of going back into government together if they get an election majority. Up to the 1998 election the key players were the Free Democrats (FDP), a small party whose support was essential to put one of the big players, the Social or Christian Democrats in office. In line with this role the FDP occupies a centrist position, frequently leapfrogging Christians and Socialists. The Christians and Socialists themselves are clearly distinguishable and never leapfrog.

Two particular events in German political history can be checked to see if they are mirrored in this map. One is the famous renunciation of Marxism made by the SPD in pursuit of power at their Bad Godesburg Conference of 1959. This touched off assertions of 'The End of Ideology' (Bell 1962) and the emergence of a catch-all party (Kirchheimer 1966; Krouwel 1998) with no social base or ideological affiliation, dedicated only to pursuit of votes.

There was no election in 1959 but the 1961 election certainly shows a substantial Rightward shift from the previous Social Democratic position which continued in slightly modified form throughout the 1960s. This certainly meshes with the effects of the Bad Godesburg decision and the SPD's pursuit of power at that time with a fairly pragmatic and moderate programme.

However, our map also cautions against seeing Bad Godesburg as more than a temporary tactical change, since by the late 'eighties the SPD had moved to an even more Leftish position than in the early 1950s! As commentators have noted, the effect of adopting Schröder as candidate for the Chancellorship in 1998 was to associate the party with an unprecedented pro-business, financially orthodox stance mirrored in the sharp rightwards shift shown by our map in that year.

In common with other conservative-leaning parties the CDU moved sharply rightwards in the later post-war period. The only exception was the crucial 1990 election related to reunification, where sure enough the CDU's emphasis on government intervention to carry through the change is mirrored in its dash to the Left.

All in all therefore the German policy map convincingly mirrors post-war political history, while lending it additional exactness and precision. Once could say the same for Austria (Figure 1.13), whose three party system reflects the same ideological influences as experienced in Germany, but where, until recently, the Freedom Party was a crucial governmental partner only in the early 1980s. Socialists and Christians (The Peoples' Party, OVP) preferred generally to cut out the middleman by forming 'Grand Coalitions' themselves, if necessary. In reaction the Freedom party aimed to challenge the whole *proporz* system, in which the large parties divided up power by appealing to the Right-wing vote. This move is well charted from 1986 onwards in our map.

The two main parties generally keep to their own ground on Right and Left, with only one leapfrog by the OVP in 1979, under the stress of the intense electoral competition of the 1970s. In times of their Grand Coalitions (1949–66 and 1986–98) the two tend to move closer.

In contrast to the limited numbers of parties competing in Germany and Austria, Norway has many (Figure 1.14). Diversity masks the fact that elections offer a clear-cut alternative between a Labour government generally supported by Left Socialists, and a 'bourgeois' government consisting of the Conservatives or a combination of Conservatives, Centre, and Liberals. Thus the obvious policy distinction to look for in Figure 1.14 is that between the two Left parties and the 'bourgeois' parties. This is clearly there. Only the Liberals leapfrog, but only twice, with the Left parties.

Even the individual bourgeois parties are quite well distinguished in the

Left-Right Party Position

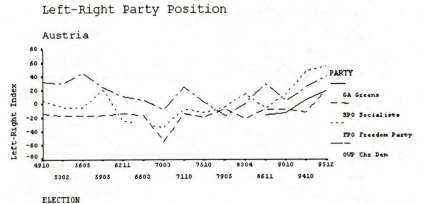

Figure 1.13. Austria

Left-Right Party Position

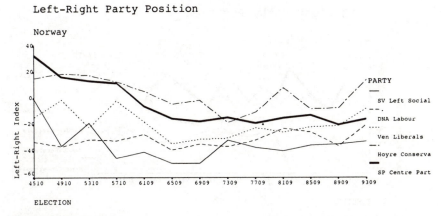

Figure 1.14. Norway

Left-Right Party Position

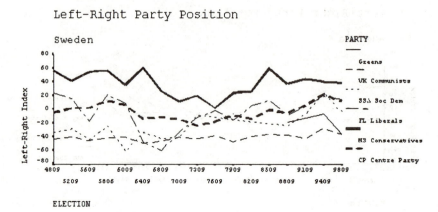

ELECTION

Figure 1.15. Sweden

Left-Right Party Position

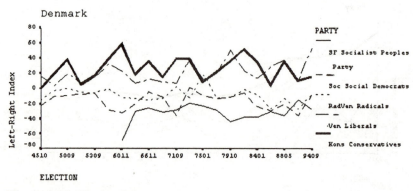

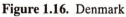
ELECTION

Figure 1.16. Denmark

Figure. The Conservatives are scored as less to the Right than many specialists would place them (c.f. Chapter 6 below). In terms of the logic of party competition in Norway, however, it makes sense for them to remain reasonably close to their potential coalition partners, particularly in elections which may precede the formation of a government. They probably get more votes that way too. So the policy map is not unconvincing.

On the Left too the need of Labour for Communist-Left Socialist support explains occasional leapfrogging between the parties, which, on the whole, fall into their expected more extreme and more moderate Leftist positions.

The Swedish Social Democrats (Figure 1.15) have the same need for the support of Communists to sustain their government, which underpins leapfrogging between the two in the earlier post-war years. With the breakdown of their hold on government in the 1970s the Social Democrats move more to the Right, especially after the emergence of the Greens in the 1990s.

This has brought them closer to the smaller 'bourgeois' parties, the Liberals and the Centre Party. They are still clearly distinguished from the Conservatives, however, who are characterized by a generally stronger Rightist stance than their Norwegian counterparts, which is one reason for the difficulties bourgeois parties have experienced in keeping their coalitions going, and by the often tolerant attitude of the smaller parties in opposition to Social Democratic governments.

The Danish party system (Figure 1.16) is even more complicated than those of its Nordic partners. For simplicity Figure 1.16 does not include all the parties but only the major competitors. Danish governments alternate between Social Democrats, the largest party, and combinations dominated by a Liberal-Conservative partnership. Most governments are minority ones, dependent on the support of the Radicals and, in the case of the Social Democrats, of the left-wing Socialist Peoples' Party (SF).

Figure 1.16 mirrors these realities. Conservatives and Liberals tend to locate near each other and to move in tandem, particularly in the later post-war period when they were at the core of the bourgeois 'four leaf clover' and 'five leaf clover' coalitions. They never overlap the Left-wing parties and only once cross over the Radicals. This was after the shock election of 1973 with the entry of three new parties including the anti-tax and anti-system Progress Party (not shown in the Figure), when all the existing parties came closer together in self-defence This moment is captured on the map.

The Socialist Peoples' Party, ecologist and pacifist, appears as the most distinctive—as it should be. It draws closer to the other parties of Centre-Left in the mid 1990s in face of continuing bourgeois coalitions. The Social Democrats occupy a more moderate position on the chart, frequently overlapping with the Radicals. All of these positions are quite plausible.[1]

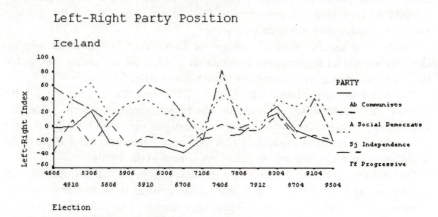

Figure 1.17. Iceland

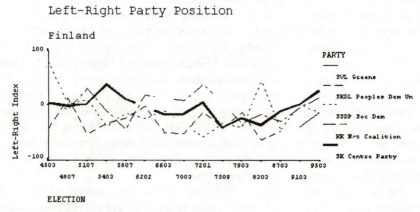

Figure 1.18. Finland

POLICY CHANGE UNDER PR WITHOUT ELECTORAL ALLIANCES

Iceland (Figure 1.17) has more of a classic multi-party system than its Nordic counterparts. No party gets a majority. Which coalition forms is not determined by pre-election agreements but by post election negotiations. For most of the post-war period the two main competitors for government office have been the Independence and Progressive parties. These are ideologically very similar. Their rivalry has meant that they often formed coalitions with ideologically dissimilar parties, notably the Social Democrats. But equally they have often formed coalitions with each other. Some of the more striking changes of policy position, notably by the Progressives in 1971, can be explained by strategic imperatives.

Right and Left are broadly distinguished in Figure 1.17. However all parties tend to come more together in the later post-war period as major points of division like the American base at Keflavik were overtaken by the end of the Cold War.

The Finnish situation (Figure 1.18) is complicated by its semi-Presidential regime which often saw the holder of the office, particularly Kekkonen, intervening in government formation in favour of his own party (up to the 1980s the Agrarians or Centre). The diverse coalitions formed with the Centre as pivot perhaps accounts for its path through the middle of the Left-Right spectrum. The National Coalition, the Conservative party, was generally excluded from governments by Presidential and Soviet influence. This is reflected by its more distinctive policy profile until Cold War influences ceased to be so potent in the 1980s. Otherwise the frequent association of parties in short-lived coalitions seemed to have produced ideological and policy confusion, mirrored in the substantial overlapping shown in Figure 1.18.

The Dutch party system (Figure 1.19) was simplified considerably by the amalgamation of the Calvinist parties (ARP and CHU) with the Catholic Party (KVP) in the early 1970s, under the name of the Christian Democratic Appeal (CDA). The new party succeeded to the brokerage role performed by its predecessors, in choosing between Labour (PvdA) and Liberals (VVD) as government partners. Figure 1.19 illustrates its centrist position which supported this role. The ideological distinctiveness of Liberals to the Right and Labour to the Left, which rendered them unable to cut out the CDA, is also well shown in the Figure. The Libertarian or Progressive D'66 generally moves in close tandem with the PvdA.

Eighty years of Christian-based government came to an end in 1994. Two dramatic events occurred. The secular parties gained enough votes to form a government on their own, without the Christians. And Labour moved dramatically to the Right, making a policy agreement possible with the VVD.

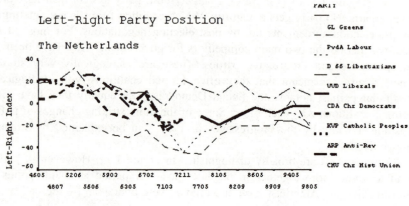

Figure 1.19. Netherlands

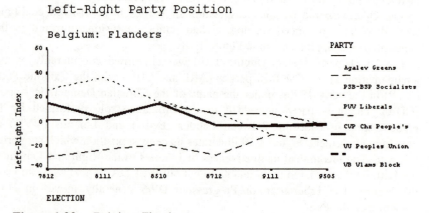

Figure 1.20a. Belgium Flanders

Left-Right Party Position

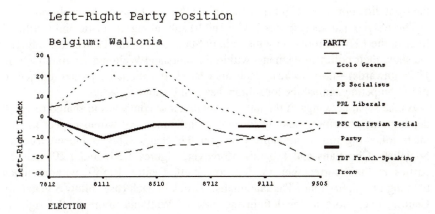

Figure 1.20b. Belgium Wallonia

Left-Right Party Position

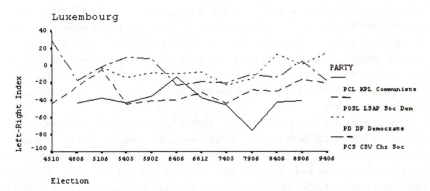

Figure 1.21. Luxembourg

This most dramatic conjuncture in modern Dutch politics is captured in our chart of policy movements with the unprecedented leapfrogging of the CDA by the PvdA. Clearly this is a major postdictive validation of the policy estimates, which show the generally distinct PvdA making a unique leapfrog in precisely the right direction at the right time to explain the new basis of the coalition.

The Belgian parties (Figures 1.20 a and b) split along linguistic and territorial lines in the 1970s, followed by the unitary State itself in the 1980s. Accordingly, we show their policy movements within Flanders and Wallonia separately (from 1978 onwards)—also because each area has had nationalist parties unique to itself competing against the local branches of the national parties.

As the separate wings of the latter maintain close contacts and shared research departments contribute heavily to their programmes, we would expect to find them following much the same paths on the charts. This is indeed true for Socialists, Christians and Liberals Moreover, Figures 1.20a and 1.20b put the parties in their correct general location (Left, Centre, Right), without much blurring or leapfrogging. The Nationalist parties in each case follow a generally Centrist line, more to the left in the case of Wallonia, more to the right in Flanders, as might be expected of them when Left-Right divisions are not their main concern. The only possible anomaly is in Figure 1.20a where the extreme Vlaams Blok is shown as shadowing the VU. Gabel and Huber (2000) have noted a tendency for our Left-Right scale not to place such parties so far out as they are perceived by electors and party experts to be. On the other hand it is perfectly possible that extreme parties choose to tone down their stand in their election programmes, in order to attract more moderate voters. So this may not after all be evidence of error in their *statements* of policy.

In Luxembourg (Figure 1.21) market Liberals, Christians and Socialists are joined by Communists which is by far the smallest party and known for its idiosyncratic support of strict financial orthodoxy in the earlier post-war period. This perhaps accounts for its lurch to the Right in 1964. The Socialists remain fairly distinctive, never leapfrogging any party other than the Communists. The Christians remain broadly centrist, enabling them to partner either Socialists or Liberals in coalition, but inclining towards the latter as their frequent policy leapfrogging shows.

Despite their common partnership in the permanent Federal Coalition, a sharp distinction opens up between the Swiss Socialists and the three 'bourgeois' parties (Figure 1.22). With some variation, the former remain at roughly the same position on the Left, never leapfrogging with any of the others. The other three frequently overlap and leapfrog each other. This is consistent with the Socialist opposition to the existing system and their boycott of the coalition arrangements in the 1950s. In the late eighties and nineties the Greens join them on the Left.

In contrast the Portuguese Socialists (Figure 1.23) are not well distinguished in terms of policy from their bourgeois competitors (who confusingly term

Left-Right Party Position

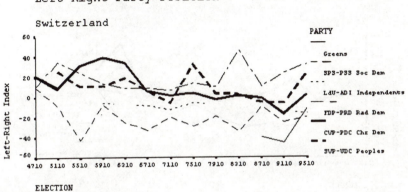

Figure 1.22. Switzerland

Left-Right Party Position

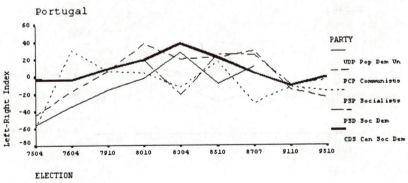

Figure 1.23. Portugal

Left-Right Party Position

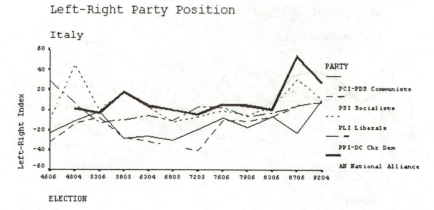

Figure 1.24. Italy

Left-Right Party Position

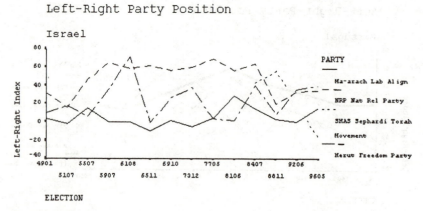

Figure 1.25. Israel

themselves Social Democrats). There are possibly two reasons for this. In the aftermath of the Revolution of 1973 it took time for party differences to sort themselves out, especially since a fully democratic system was not in place till 1983 with the abolition of the Army Council. Secondly, our scoring method regards support for the military as a Right wing issue. In Portugal where the coup was carried through by Left wing officers, left-wing parties also offered support. Indeed it might have been indiscreet not to do this in the early years! Whatever the reason, our chart does not distinguish the Portuguese parties very well, and hardly reflects the period of intensified party competition which began in the 1980s.

Italy (Figure 1.24) in contrast shows a much more interpretable pattern of party movements and differences. These are shown over the period of the 'First Republic' till 1992. Although the dominant Christian Democrats maintain a resolutely centrist position, this is clearly distinguished from those of the parties of the Left, the Socialists and Communists. It overlaps frequently with its minor ally, the Liberals, but rarely with the heir of the Fascists, the National Alliance, which is clearly on the Right of the system.

The problematic part of the representation is the relationship between Communists and Socialists. The latter appear more generally to the Left than the former even though they were permanently in opposition while the Socialists participated frequently in government from 1963 onwards. There is no problem with their leftwards position in the 1950s when they were in relatively close relations with the Communists. Conversely, in the 1970s the Socialists were generally out of office while Communists sustained a minority Christian Democratic government. All parties drew closer in the 'years of lead' in reaction to left wing terrorism. In the 1980s when the Socialists shared power with the Christians the Communists are shown more to the Left. The real problem is the 1960s, even though differences between the parties at that time are not shown as large.[2]

The main Israeli parties (Figure 1.25) are notably more Right-leaning than in most systems examined previously, reflecting both the politics of coalition-building and the national need for strong defence. The two contenders for governmental dominance, Labour and Herut/Likud, are thus pushed together near the Centre in the later post-war period, while the main contrast opens up with the (Ashkenazi) National Religious Party on the Right The populist (Sephardi) religious party Shas varies its position considerably.

In spite of their closeness however, Labour and Herut/Likud are quite well distinguished, with only two instances of leapfrogging. The first is a marginal case in 1955 whilst the second, in 1981, occurs when they were moving towards shared government. The strong contrast between the secular and the religious parties is expected. Herut/Likud's shift towards the religious position in the 1990s, as it intensified its opposition to Palestinian demands, is also in accord with contemporary analyses of the Israeli political situation.

CONCLUSIONS: VALIDITY AND ENLIGHTENMENT

This chapter has had three tasks. The first is primarily presentational—to show how the Manifesto estimates can be used to place parties on a Left-Right continuum and to trace their movements directly and graphically. Clearly they can, as the 26 'maps' of the Chapter attest. The Figures are interesting in themselves for the pictures they give of national politics. They can also be used as direct operationalizations of theories of party competition, as Chapter Two illustrates.

Representations of policy movement can be created but are they correct? The question of validity is the second one addressed in the chapter, involving not just the spatial plots themselves but also the whole range of Manifesto estimates upon which they draw. We have been concerned above all with predictive or postdictive validity, i.e. to what extent do the party positions and movements we trace anticipate or correspond to other political events? Operationally we have tried to answer three questions. Are the parties located in appropriate sectors of the policy space—appropriate that is in terms of their party family and known historical record? Are they clearly distinguished from each other? And are dramatic changes in their position correlated with public political events such as a particular candidacy or change of coalition arrangements?

In regard to the last question we found that dramatic candidacies and political initiatives in the US, UK, Germany, Austria and the Netherlands were well picked up in the corresponding representations. Elsewhere less dramatic matches were found, more subject to interpretation. Turning the question around, quite dramatic changes in party position do not always have obvious public correspondences. Why, for example, did Herut/Likud in Israel make such a dramatic switch in 1961? (Figure 1.25) Why did the AN move sharply in 1987, a relatively quiet time in Italian politics? It is possible of course that the party intended the change to have certain effects which did not materialize? Or it was responding to internal pressures at the time of a change of leadership?

This raises the question of how far such anomalies are really fresh and challenging new information which modifies old political interpretations, or how far are they proofs of the invalidity of the estimates? Ideally we would like the representations to produce results which are generally but not entirely what we expect. That might well be a reasonable judgement of the spatial representations of this chapter.

In assessing overall validity we are on safer ground in requiring parties to stick to a limited range of the policy spectrum and to their appropriate ideological position. For multi-party systems (all countries except the US) this is an expectation promoted by all the leading theories of party competition (Lipset and Rokkan 1967: 1–67; Downs 1957: 122–7). We can add to this the ability of our representations to distinguish fairly clearly between parties, in terms of either overlap or leapfrogging.

Here we can say that almost all of these representations over extended periods of time and many countries, pass the test. Naturally as we move from systems with two clearly competitive parties to situations with greater numbers of significant parties, locations become more entangled with each other. Any overlapping generally takes place between ideologically close parties however. Generally Socialists and Communists are well distinguished from the rest, as are major parties of the Right. Only in the case of Portugal did the representation fail to sort out the parties satisfactorily. This may raise questions of validity. But it is of course also possible that the failure does reflect aspects of Portuguese politics which distinguish them from the generality of Western European systems.

The well-behaved US representation cuts across the expectations of pragmatic, convergent, non-ideological competition held by many commentators and analysts. This seems a genuinely informative and original contribution of our estimates rather than a mistake. The US does seem to experience a form of party competition which is as ideologically (or non-ideologically) driven as the other countries we have studied and can be put easily into this comparative framework.

This brings us to the third concern of this chapter—do our estimates provide any fresh and useful information? There is always a tendency, less marked nowadays than it used to be, to say that estimates and charts of the kind presented here simply tell us in excessive detail what we already know. Certainly if the representations went totally against established knowledge we would doubt their validity. As the American example shows, they do have something fresh to say. They may also stimulate a rethink on other, more controverted questions. Are the policy estimates necessarily wrong when they represent certain parties as more moderate than specialists and public see them? (Gabel and Huber 2000; Chap 6 below). It must be remembered that we are talking about public statements of preference rather than government behaviour or other public acts of the parties. Is it not plausible that when they present their 'five year plans' to public view they have to tackle a whole range of questions outside their core concerns? If the latter might alienate potential support they need not say much about them.

We do not need, however, to rely solely on predictive validity to assess the worth of the Manifesto estimates. All the chapters of this book are concerned to assess this from various angles, starting with the review of research applications (their range and usefulness) in Chapter 2. This series of concurrent assessments reported in the chapters of the book may leave our estimates the most tested and tried in the whole of the policy field. What is clear from this discussion is that they flesh out our existing knowledge of party politics with numbers and spatial representations which render it at the same time more detailed and more accessible.

1 But not to Kitschelt (1994: 139), the severest critic of the MRG placements. He finds the maps of Swedish and Danish party movement 'too volatile', a rather surprising objection given the shocks the latter particularly has been subject to. His solution is to dispense altogether with party volatility, methodological or substantive, by opting for one-point estimates of party position over the whole post-war period (Laver and Hunt 1992)—really cutting the Gordian knot! Such a solution, unfortunately adopted by some other party specialists as well, relieves them of the necessity of analyzing or interpreting party change, but at a great cost. One wonders if they really think of parties as static monoliths rooted in time, or as having any policy flexibility at all.

2 Italy is one of the countries recoded under the CMP programme of updating and checking estimates. The original MRG estimates (Mastropaolo and Slater 1987: 364; Mastropaolo and Slater 1992: 320–1) showed the PCI to the left of the PSI in the 1960s, though not consistently at other times. The discrepancy indicates some need for re-examination of these party programmes.

2

Manifesto-based Research: A Critical Review

Ian Budge and Judith Bara

INTRODUCTION

The graphs of party policy movements presented in Chapter 1 demonstrate the range and flexibility of our policy estimates more dramatically than any detailed review. Similar 'maps' can be produced for specialized policy areas such as the 'planning' and 'peace' scales incorporated in the data-set, or for individual policy-variables such as attitudes to the EU (Evans and Norris (eds.) 1999:12–19).

A whole range of questions can be raised and answered on the basis of this information. We can start with simple descriptive concerns—for example, have parties become more or less distinct in policy terms over the post-war period?

Although simple, assumptions about what is going on in this regard have touched off the most heated debates. The 'End of Ideology' (Bell 1962) has been predicted every time a party has altered its policy position dramatically—only to drift back to its previous positions over time, as the German Socialists did in the 1980s after their famous renunciation of Marxism at Bad Godesburg in 1959 (Figure 1.12 above).

Another thesis touched off by this event was the idea of the catch-all party, dedicated to the pursuit of votes and abandoning its mass base and anchoring ideology (Kirchheimer 1966; Krouwel 1999). Again, the MRG graphs give little credence to this idea as they show all the parties, even American ones, sticking to very much the same ideological segment over time. Indeed, one might venture to say that if Bell and Kirchheimer had had access to our estimates, they might never have come up with these rather misleading generalizations.

As well as over-time movements it is also interesting to examine cross-national differences. Do multi-party systems show different patterns and movements from two or three party ones? Are such differences associated with other contrasts in national politics such as the stability and effectiveness of governments?

Description can thus be pressed into the service of theory. It can aid theoretical development in two ways—by suggesting hypotheses or by testing them. The graphs of party movement shown above display patterns which can be generalized into rules of party electoral competition (Budge 1994). Alternatively such patterns can be used to test formal models generated independently (Adams and Merrill 1998). The graphs also show how parties may move together to form coalitions—or move apart as they break them up (Baron 1991; Laver and Budge (eds.) 1992; Schofield 1993). Nor need only one-dimensional representations be used to test coalition theories. The data-set also lends itself to multi-dimensional modelling within which theories and models can be set (Grofman 1982; Laver and Budge (eds.) 1992).

Relating party policy positions to other developments—class (Evans, Heath and Payne 1999), economy (Keman 1997), government policy change (McDonald et al, 1999) or expenditures (Klingemann *et al.* 1994)—provides hitherto neglected explanations for political events. Indeed party policy might be characterized as the missing element in econometric models of voting (e.g. Sanders and Price 1993). Estimates of policy are certainly necessary to check whether party-based representative democracies actually fulfil their promise of carrying through the election programmes endorsed by the people (Klingemann *et al.* 1994).

This chapter reviews the uses to which the manifesto estimates have been put, starting with their descriptive applications (Section 2) then going on to the nature of the political space their analysis reveals (Section 3), studies of party competition set within such spaces (Section 4), coalition and government formation (Section 5) and relations between party programmes and governmental policy-implementation (Section 6). A concluding section (7) considers potential future applications of the Manifesto estimates.

DESCRIBING THE POLICY POSITIONS OF PARTIES

Surprisingly, these have not been much used in comparative summaries of policy positions of parties in the post-war era (though they have been widely used in single-country studies (c.f. Mair 1987; McAllister and Moore 1991; Strom and Leipart 1989; Evans and Norris (eds.) 1999; Gibbons 2000; Webb 2000—and in specialized comparative studies—Hearl 1988; Bartolini and Mair 1990; Klingemann and Fuchs 1995; Krouwel 1999). This oversight is surprising because of the very rich information the manifestos provide (Figures 1.1–1.25 above). Their very richness, however, may also explain their relative neglect. Books on party systems (von Beyme 1985; Ware 1996) have traditionally had to rely on such impoverished information that they hardly know how to cope with richer and more differentiated material. Change over time has been bypassed in favour of static characterizations of policy positions over some vague post-war period (Ware 1996: 27–49; Kitschelt 1994: 139). The fact that such characterizations, usually based on expert judgements, generally conflate overt party behaviour with their policy preferences does not particularly concern institutional writers, as they are not by definition concerned to explain one by the other. They have no reason to keep them strictly apart—though the overlap should very much concern rational choice theories which aim to explain behaviour by party *preferences* (Budge 2000).

To render use of the Manifesto data easier in this regard we present here the mean Left-Right positions of the major political parties in 25 countries both for the whole post-war period and the later period from (1970–98 inclusive). (Figure 2.1). These can be used as a convenient summary of parties' preferred policy positions as distinguished from their actions or record in government. The reason for breaking at 1970 is that the second half of the 1960s formed the great watershed of the post-war era in terms of society and economies as well as (party) politics. All recent political developments emerged around or after this date. In spite of this it will be seen that most party positions remained relatively stable over the whole post-war period so there was rarely a major break at this point. Figures 1.1–1.25 above also demonstrate this, controverting some of the New Politics and post-materialism theses popular in the 1980s and early 1990s (Inglehart 1977; 1990; 1997).

Figure 2.1 is supplemented by Appendix V which provides similar information about average party policy positions on four more detailed policy scales—reliance on (free) markets, government planning, welfare provision and international peace. Again, differences between party positions on these over the whole post-war period, and in the later period, are neither widespread nor particularly marked—which may tell one something about the rigidity of party ideology and their lack of responsiveness either to external problems or electoral concerns.

Some tracking of party policy changes has, of course, been done in all the studies based on the Manifesto data, as a comparison between the 'maps' they produce and what the general historical record tells us is an essential element in validating the estimates. Thus, Robertson (1976) in his pioneering study charted out British parties' changes of position from 1922–74 on the principal dimension of his two-dimensional policy space—a primarily economic Left-Right confrontation. Budge and Farlie (1977: 424–5) covered the same period for both Britain and the US in terms of a 'party-defined' space, to which every policy difference between the parties (plus demographic characteristics of the leaders) contributed. Such graphs can be examined to see if greater differences between the parties correspond to periods like the New Deal in the US or post-war reconstruction in the US, when on general historical grounds they would be expected to move apart. Generally they do.

The first broad comparative study of election programmes (Budge, Robertson and Hearl (eds.) 1987) was perhaps more concerned with the extent to which parties were different rather than when. Its general concerns lay with the nature of the policy cleavages underpinning party competition and whether these were disappearing over time—thus fostering a general convergence between parties—or sustaining themselves and producing divergence.

The operationalization of these concerns in terms of factor analyses also hampered a detailed over-time investigation. Typically the factor-analyses produced a four- or five-dimensional policy space for each country. This

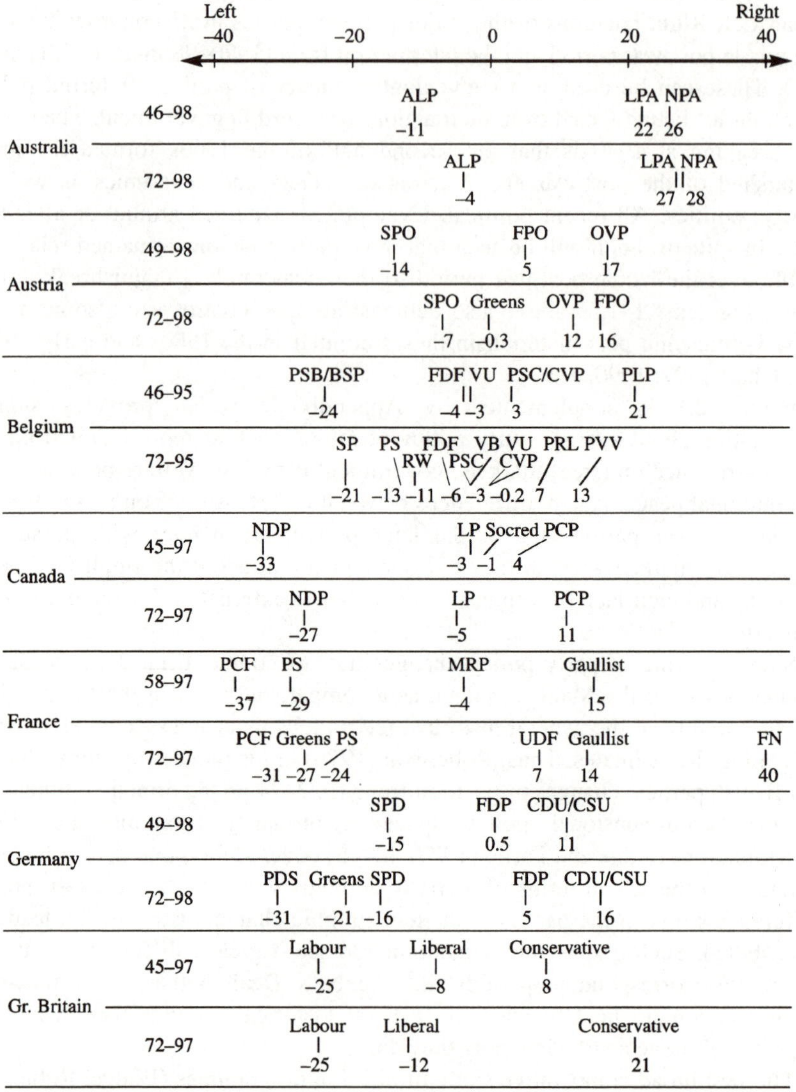

Mapping Policy Preferences

Left
-40   -20   0   20   Right 40

Australia

46–98   ALP −11   LPA NPA 22 26

72–98   ALP −4   LPA NPA 27 28

Austria

49–98   SPO −14   FPO 5   OVP 17

72–98   SPO −7   Greens −0.3   OVP 12   FPO 16

Belgium

46–95   PSB/BSP −24   FDF VU −4 −3   PSC/CVP 3   PLP 21

72–95   SP −21   PS −13   FDF −11   RW   PSC   VB −6   VU −3   CVP −0.2   PRL 7   PVV 13

Canada

45–97   NDP −33   LP −3   Socred −1   PCP 4

72–97   NDP −27   LP −5   PCP 11

France

58–97   PCF −37   PS −29   MRP −4   Gaullist 15

72–97   PCF −31   Greens −27   PS −24   UDF 7   Gaullist 14   FN 40

Germany

49–98   SPD −15   FDP 0.5   CDU/CSU 11

72–98   PDS −31   Greens −21   SPD −16   FDP 5   CDU/CSU 16

Gr. Britain

45–97   Labour −25   Liberal −8   Conservative 8

72–97   Labour −25   Liberal −12   Conservative 21

Figure 2.1. Mean party left-right positions, 1945-1998 and 1972-1998

Figure 2.1. *(continued)*

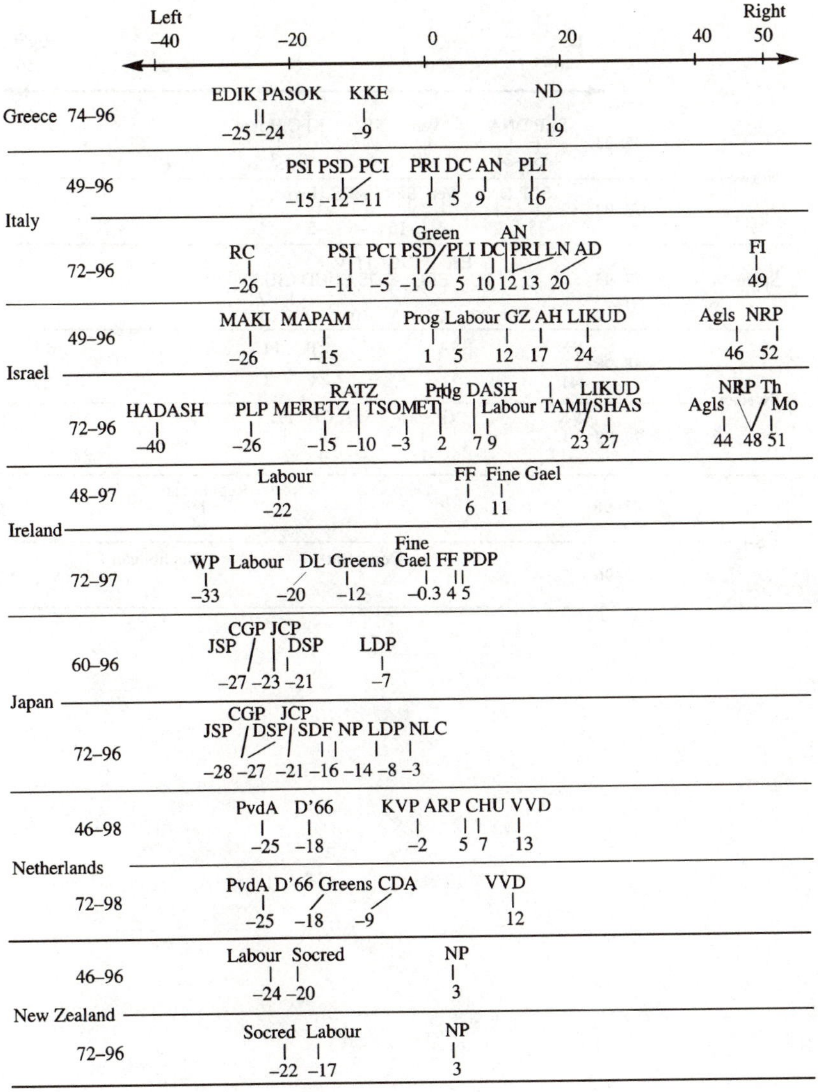

Left ... Right
-40 ... -20 ... 0 ... 20 ... 40 50

Greece 74–96
EDIK PASOK KKE ND
-25 -24 -9 19

Italy

49–96
PSI PSD PCI PRI DC AN PLI
-15 -12 -11 1 5 9 16

72–96
Green AN
RC PSI PCI PSD/PLI DC PRI LN AD FI
-26 -11 -5 -1 0 5 10 12 13 20 49

Israel

49–96
MAKI MAPAM Prog Labour GZ AH LIKUD Agls NRP
-26 -15 1 5 12 17 24 46 52

72–96
RATZ Prog DASH LIKUD NRP Th
HADASH PLP MERETZ TSOMET Labour TAMI/SHAS Agls Mo
-40 -26 -15 -10 -3 2 7 9 23 27 44 48 51

Ireland

48–97
Labour FF Fine Gael
-22 6 11

72–97
Fine
WP Labour DL Greens Gael FF PDP
-33 -20 -12 -0.3 4 5

Japan

60–96
CGP JCP
JSP DSP LDP
-27 -23 -21 -7

72–96
CGP JCP
JSP DSP SDF NP LDP NLC
-28 -27 -21 -16 -14 -8 -3

Netherlands

46–98
PvdA D'66 KVP ARP CHU VVD
-25 -18 -2 5 7 13

72–98
PvdA D'66 Greens CDA VVD
-25 -18 -9 12

New Zealand

46–96
Labour Socred NP
-24 -20 3

72–96
Socred Labour NP
-22 -17 3

Figure 2.1. *(continued)*

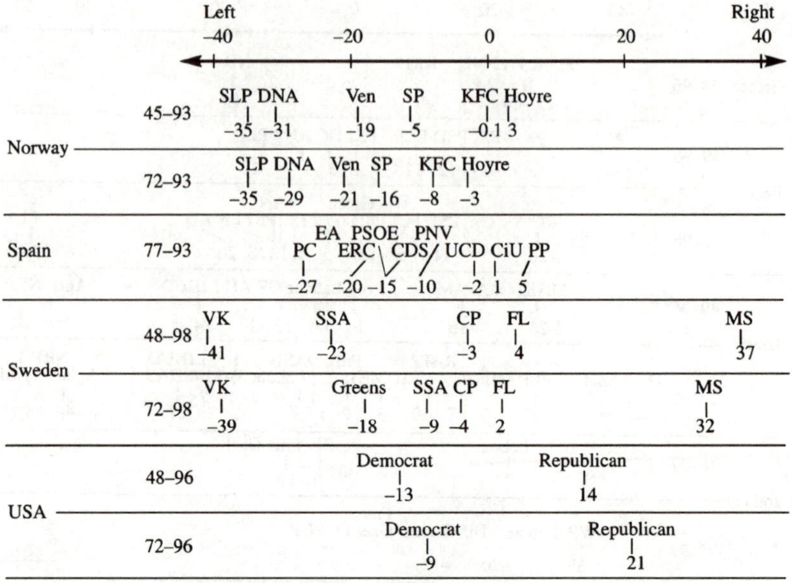

		Left −40	−20	0	20	Right 40
Norway	45–93	SLP DNA −35 −31	Ven SP −19 −5	KFC Hoyre −0.1 3		
	72–93	SLP DNA −35 −29	Ven SP −21 −16	KFC Hoyre −8 −3		
Spain	77–93		EA PSOE PNV PC ERC\ CDS/ UCD CiU PP −27 −20 −15 −10 −2 1 5			
Sweden	48–98	VK −41	SSA −23	CP FL −3 4		MS 37
	72–98	VK −39	Greens −18	SSA CP FL −9 −4 2		MS 32
USA	48–96			Democrat −13	Republican 14	
	72–96			Democrat −9	Republican 21	

combined a leading Left-Right dimension which contrary to the investigators' expectations emerged practically everywhere—and a second 'New Politics' dimension in some countries, with country-specific dimensions which had little in common with each other.

Attempts to trace movement in a two- or three-dimensional space gave rise to a less interpretable time-line than in the earlier studies. What was of interest was the extent to which parties stayed within one policy sector over time and how far different parties within the same family resembled each other rather than their co-national parties (as in fact they did).

The strong finding of this first fully comparative study, that the Left-Right dimension was the dominant and most generalizable policy continuum, across countries and over time, did however give rise to the Left-Right index used in Chapter 1 to create the graphs of party movement reported there. This was developed in order to produce a simplified space within which to represent policy-closeness, a key element in all theories of coalition-formation. It could be used as an alternative measurement-setting to the twenty-dimensional space also employed in the study and as a way of simplifying presentation. (No reduced dimensional space greater than one or less than twenty dimensions proved to generalize across countries (Laver and Budge (eds.) 1992: 15–40).

The Left-Right index was primarily powered by theory—what were the main policy differences one would expect between Left and Right? However the constituent items were then tested for unidimensionality and other items added where they proved to co-vary with those originally chosen. The result of these 'directed' factor analyses was a very generalizable comparative and over-time measure which captured central policy tendencies of the parties involved.

To substantiate this claim, both the studies which used it (Laver and Budge (eds.) 1992; Klingeman, Hofferbert, Budge *et al.* 1994) examined party movement on the Left-Right index over time, as a further way of validating the claim of the measure to get at central party policy differences. If this were the case movements along it should correspond closely to the historical record. The analyses carried out in these studies did not differ essentially from those of Chapter 1, except that shorter time series were involved. And they reached the same conclusion—that by and large party Left-Right movement, as measured by the MRG scale, corresponded surprisingly well with what one would expect from the historical record.

This is not to say that they did not on occasion weigh on the side of one historical interpretation as opposed to another, as in the case of the SPD's formal renunciation of Marxism at Bad Godesburg in 1959. The Left-Right map shows that this was neither as permanent nor so far reaching as some observers (e.g. Kirchheimer 1966) thought at the time. By the 1980s the SPD was as Left-wing as it had been in the early 1950s. Most contemporary historians of German politics would agree with this.

Parties oscillate in terms of their ideological position. But their movement is just that—oscillation and not a one way trend to the centre. The same may be said of British Labour's and US Democrats moves to Centre-Right in the 1990s: they came after earlier moves leftwards on the part of both and are quite likely to be succeeded by other Leftist moves (Evans and Norris (eds.) 1999).

In terms of the 'Big Questions' raised regularly in the post-war period about the 'Decline of Ideology' (Bell 1962) or of the Left or of the Right, one can say from these descriptive analyses that party differences along these lines continue more or less unchanged. Left-Right movement may be purposeful in particular cases (dictated by strategic and internal considerations) but overall it is also trendless. Parties are neither diverging nor converging consistently and seem overall to inhabit much the same policy sectors now as they did immediately after the war.

DIMENSIONS AND DIMENSIONALITY: THE NATURE OF PARTY SPACE

Any discussion of policy space raises the vexed question of whether it is one-, two-, three- or many-dimensional—a point which comes up even at a descriptive level. For how is one to accept a picture or a map as accurate and correct without first knowing the relevant policy dimensions to set it in?

There are obviously strong pressures towards simple and direct presentation of party movement over time along one dimension—which then has to be a Left-Right one, given its general predominance in party politics (Chapter 1). Equally, however, investigations of the Manifesto data have often produced two- (Robertson 1976; Schofield 1985), three- (Warwick 2000) and even five- (Budge, Robertson and Hearl (eds.) 1987) dimensional solutions to factor analyses. Laver and Budge (eds.) 1992) even ran parallel analyses of one-dimensional (Left-Right) and twenty-dimensional representations!

The question of which number of dimensions should be used to represent party policy space, rather than being a purely presentational one, is of fundamental theoretical importance. It has been shown (McKelvey 1976) that any set of policies party agree on is subject to defeat by an alternative combination of parties in spaces of three dimensions and above, and highly vulnerable to subversion even in two dimensions (Schofield 1985). The differing dimensionality of policy space at different times, and between politics, has thus been suggested as one explanation for differences in government stability and effectiveness (Nagel 1998).

Theoretically, analyses of the Manifesto data—the parties' own statements of policy preference—should be able to give a conclusive answer to the question of dimensionality. But as we have seen, different analyses have produced representations with varying numbers of dimensions from the same data. Our policy estimates do not speak directly to us: the answer they give depends at least in part on the way we frame the question and the techniques used to operationalize it.

This is not to say however that these data-sets cannot help. All analyses give strong indications that Left-Right divisions are the most important and strongest practically everywhere—even when the investigators were strongly sceptical of their existence (Budge, Robertson and Hearl (eds.) 1987). However, we cannot just proceed by induction from the data. We need first to step back and consider what it is we want from it.

Most investigators in this area would probably agree that the 'true' policy space is composed of as many dimensions as there are political actors and public preferences held by them—forming an underlying space of almost infinite dimensions therefore (especially if we take private preferences into account, whose translation into public ones is difficult and chancy (Budge and Farlie 1977: 172–7). Any attempt to measure this space is bound to have built-in distortions, whether the representation is one-dimensional, two-dimensional or has as many dimensions as we can handle. Indeed, compared with the leap we make from the underlying policy space to any measurable one, differences between our operationalizations of it probably fade into insignificance.

This might seem like a recipe for complete subjectivism—whichever dimensionality we choose to accept is as good as any other. And to some extent it may be true that the choice of an appropriate dimensional space depends on our own research purposes, as we can never directly examine the 'true' space.

Three considerations however impose some objectivity on our choice of representation. The first is that we want to use the space which most accurately (or with least distortion) represents the underlying one. The second is that our chosen space should be generalizable and stable across countries and time. The third is that for most research purposes we want to reflect the way that politicians and electors themselves view the world. After all it is their locations and movements that we wish to represent.

Viewing distortion as inevitable and relative frees us from the need to debate the 'true' dimensionality of the space. In one sense spaces with higher dimensionality must give a more refined picture of the underlying policy matrix as they include more detail. If they project down to a space of more limited dimensions—say from two to one—without materially affecting the relative positions of the actors, however, this greater level of refinement is irrelevant and we would on grounds of parsimony prefer the simpler representation.

The only systematic comparison between spaces of higher and lower dimensionality was to our knowledge that carried through in Laver and Budge (eds.) 1992. Not only was a search carried out to see which spaces were generalizable across ten countries—as it turned out, only the Left-Right and a twenty-dimensional representation. But these two representations were used in parallel to measure policy distances and test a whole range of theories. In these comparisons the Left-Right continuum used in Chapter 1 performed equally well as the twenty-dimensional representation. This investigation also added two important new measurement considerations to the dimensionality debate:

(a) How should one measure policy distance in a multi-dimensional space. Usually Euclidean distance is just assumed so we define the shortest distances between two points as a straight line. Experiments (Laver and Budge (eds.) 1992: 32–8) showed however that the best choice (at least for looking at coalitions with Manifesto data), was a 'city-block' metric, in which distances between parties were calculated independently for each dimension and then added up. This has implications for the stability of party policy agreements and coalitions. Separable dimensions of this kind always have a median point which is preferred by a majority of actors to all others (Ordeshook 1986, 250).

(b) How one constructs a policy space from relevant estimates affects its stability and comparability. Van der Brug (1999) among others has pointed out that factor analysis may be useful for exploring the dimensionality of data sets. As a basis for constructing scales however the resulting factor scores are highly dependent on the particular set of cases included. To take an extreme example, the factor analytic estimate for Swedish Social Democrats in 1992 depends in part on the position of Italian Neo-fascists in 1948. This is because the scores are inductively derived from the overall configuration of the data. Add or subtract parties or time points and the configuration and resulting scores may change. This is a weakness both of the factor-analytic scores used in earlier work by the Manifesto Research Group and of some later analyses (Robertson 1976; Budge, Robertson and Hearl (eds.) 1987; Gabel and Huber 2000; Webb, 2000).

The solution to creating a Left-Right dimension adopted in Laver and Budge (eds.) 1992) is elaborated in Chapter 1 and summarized above (see Table 1.1). This was to use the simple percentage frequency for each individual policy-item, subtracting the sum of Left percentages from the sum of Right percentages. Factor analyses were used to *test* the unidimensionality of the scale and to search out other items which might relate to it. But they were not used in its construction which was basically theory-driven: what, on the basis of ideological writing and commentary, would one expect Left-Right differences to be?

So far as our data are capable of settling the dimensionality question therefore, the tendency of the various investigations has been to evolve towards a Left-Right, unidimensional solution. The real answer however may be procedural rather than substantive. Induction based on factor analysis or similar techniques is bound to give different answers when different data-sets are involved. Thus different policy spaces will be produced for different countries and even analyses of the whole set of estimates for the entire post-war period will be liable to change from the addition of new election material. And elections are always recurring.

To some extent this is of course what we would expect from analyses of party systems: both from the effect of different electoral rules and from the existence of different social cleavages, as in Lipset and Rokkan's (1967) classic treatment. Their specification of religions, urban-rural, centre-periphery or ethnic divisions in addition to class points to multi-dimensionality of the policy space, along with national variations in cleavages and thus in the number of important dimensions, which explain the different shapes of national party systems.

It is significant however that Lipset and Rokkan (1967: 20–1, 46, 50) also recognize the dominance of the Left-Right, class-based cleavage. The major systematic check on Lipset and Rokkan's ideas (Bartolini and Mair 1990) also conducts its analysis exclusively in terms of this one dimension on the grounds of its centrality to electoral politics, generalizability and stability. These are precisely the criteria which we want to apply to spatial representations in general, and they do seem to argue in favour of one-dimensionality and the Left-Right dimension.

Besides the way analysts view policy we should also include as a central consideration—if not *the* central consideration—the way politicians, electors and media regard it. This is certainly given in part by the manifesto evidence, but only in part, since as we have noted theoretical perspectives shape the interpretation of the estimates. Budge (1994) has suggested that the electoral debate becomes increasingly simplified and consolidated into Left-Right differences during the run up to polling day. Only in terms of a single dimension of differences can complex issues be rendered intelligible for mass debate. Left-Right ideology is already there to focus current differences and the media in particular use it and practically force it on electors and parties alike.

The tendency is reinforced by the fact that the major national parties by definition have well defined locations on this central aspect of politics. It is generally not in their interest to let new issues like minority grievances or environmentalism increase the electoral uncertainty they are already in. So they generally accept and reinforce the Left-Right framework of election debate. Votes then have their choices defined for them in Left-Right terms. Other issues are either confined to particular minorities and thus separated from general discussion; or more likely slide into the Left-Right dimension as particular instances of traditionalism or maldistribution or other concepts familiar from ideological discussion.

Once the elected government gets going this election synthesis may fall apart, as policy debates tend to mirror bureaucratic and legislative organization, focussing on the concerns of particular ministries such as Finance, Environment, Foreign, Transport, etc. But if policy space thereby becomes multi-dimensional the dimensions are debated each on its own and are therefore separable. They are only drawn together, imperfectly but compellingly, into a new Left-Right confrontation for the next election.

These thus seem good grounds for shifting the debate over dimensionality from a straightforwardly inductive to a hypothetical approach. The compelling reasons for representing policy space as a unidimensional Left-Right continuum should be accepted until the latter can be conclusively shown to be untenable. The advantages of the Left-Right representation are clear. It produces stable majorities (Black 1956). It produces a simple and direct picture of party systems and of party competition (Downs 1957) generalizable like no other over time and space (Chapter 1 above). It taps into the central issues of politics even if it distorts or omits less central and more transient issues. It bases itself theoretically on the major ideological and social cleavage of the modern world (Bartolini and Mair 1990) and subsumes many of the minor ones.

Acceptance and use of Left-Right unidimensionality should not however form an article of faith. If it can be shown to work badly over a majority of comparative cases it should be rejected in favour of a better alternative. Its current advantages and empirical support—from, but not solely from, the Manifesto data—are such however that a very strong case needs to be made for rejection or substitution. Where the evidence against its general use remains as partial and inconclusive as it is now, the derived spatial representation should remain as the setting for studies of party competition and government formation. Such, at any rate, is the lesson to be taken from Manifesto-based studies.

PARTY COMPETITION AND POLICY EQUILIBRIA

This conclusion is opportune for comparative studies of party competition, which—carrying on from Downs (1957)—have usually been set in Left-Right space. As noted in our introduction, the ability to operationalize and check Downsian theories of policy convergence and divergence was one of the driving forces behind textual analysis and led directly to Robertson's (1976) pioneering analyses of British party manifestos between 1922 and 1974 and of candidates' constituency addresses for two post-war elections.

A Left-Right 'map' has the additional advantage of clear visual presentation, which aids theoretical induction from parties' patterned movements over time. Its power is such that Robertson, who as we have seen proposed a two-dimensional representation for British policy space, conducted most checks of his theory in terms of the dominant Left-Right continuum.

Apart from his modified Downsian hypothesis about party policy movement, examined below, the saliency theory underlying his and the derived MRG codings is also, in a more general way, a theory of how parties interact and compete. We shall examine this set of ideas more explicitly in the next Chapter (see in particular Table 3.1). Summarizing, this theory sees parties as trying to make 'their' issues prominent in an election (by highlighting them in their manifestos) and de-emphasizing rival issues. The issues parties 'own' are those on which they have a track record of carrying out the most popular preference— cutting taxes and observing financial orthodoxy in general, extending social services, seeking peace et cetera (c.f. Saglie's (1998) use of MRG estimates to map 'Norwegian Parties and the European Issues' 1989–95). If parties are indeed tied to particular issues one overwhelming consequence follows—they cannot change policy very much and hence will not move a great deal in policy space. They will stick to the segment in which they are located in terms of underlying ideology. Any movement they do make by selective emphasis and de-emphases of certain of their issues will be confined within that segment. Consequently they will not 'leapfrog' a great deal and then only over contiguous parties. All these expectations are empirically confirmed by analyses of the Manifesto data over 20 post-war democracies (Budge 1994). They constitute more evidence for the validity of Saliency ideas, which are put in context in Chapter 3.

Robertson's (1976) modified Downsian hypothesis added dynamic detail about the type of party movement to be expected under different election circumstances. Parties would only need to gain votes, and thus move to the centre, when they saw the election as competitive so extra votes were needed to win. Where they expected to clearly win or lose they had no need for extra votes. Their priorities then shifted to reassuring their own supporters by reaffirming traditional priorities, and moving to the extremes.

The weakness of Robertson's test of these ideas was his lack of a measure of party expectations other than the subsequent election result itself. He had to assume perfect information and certainty on the part of strategists who could fine tune the manifesto in light of this. This is surely unrealistic. A counter hypothesis would be that politicians are incorrigible optimists who always think they have a chance otherwise they would not be in the game at all, thus they would always wish to pick up votes. This brings us back to the original Downsian hypothesis of general convergence at the centre under two-party competition (Downs 1957: 90–120).

However, the modified assumption about policy convergence depending on electoral circumstances was supported in the case of the Conservative Party in Britain, though less so in the case of Labour from 1922–74 (Robertson, 1976, Chaps 4 and 6). A later analysis by Budge and Farlie (1977: 428–33) for both British and American parties over the same period, set within a 'party-defined space', found support for the idea ranging from 55% of party moves to 77%.

A subsequent manifesto-based study by Budge (1994) modified Robertson's (and Downs') assumption of almost total certainty and perfect information among party strategists to one of almost total uncertainty. This was felt to account for the relative immobility of parties in general. In the absence of any reliable information about popular preferences it was best to move little and incrementally, for fear of losing the votes one had last time.

Previous election results were in fact the best indicators politicians had of how their moves were being received by the public. Where their vote went up, their reaction was either to stay in the same place or more cautiously further in the previous direction. Where vote had gone down they changed direction. This hypothesis is supported in an analysis of overall correlations between all 54 standard manifesto categories in the previous and present election programmes, carried out for Britain, Germany and the US from the 1950s to the 1980s (Janda, Harmel, Edens and Goff 1995). Programme content was found most likely to change after a bad election result.

Under radical uncertainty however some politicians might even discount previous results on grounds of the (unknown) changes taking place among electors. In the absence of any trustworthy external indicators at all, the risk averse might choose to stay where they were and never move, while risk-acceptant strategists might always move in the opposite direction from last time, producing a zig-zag pattern of policy changes without reference to election results.

All of these decision rules are rational under near-total uncertainty. Budge's investigation was directed therefore not to checking which applied overall, but which was used by different parties over the various countries. Robertson's rule was admitted as an alternative which might be used in some cases, as the electoral situation might allow for more predictive ability under certain rules and party systems.

Overall the alternation model (change policy direction each time) fitted the largest number of parties, followed by the 'past results' model and Robertson's 'rational expectation' model. The general level of predictive success for the models in the cases where they fitted best was around 0.68. While these are reasonably impressive results, Burt (1997) has pointed out that the results obtained from the alternation model are not clearly distinguishable from what might appear by chance.

A follow-up to Budge's analysis (Adams 1998) seeks to unify party decision rules by postulating that in addition to policy preferences, voters are motivated by non-policy considerations arising from leadership or candidate attractiveness, predispositions rooted in class and religious or organizational affiliations, strong identification with parties and so on. On this basis parties are motivated to differentiate their policy proposals from each other, and to vary them over time, but incrementally and without leapfrogging—just as appears empirically in Figures 1.1 to 1.25.

In operational terms, outer parties tend to move up on centre parties, especially when they are further away from them. By doing so they can detach a certain number of centrist policy-oriented votes from the centre party. Gains, however, are limited because many centrist supporters continue to vote for that party on non-policy grounds. To staunch the flow of policy-oriented electors who do leave, the centre party also moves towards the position of the challenger who then loses votes, making it advisable to retreat to a more extreme (Left or Right) position. This, however, gives parties on the other wing the chance to move in on the Centre, to which the centre party responds by moving to the other side of its range.

There is thus a continued oscillation of policy positions in a characteristic zig-zag pattern but little major change owing to the ability of each party to check the others, helped by the continuing support of biased voters.

This model produces plausible patterns of movement for both the British and French cases. In the British case it obtains a postdictive success of 0.66 or two-thirds of actual movements made. The explanation is appealing—both because it is unified, and because it fits in with many models of voting which combine long term predispositions with short-term issue-attractiveness.

All of the analyses of competition applied to the MRG produce expectations and outcomes of non-convergent policy equilibria. This is in contrast to a whole tradition of theory and (non-empirical) modelling stemming from Downs' analysis of two-party competition which expects parties to move towards the same policy position, even under imperfect information (c.f. McKelvey and Ordeshook, 1985a) and b)). So powerful is this expectation that many analysts in the field are not prepared to accept non-convergent positions as an equilibrium (in the sense of a point of rest or a situation which parties tend towards in the long-run) (c.f. Coughlin 1992; Calvert, 1986; Ordeshook, 1986).

It matters not that Downs himself (1957: 112) described the expectation of convergence under two-party competition as merely a hypothesis subject to testing, nor that in a multi party system (1957, 122–3) (which most are) he expects a non-convergent equilibrium to be reached. Contemporary economic theories of competition and mathematical modelling have as their criterion of success the achievement of convergent equilibria based on the position of the median voter. There is an implicit normative assumption built in here, that as only the position of the median voter maximizes satisfaction for everyone, this is the only truly democratic outcome to the process and any other outcome is suboptimal (Budge *et al.* 1998: 664–7).

However this may be, the weight of evidence from the Manifesto data among others, is that non-convergent policy-equilibria are the norm in party competition. Where they occur in a multi-party system with coalition governments however, this may result in the middle or median party almost always becoming a member of the government. We look at this possibility and what analyses of our data say about it, in the next section.

PARTY POLICY AND GOVERNMENT COALITIONS

Most explanations of how coalitions and other governments form base themselves on policy relationships in some shape or form. Even 'minimal winning' formulations founded on the desire to maximize participant payoffs (Riker 1962) rapidly incorporated policy considerations (c.f. Budge and Laver 1986, for an analytic overview).

The policy estimates provided by the Manifesto data are thus ideal for operationalizing and testing coalition theories. Being based on government programmes and declarations they provide an exceptionally pure indication of agreed coalition policy. From a comparison between this and the position of individual parties we can get an idea of the payoffs awarded to winners and losers in the system. From this we can check the assumption implicit in most rational choice accounts that parties join coalitions because they get something out of them.

Our estimates have been drafted into the service of coalition theory in two ways. The first is to check current models of government formation and policy payoffs to coalition partners. Here the emphasis has been on the extent to which the models, (generally fairly simple ones, operationalizable in one-dimensional space), have successfully and uniquely predicted the governments which form. The second use has been to illustrate more complex mathematical theories grappling with problems of government formation in two dimensions (Baron 1991; Schofield 1993). Here the Manifesto data have been employed illustratively and heuristically to show that the theory is capable of generating results applicable to the real world. However, strong predictions have not been generated because of the complexities involved.

Tests of a variety of coalition theories are reported in the second 'book report' of the Manifesto Research Group edited by Laver and Budge (1992). Results are summarized in Budge and Laver (1993). Theories range from minimal (connected) winning models where contiguous parties on the Left-Right continuum join up to form the smallest majority government they can, to a 'cluster tree' (Grofman 1982) in twenty dimensions, where the idea is that parties join the first majority coalition that forms on the basis of proximity. Only two theories were predictively successful: that Governments are formed by 'connected parties' on the Left-Right continuum and that governments contain the median party defined either in terms of position on the Left-Right continuum or on a majority of twenty separable dimensions.

The problem with both these theories is that their postdictions are successful but not unique: that is, they do identify the governments that formed but at the same time predict many governments that did not form. Blunderbuss predictions have more chance of success but are also of course less informative than unique ones.

However the finding that four fifths of (mostly coalition) governments include the middle party is interesting in light of the previous discussion. One may not get convergence to the median through electoral competition but one does get it through coalition negotiations, which often proceed in complete independence of the election result. A median party in government is in a powerful bargaining position as it is essential to both cabinet and/or legislative majorities and should normally be able to bargain to get the majority supported policy close to its own (median) position (otherwise it can go over to the opposition and achieve this result with them). Through giving power to the median party governments may produce the best policy outcomes for everybody in a way that straight election competition may not (Lijphart 1984).

The second way the estimates have been used is to illustrate, rather than test, mathematical theories. These try to identify policy points which an unchallengeable majority of parties could agree as government policy, given various configurations of their own preferences in multi-dimensional Euclidean space. The Manifesto estimates are useful in indicating what configurations emerge, empirically, and whether they are ones that would give rise to a stable equilibrium point or area.

Two major articles have used the estimates in this way. In the first David Baron (1991) developed a theory of government formation in parliamentary systems from a model which incorporates policy-oriented parties with spatial preferences and a formation process in which parties are selected in sequence to attempt to form a government. A two-dimensional policy space is assumed. A government is formed when the policy proposed by the party selected is sustained on a vote of confidence. The policy equilibria identify the government and the policy it will implement and depend on the configuration of party preferences and on the government formation process. For example, in a political system with two large parties and one small party where one of the large parties will be selected to attempt to form a government, the government will be formed by a large party with the support of the small party. The policy will reflect the preferences of the small party but will be closer to the ideal point of the large party.

In equilibrium, parties make proposals that reflect their and other parties' future opportunities to make and to support or oppose policy proposals. The theory thus provides a set of internally consistent predictions about government formation. Those predictions are in general probabilistic and institution-dependent and the theory indicates that a variety of governments could form depending on preferences and on the structure of the formation process. The predictions are thus induced by preferences and by institutional structure. Although equilibria depend on structure and preferences they share several qualitative features:

1. Equilibrium policy proposals reflect the preferences of the parties both in and out of government

2. A small party is very likely to be in government under a selection procedure or fixed order involving the two larger parties

3. A centrally located party is highly likely to have the government policy located at or near its ideal point, establishing another version of the median voter theorem already supported by the empirical findings above.

Schofield's (1993) article on Political Competition and Multiparty coalition governments does not take sequential bargaining into account. It focuses instead on a competitive two-dimensional model of multiparty coalition behaviour in which parties are concerned with policy outcomes but choose party positions both with a view to electoral consequences and as a basis for coalition bargaining. The *political heart* is proposed as the set of possible coalition outcomes. The heart is either the core of the political game or is determined by a small number of party positions. Under certain circumstances an equilibrium in the choice of party positions can be shown to exist. The model suggests that parties can be categorized as either weak or strong core parties, anti-core parties or peripheral parties. This implies a typology of party systems which gives some theoretical foundation for the occurrence of minority, minimal winning and surplus coalitions in many European countries in the post-war period. The data used is largely derived from the MRG dataset which is essentially factor analyzed to provide two-dimensional representations of the main political issues in the states under investigation. Schofield's interpretation assumes that the estimates are subject to considerable error.

Three patterns emerged from the analysis:

i)   In unipolar or unbalanced systems a strong left wing party faces several bourgeois competitors. Governments are either minority social democrat or a bourgeois coalition.

ii) In multipolar systems a centrally located Christian party is able to determine negotiations for government formation which leads to minimal winning coalitions.

iii) In fragmented core systems a Christian party typically faces four others, giving it a strong position for negotiation.

Given the assumptions regarding error, the manifesto data yielded stable party patterns of these kinds over many years.

European party systems have, of course, been frequently characterized in terms of a rather similar typology (Sartori 1976). However, Schofield's argument gives a theoretical underpinning to these descriptions, provided that the assumption of two dimensions to the (Euclidean) policy space is accepted. One-dimensional assumptions would not of course generate the problem of unstable equilibria in the first place.

The earlier MRG study (Laver and Budge (eds.) 1992) also found that party payoffs varied with the party system. Where the centrist Christian democrats were almost permanently in government, other parties did not see their preferences being implemented to any great extent (at least as far as the formal programme was concerned). Sometimes parties out of government saw more of their preferences being reflected than those within. Only the Christian democrats got a constant payoff. Where, however, electoral alliances alternated in government, as in Scandinavia post-1970, the partners did decrease the distance between their own and the government programme. Presumably getting more rewards improved coalition satisfaction and stability, although this question was not followed up in the study.

Relating party programmes to government ones begins to raise the question of how far parties can and want to carry through their election promises in government. The Manifesto estimates have also been used as a basis for mandate and output studies relating party priorities to government expenditures. We review these studies in the next section.

PARTY MANDATES AND GOVERNMENT OUTPUTS

Democracy is justified normatively as a system which makes public policy responsive to the wishes of citizens. Studying responsiveness involves relating election programmes to survey responses, or public opinion polls, which are the pre-eminent source of information about the wishes of the electorate. Surrogates for the latter are general economic indicators, as one can assume that prosperity will please electors and downturns worry them. The studies which have related such indicators to manifesto emphases have come to somewhat contradictory conclusions. On the one hand Keman (1997: 197) finds that party policy emphases are generally responsive to labour and market conditions: when these deteriorate the parties mention the economy more. Pennings (1998) also using MRG data found on the other hand little variation in parties' emphasis on their main economic policies of planning and market reliance, in response to economic conditions. Of course, it would be quite consistent for parties to increase emphases at a general level in response to electoral concerns while remaining committed to their characteristic policies for dealing with them at a more specific level. This would be consistent with evidence cited earlier that they do not change their ideological positions very much over time. Klingemann (1995) examining parties' mean policy positions on a Left-Right dimension over the post-war period, also found them very stable.

Government responsiveness to electoral preferences could be secured not by parties responding directly to these but by them paradoxically offering a fixed and stable policy choice. Electors could then choose the party whose programme seemed best adapted to prevailing conditions. This would satisfy conditions for the operation of a party mandate, which Sullivan and O'Conner (1972) have summarized as involving four conditions for public control over policy:

1. Parties offer votes a policy choice

2. Voters are aware of that choice

3. Electors vote on the basis of their policy choice

4. The parties in control of government follow policies consistent with the policy option they placed before the electorate.

Analyses of manifesto data clearly cannot address conditions 2 and 3, about electoral control, very directly. But they can address the questions of whether parties do offer a choice and whether they carry through the policy choice they have offered to electors in government.

On the nature of the policy choice they offer, Chapter 1 has already demonstrated a main finding based on our estimates, that in general Left-Right terms, parties keep themselves very distinct (see also Budge 1994). Klingemann's (1995) analysis of West European parties' mean policy positions as shown by Manifesto data also demonstrates this. Members of the main party families (Communist, Socialist, Christian, Liberal and Conservatives) have clearly differentiated policy positions. Moreover these correspond quite well to the ideological preferences of their supporters, as estimated on *Eurobarometer* responses.

Parties' relative inflexibility and commitment to their underlying ideology both clarify choices for electors and give them a concrete incentive—quite distinct from and perhaps more powerful than their moral requirements under the mandate—to carry through their policy priorities in government. Various manifesto-based studies have tried to estimate how this works out in practice. Doing so, however, requires the collection of information additional to that in the manifestos themselves, which can be very difficult for comparative study over an extended time-period. Basically three research strategies have been pursued up to this point (this is apart from the separate studies of specific election pledges, mentioned in the introduction):

(a)   The actual government programme, announced either annually or at the beginning of the term of office, can be coded into categories comparable to the manifesto ones and the congruence between the two estimated (Laver and Budge (eds.) 1992). One set of estimates contained in the accompanying disk actually provides such estimates for ten countries for a thirty year period in the post-war era.

The problem with seeing how far emphases get carried over by each party into the programme is twofold. First of all the government declaration itself relates only to intentions, not completed acts. We need also to know how far the programme gets effected in legislation or other government actions.

Secondly parties' failure to get their policies into a programme may in the case of coalition and minority governments reflect their weak bargaining position rather than any failure of intent. Indeed, Laver and Budge (1992) found that policies got into the programme more effectively where there was alternation of electoral alliances rather than classic negotiated coalitions.

(b)   These two problems have inhibited the use of government declarations to check mandate theory. The obvious alternative is to compare manifesto priorities with legislation and important administrative decisions. The problem here relates to coding and processing the vast mass of texts in which such decisions are summarized. Here computerization may help, provided we can validate the procedures (Chapter 7 below). At the moment however manual codings have to be employed. The expense and time needed for these has limited development of an index of legislative/administrative output to just one country, the United States (Stimson, McKuen and Erikson 1995). The relationship between the US parties' Left-Right positions and the relative 'liberalism' of their actions in government is very strong and significant (r=.81), indicating that they do carry through their election priorities in government. We can probably generalize this relationship elsewhere, though we have as yet no direct evidence for it (McDonald, Budge and Hofferbert 1999).

(c) The most readily available measure of government output on a comparative basis are expenditures in various policy areas. These can be related to manifesto emphases on the corresponding areas, so party priorities can be matched directly to government ones. Of course, expenditures are far from the whole of policy, but they are a good indicator of government seriousness and commitment.

The studies of the relationship carried out for single countries (Budge and Hofferbert 1990, 1992; Petry, 1988; 1991; 1995; Gibbons, 2000) and comparatively (Klingemann *et al.* 1994) all show a good correspondence between variations in emphasis and fluctuations in policy expenditures. Not all of the relationship is accounted for by government party(ies)' emphases anticipating expenditure trends. In some countries and policy areas 'agenda' effects are equally important: that is, party emphases anticipate expenditures whether the party is in or out of office. One might be tempted to attribute this to the lack of clear distinctions between government and opposition in coalition systems, but in fact 'Westminster type' systems are not clearly distinguishable from the latter in regard to 'agenda' and 'mandate' effects (Klingemann *et al.* 1994: 256–61).

King and Laver (1993) have pointed out that the relationship between platform emphases and expenditures cannot be regarded as causal, since there is no statistically significant effect once the previous years expenditure is related to current expenditure. Three points can be made in relation to this:

(a) their 'control model' may have been mispecified in the sense that the use of previous expenditure to 'explain' present expenditure vacuums up all previous effects including possible past effects from manifestos (Thorne, 1999) and accepts anomalous results (Hofferbert, Budge and McDonald 1993). Gibbons (2000: Chapter 9) using alternative control procedures, upholds manifesto effects for Britain and New Zealand.

(b) expenditure changes may be too slow from year to year to show clear party influences on them (owing to constraints such as contracts, half-finished building work and so on). However, causal effects can be demonstrated for expenditure targets, which are more susceptible to change from government to government (McDonald, Budge and Hofferbert 1999).

(c) in any case the mandate model as summarized above (Sullivan and O'Conner 1972) does not require causal relationships to be established between manifesto emphases and policy changes—only that government parties follow policies consistent with manifesto commitments.

Direct effects from parties entering government would of course be sufficient to establish the existence of a mandate but are not necessary for it. The literature on power (Easton (ed.) 1966) is replete with possibilities of anticipated reactions (bureaucrats read party programmes and institute actions they think will have popular support) or of concurrent action (manifestos identify problems in the same way and at the same time or slightly later, than bureaucrats).

Claiming that manifestos have a signaling rather than strictly causal function (at least as far as current expenditures are concerned) might imply that government policy could as well be predicted by baseball scores as manifesto emphases (King and Laver 1999). But, of course, electors do not look to baseball scores to get some indication of what they are voting for. They read platforms and manifestos—or more likely, respond to media comment based on these.

The debate about whether mandates work, and the manifestos role in regard to Government policy, cannot therefore be resolved on purely statistical grounds— particularly as testing is hampered by sluggish expenditure changes. As legislation and administrative practices can be altered drastically without the same constraints it is here that we probably ought to look for statistical effects. One can anticipate future research concentrating on this area, with or without computerized textual analysis. Any testing of party influence on policy, whether in terms of a popular mandate or simple agenda setting, will certainly have to base itself on manifesto based estimates of party preferences however, since manifestos are the only statement of policy that parties as such ever make.

THE MANIFESTO DATA: FUTURE RESEARCH

This last observation already indicates one direction in which manifesto research will go—relating party programmatic estimates to legislative and administrative policy-making. Whether coding is manual or computerized, research in this area will go ahead, and will clearly draw on the estimates reported here.

Relating party preferences to government output fills in one end of an overall model of democratic policy-making. At the other end we want to know how party policy is shaped—in response to electoral preferences, to developments in society and economy, or to the emphases both get in the media. Some of these relationships, plus other interactions between social developments such as the impact of public opinion on media coverage, have already been modeled in a single country context (Kleinnijenhuis and Rietberg 1995; Evans, Heath and Payne 1999). Comparative analyses would sort out what is common to democracies everywhere in these relationships and what is peculiar to specific countries. The cross national over time estimates reported here offer a stimulus to, and a basis for, such an extension of the analyses.

The analysis of vast numbers of texts—legal, administrative, journalistic—cries out for computerized analyses and will surely be only partially carried through without them. Our estimates offer a standard for validating computerized results as we explain below (Chapter 7). Of course the policy estimates we examine below derive from party policy programmes not other types of texts. So thoroughly have these programmes been analyzed by manual techniques, however, that the ability of computer processing to produce close matches would constitute convincing evidence of its likely validity when applied elsewhere. Our estimates would thus retain a useful validating function even if computers were turning out similar estimates—which is still not the case unfortunately (Chapter 7).

Other extensions for the existing estimates are suggested in Chapter 8, where median voter and government preferences are mapped on their basis by Kim and Fording (1998). Having precise indications of voter, government and party preferences will help provide measured time series, for econometric models for example, which have so far had to infer political variables from discrepancies between economically predicted, and actual results (c.f. Sanders and Price 1993). With measured variables based on the manifesto estimates such models could now incorporate political variables on *a priori* theoretical rather than *ad hoc* grounds, thus improving both the quality and (hopefully) the predictive capacity of the models.

Thinking of new uses for the estimates is not, of course, to imply that the applications reviewed in this chapter could not be extended. We have indicated how much more could be done in relating programmatic intentions to other types of government output. Spatial models of competition could also be refined and unified into a general theory (Adams and Merrill 1998). Policy-based models of coalition formation have so far failed the checks we have been able to mount with our data. They need improvement, possibly by incorporating factors such as party size and long-standing cleavages (Budge and .Laver 1993). There is in short still much fruitful work to be done on the basis of the measurements reported with this book—indeed, their full utilization has only just begun in a discipline crying out for validated, over time comparative policy time series.

3

Theory and Measurement of Party Policy Positions

Ian Budge

THE IMPORTANCE OF HAVING A MEASUREMENT THEORY

Previous chapters have reviewed the results of coding party election programmes, and the various ways estimates have been applied. As we have pointed out however documents do not speak for themselves, at least if one wants to summarize them statistically as we have done. Assumptions have to be made about what is important in the text and what can be left out. These, if traced far enough back, turn out to involve a whole theory of party competition about what we think are the major aims of the party strategists writing these programmes and how they seek to effect them.

Too often measurement procedures are taken as 'obvious' when in fact they are anything but. The whole history of 'expert judgements' of party policy positions demonstrates this. Political scientists and practitioners were asked to locate political parties across countries on Left-Right or other policy scales with no reflection as to how these 'experts' were going to make such judgements (Castles and Mair 1984; Laver and Hunt 1992). Were they all going to use the same criteria? (Huber and Inglehart 1995)—if so, what criteria? Were these appropriate for the tasks for which the measures would be used, e.g. tracing movement over time (Knutsen 1998)? Were they measures of preference, of party behaviour in government, or were both conflated? What time point did they actually refer to—the year they were made, the whole post-war or the relevant decade (Budge 2000)?

Similar considerations apply to the question of how parties make their issue appeals to voters. Many have felt, since parties are in competition, that they must go in for yah-boo responses over the whole range of issues. Thus once one party takes some stand on a particular issue, e.g. taxes, others will oppose it by taking up alternative stands. In the case of taxes this would mean some parties advocating cuts and others supporting increases.

Once the gut feeling that parties must oppose each other on everything is really examined and applied to particular issues like taxes, the choice of appropriate competitive strategies ceases to appear quite so obvious, however. Most electors oppose tax increases. Is a party going to stick its neck out by committing itself to a policy which an overwhelming majority oppose? Certainly a range of policies is theoretically open to endorsement but does prudence not point to endorsing only one? The same might be said for other issues involving, for example, services. Given that large numbers benefit from health and welfare provision, are there voting gains in directly advocating cuts simply to distinguish oneself from rivals who say 'preserve them'? What about drugs and criminals? Of course, one could, theoretically advocate 'soft' positions to contrast with a rivals' hard-line, but would this pay off electorally?

Some counter-intuitive arguments (notably Downs 1957; Stokes 1966), see competitive pressures, at least in a two party competitive situation, as driving all parties to endorse the same position inside each issue area, ending up with a situation in which all parties have the same overall policy stand. Most actual findings however—including those based on the Manifesto estimates, find parties differentiating themselves consistently from each other in Left-Right terms (Chap 1) and on other aggregate policy scales (Evans and Norris, (eds.) 1999; Klingemann *et al.* 1994).

Does this mean that parties do in fact take up contradictory stands, however unpopular, across all specific issue-areas? Does this confirm gut feelings that the essence of party strategy must be to oppose contrasting policies whenever and wherever they can? There is an alternative, which involves distinguishing between party positions at the level of specific issues and their general political priorities across issues (Section 5 below). Parties may by and large endorse the same specific issue stands but still prioritize them differently. This is a tactic which also fits general common sense impressions Left wing parties do not emphasize tax-cutting but stress the expansion of welfare, while Right wing parties do the opposite. Other oppositions such as those between a war-like and pacific stance also occur. No party wishes to be accused of leaving the country weak and unprepared—but neither will it wish to be seen opposing peace. One can nevertheless differentially emphasize threats to security compared to opportunities for negotiation, and such varying priorities do quite clearly differentiate *overall* party stands.

QUALITIES OF AN AUTHORITATIVE MEASURE OF
PARTY POLICY POSITIONS

This saliency theory of party competition is the one the manifesto codes and estimates are based on. It is less intuitive and 'obvious' than a belief in party confrontation at all levels, but seems to fit the textual evidence better—as we shall see below. The important point to emphasize however is that there is no getting away from theory in this kind of measurement. The most seemingly intuitive and obvious measures base themselves on some kind of general assumption, however implicit it may be. The only way to evaluate a measure properly is to take account of its theoretical justification and evaluate this along with the other properties which contribute to its measurement standing.

We can generalize this point to ask what are the qualities which we would desire in a good measure of party policies? Making these explicit will guide discussion not only in the present chapter, which is largely concerned with the theory on which measurement is based, but also in the three following chapters—concerned with more conventional tests of validity and reliability. A set of useful measurement qualities is briefly summarized in Table 3.1.

Table 3.1. Desirable qualities of an authoritative measure of party policy positions

---

1. A clear accompanying explanation of why and how it is derived and what it measures (an underlying measurement theory).

2. Reduction of subjective judgement—aimed at reflecting as closely as possible the way the party spontaneously presents itself (described in the theory).

3. Validation of the measurement theory through direct inbuilt checks.

4. Face validation through its good operationalization of general models and plausible results.

5. Desirable measurement properties e.g. invariance of measure over time and space, suitability for statistical analysis (including graphs) creation of useful indicators, particularly a Left-Right scale.

6. Supports controlled development of its measures (e.g. computerized text processing).

This re-confirms what we have said about the importance of theory. The first and most important aspect of measurement (1) is to have a clear account of what aspect of the text one wishes to measure, and why. Specifying what is being done and how, reduces the element of uncheckable subjective judgement in the measurement (at its maximum in expert judgements but also present for example when analysts are determined to identify specific confrontations however much parties may try to avoid them) (Laver and Hunt 1992; Harmel, Janda and Tan 1995). In contrast a good measurement theory should aim to reflect the strategic intentions of the authors of the text (2). That is, if we think parties do compete in terms of issue priorities and avoid taking minority stands on specific issues, we should say so and base our procedures on this point—as our coding here by and large does.

A measurement theory, like all empirical theories, should expose itself to empirical checks so far as possible (3). It is not always in fact possible to do this since we face a chicken and egg problem. That is, if the measurement theory seems plausible, measurements are then constructed to be in conformity to it. The only way one can check that they work is if they then produce generally plausible results and successfully operationalize other general theories and models of the phenomena they are dealing with. To a large extent the MRG coding has already passed this general check with the charts of Left-Right movement in Chapter 1.

However, as we shall see, our coding has also had built-in checks put in at a certain cost in terms of consistency and reliability. Scepticism on the part of certain members of the Manifesto Research Group at the very beginning of the coding operation resulted in 'pro-con' codings being put in for certain issue areas where confrontation between parties was thought most likely. Thus the theory has indeed been 'validated through direct and indirect checks' (3 and 4). Had different parties ganged up on opposite sides on these issues, we would have had a vindication of confrontational ideas and a rejection of saliency ones. Instead endorsements were made by all parties of (usually) the pro side (and only that side) on each of these twelve issue areas. Endorsements of that stand by the different parties were however not equally emphasized, confirming saliency ideas about different parties emphasizing different areas to the extent that they have a credible record in regard to them.

We shall expand on these points below. Suffice it to note here that the invariance of the main general measures (Left-Right and other policy scales) over time and space has been impressively demonstrated in Chapter 1 (5). The usefulness of the Manifesto codings for supporting further developments such as computerization and extension of estimates (6) is demonstrated in Chapters 7 and 8.

SALIENCY THEORY AND THE MEASUREMENT OF PARTY POSITIONS WITHIN SPECIFIC ISSUE AREAS

On the basis of the arguments put forward above, the Manifesto Research Group coded programme sentences into the original 57 policy categories—representing the specific issues discussed above—which are summarized in Table 3.2. The percentages of sentences coded into each category constitute the data used in further statistical analyses, such as the Left-Right scales in Chapter 1. To recapitulate, these identified certain categories as belonging theoretically to the right ('free enterprise', for example) and certain to the left (such as 'economic planning'). Exploratory factor analyses were carried out to see if the selected categories hung together—which they did—and to investigate whether any others belonged with them on the same dimension. Percentage scores for 'Right' and 'Left' categories were added up separately, and the total 'Left' score subtracted from the total Right one to give the final locations in Figures 1.1–1.25. This procedure has been summarized in Table 1.1 above.

Some of the contrasting Left and Right scores derive from directly opposed positions (pro-military and anti-military, for example) which as noted above were put in as a check on the basic saliency assumptions. The pure saliency categories however find no such direct contrast on the other side: pro-peace on the Left is not contrasted with anti-peace on the Right, because there was no 'Peace: negative' category in the MRG scheme. By contrasting mentions of peace on one side with a lack of mentions on the other side the measure is recording 'saliency' or the selective emphasis given to issues by parties, rather than directly contrasting stands. This is counter intuitive in terms of simplistic conceptions of parties opposing each other all along the line and requires a more detailed justification than we have given it above.

In order to pursue the argument we have to go back to the original MRG codings and see why they take the form that they do. The aim is to count all sentences in a text whether they seem to have a direct policy content or not (thus the 'count' for each category includes vague historical generalizations about a problem or simple references to its importance). The justification for doing this is that party programmes are carefully considered and finely honed documents, so no sentence appears in them without a purpose.

Including all such references to an issue-area does make it difficult to tie most sentences down to specific pro- and con- positions however. Long digressions on the growth of unemployment are presumably saying it is a bad thing and the party would do something to counter it. Is any party gong to say explicitly that it is *for* unemployment? Immediately the question is put it seems unlikely. A party might however *say* very little about unemployment and devote a lot of attention to the evils of inflation, implying that all other considerations should be subordinated to fighting this problem.

These tricks of party rhetoric are no doubt familiar to every reader. They do not leave much room for parties to line up for and against each other on each issue. What party wants to appeal for votes by extolling either unemployment or inflation—or supporting war against peace?

It was the seminal finding of the pioneering analysis of party manifestos made by David Robertson (1976) that parties do *not* in fact directly oppose each other on an issue by issue basis. They rarely take specific policy stands at all or mention any other party or its issue-positions. Instead their programmes assume there is only one tenable position on each issue and devote their energy to emphasizing the policy areas on which their credibility on that position is strong enough to pick up votes. This is a discovery which has been repeated in subsequent analyses of party rhetoric (Riker 1993: 81–126) and computer word counts of manifestos (Laver and Garry 1998).

It is not of course that either Robertson's original coding, or the MRG coding so far as it is derived from Robertson's, are blind to questions of party position. Rather they *are* positional in nature but only one-positional so far as most issue-areas are concerned. This is because the texts themselves are one-positional. The actual coding categories are theoretically guided but inductively derived— basically formed by grouping related sentences in the text—and so they reflect the textual practice of only endorsing the 'obvious' position on each issue— being against environmental destruction, for example, but all for a hard line on

Table 3.2. The saliency coding of election manifestos 1945–1998

Cat No	Category title
101	Foreign special relationships: positive
102	Foreign special relationships: negative
103	Decolonization
104	Military: positive
105	Military: negative
106	Peace
107	Internationalism: positive
108	European Community: positive
109	Internationalism: negative
110	European Community: negative
201	Freedom and domestic human rights
202	Democracy
203	Constitutionalism: positive
204	Constitutionalism: negative
301	Decentralization
302	Centralization
303	Government efficiency
304	Government corruption
305	Government effectiveness and authority
401	Free enterprise
402	Incentives
403	Regulation of capitalism
404	Economic planning
405	Corporatism
406	Protectionism: positive
407	Protectionism: negative
408	Economic goals
409	Keynesian demand management
410	Productivity
411	Technology and infrastructure
412	Controlled economy
413	Nationalization
414	Economic orthodoxy
415	Marxist analysis
416	Anti-growth economy
501	Environmental protection
502	Arts, sports, leisure, media
503	Social justice
504	Social Services expansion

Table 3.2. *(continued)*

Cat No	Category title
505	Social Services limitation
506	Education expansion
507	Education limitation
601	National way of life: positive
602	National way of life: negative
603	Traditional morality: positive
604	Traditional morality: negative
605	Law and order
606	National effort and social harmony
607	Multiculturalism: positive
608	Multiculturalism: negative
701	Labour groups: positive
702	Labour groups: negative
703	Agriculture
704	Middle class and professional groups
705	Minority groups
706	Non-economic demographic groups

law and order (Laver and Garry 1998, 12). The coding scheme thus directly reflects party assumptions that there is only one tenable policy on each issue.

However, we do not need to rely simply on induction to justify this approach. A perfectly plausible theory of party competition underlies the strategists' programmatic presentations. Its constituent assumptions are set out in Table 3.3. Given the limitations of party informational and processing capacities, strategists write programmes in response to perceived majority endorsements of obvious courses of action on each issue. Parties seeking votes do not buck majority opinion. They thus do not oppose perceived popular preferences and hence mostly end up endorsing the same position. Examining 'pro' and 'con' stands on each issue thus gives little mileage in measuring party differences as parties are *all* generally 'pro' or 'con' on a specific issue. (For internal checks and empirical evidence for this assertion see below).

Dynamism is given to party competition and the construction of programmes by strategists' belief that electors see one party as more able to carry through their preferred preference in a particular policy area than others. Again this seems plausible—to cut taxes, reduce government spending, and generally impose economic orthodoxy one would prefer market liberals to socialists, and vice-versa for extending social services. To win votes therefore strategists do not argue much about policy positions, which are taken as read, but emphasize the importance of those issues where the party is ideologically committed and hence most trusted by electors. This is what enables us to contrast the Left and Right stances of parties and to trace movement in them as in Figures 1.1–1.25. If the assumption is correct that varying emphases on issues are by and large the only way that parties express their policy differences, it follows that the only way to get at these is by measuring the relative saliency given to them in the manifestos. This is what the MRG coding scheme was designed to do.

Table 3.3. Theoretical assumptions of the saliency approach to measuring party policy

---

1. Party strategists see electors as overwhelmingly favouring one course of action on most issues. Hence all party programmes endorse the same position, with only minor exceptions.

2. Party strategists also think that electors see one party as more likely than the others to carry through the favoured course of action.

3. Hence each party has a set of issues that 'belong' to it, in the sense that the centrality of these issues in an election will increase its vote.

4. A party therefore emphasizes its 'own' issues in its election programme, in an attempt to increase the salience of these for voters. It emphasizes 'rival' issues less or not at all.

5. Policy differences between parties thus consist of contrasting emphases placed on different policy areas.

Its theoretical basis is set out in the 'valency and saliency' theory in Table 3.3 which is supported by:

(a) Classical qualitative studies of party competition—see Stokes (1966) on the predominance of valence issues and Riker (1993) on the 'dominance principle' of party rhetoric. Such studies demonstrate that parties, rather than continuing to endorse a minority-supported position against a majority-supported one, shift to emphasizing other issues in line with saliency ideas.

(b) Computerized counts which show that key words relating to different issues (e.g. taxes, environment) are selectively emphasized by different parties and that this is what differentiates them (Laver and Garry 1998; 1999). (Of course this does not mean that the disadvantaged party *never* mentions an issue. Because of its importance it may lose credibility if it totally ignores it. It just means that it mentions it noticeably less than the other party).

(c) Results deriving from internal checks in the MRG codings themselves. The checks were included as noted above because some members of the original group were healthily sceptical of precisely the 'valency and saliency' ideas codified in Table 3.3. Like many others, they shared a gut feeling that party competition consists in direct confrontation between pro and con positions on each specific issue. To settle the question all issues where such confrontations seemed likely had pro and con positions assigned to them in the coding. This feature undermined the pure saliency nature of our framework. But it did allow for a continuing empirical check on the validity of the saliency assumptions, which turn out to be strongly supported. *Even where key issues were coded into opposing positions they yet turned out to be valence issues with the overwhelming number of references going to one of the possible positions* (Budge, Robertson and Hearl (eds.) 1987: 50–1). Of the twelve 'pro versus con' contrasts contained within the MRG coding for validation purposes only two show near-equal emphasis in each side— for and against Military Expenditure and protectionism (Table 3.4). The latter receives only minor mentions overall. In the case of the Military categories, the negative one has a blurred boundary with Peace—would 'beating arms into plough-shares' go into 'opposition to military strength' or 'peace'? Such blurring was the price paid for multiplying categories to accommodate early scepticism about the way a purely salience-based theory would work. On most bipolar contrasts, however, the negative side attracts such few endorsements that the codings can overall be taken as effectively one-positional. This is illustrated in Table 3.4.

Table 3.4. Mean percentages of manifesto sentences endorsing pro and con categories on specific issues over 24 OECD countries, 1945–1998

	Pro	Con
Foreign special relations	1.1	0.4
Military	1.4	1.1
Internationalism	2.3	0.5
European Union	1.1	0.3
Constitutionalism	0.8	0.4
Protectionism	0.4	0.3
Social Services expansion	6.3	0.4
Education expansion	3.4	0.1
National way of life	1.0	0.2
Traditional morality	1.7	0.2
Multiculturalism	0.7	0.2
Labour groups	2.7	0.2

While this result supports the theory underpinning MRG procedures, it means that the coding itself is not in principle a pure saliency one—a criticism made by Kitschelt (1994: 139). What Kitschelt did not notice, however, is that in practical terms it works like one, simply because one or other of the pro-con positions on individual issues are so overwhelmingly dominant. Few parties will for example propose limiting education: thus references to education are almost all for expansion.

A critic might still say that some pro and con positions *are* encapsulated in the MRG coding scheme, so why can't they be put in for all categories? That would satisfy both saliency and confrontational approaches and could be used to settle the differences between them on a comprehensive basis. They are three reasons why this cannot be done:

(a) *Consistency and continuity:* Introducing pro- and con- categories does not simply mean subdividing existing categories but revising the whole coding scheme and re-applying it to all the documents—an enormous, costly and probably impossible task at this point. It cannot be undertaken simply to meet an abstract consideration, unsupported by empirical evidence, that anything is actually *wrong* with our measurements. It may be the case that a more flexible and reliable computerized approach, basing itself on the MRG categories but characterizing these in terms of positive or negative qualifiers, might overcome these problems. The expectation would still be, however, that only positive or negative references, but not both, would dominate all parties' stands on each category; but that could then be checked empirically. The results would constitute another validity check on the procedures and theory underlying the MRG approach, which current evidence suggests they would meet.

(b) *Unreliability:* The multiplication of small, thinly populated categories makes for random error and statistical noise in the codings (Laver and Budge (eds.) 1992: 23). The blurring of boundaries which currently occurs between 'military: negative' and 'peace' discussed previously illustrates this problem and cautions against extending the confusion.

(c) *Theoretical and coding consistency:* Discussions of content analysis all emphasize the extent to which coding procedures have to base themselves on some theory about the nature of the evidence to be analyzed (Stone *et al.* 1966: 5–7; Weber 1990: 79–80). The 'saliency and valency' assumptions underlying the MRG codings have already been specified (Table 3.3). A confrontational ('pro and con') coding bases itself on a different view of the way parties compete, and of how they therefore compose their manifestos in order to attract votes (Section 4 and Table 3.5 below). The two interpretations are already somewhat confused in the MRG codings, because of the bipolar categories introduced as checks. However, we have emphasized that the coding is essentially saliency-based, as a result of the nature of most of the categories and the fact that one out of the bipolar categories generally predominates. Basing a single set of coding decisions on two contrasting theories about party competition is a recipe for increased error and confusion. So it is better to keep them separate so far as possible and decide clearly which fits the evidence better. The balance is overwhelmingly in favour of Saliency theory and its associated codings of specific issues and policy areas.

INCORPORATING VALENCY WITHIN SPATIAL ANALYSES

Saliency theory gives a picture of party competition that corresponds more closely to the intentions and strategies of the parties themselves than an approach based on a confrontation between specific party positions. The picture that emerges is more subtle and differentiated than that provided by a mechanistic counterposing of 'pro' and 'con' positions on each issue. Parties do not square up to each other, landing heavy blows on each others' strong points, like a pair of inexperienced pugilists. Instead they duck and weave, avoiding direct hits from their opponents, while seeking an opening for their own blow to a weak spot. Besides their greater fidelity to the actual mode of party competition, saliency ideas have another advantage over confrontational ones. They are capable of accommodating one of the most serious and sustained critiques of Downsian spatial analyses ever made.

Stokes' (1966: 170–6) central point is that spatial analyses inevitably miss out the major issues in politics, since these are generally valence rather than positional issues. By 'positional' issues, Stokes means ones where parties take up the 'pro' and 'con' positions assumed by confrontational codings. (It seems better to use the terms 'saliency' and 'confrontational' to distinguish the two approaches, since *both* are concerned with estimating party policy positions. Their differences relate to how this is to be done—by relative emphases on one position over the whole set of issues, in the case of the saliency approach, or by the pro and con positions taken up by parties on each individual issue, in the case of the confrontational approach). By 'valence' issues he means ones where only one position is possible, as assumed in the MRG approach, because of overwhelming perceptions of its moral superiority or obviousness or rightness. Stokes argues that the most important issues in politics tend to be valence ones, citing the famous slogan of 'Korea, Corruption and Communism' used by the Republicans in the 1952 US Presidential campaign. How could these winning themes—which everybody *had* to be against—possibly produce differentiated positions over a spatial continuum, asks Stokes? But in fact, as Figures 1.1–1.25 demonstrate, valence issues can be used to locate parties and trace their movements in space—once we recognize that parties differentiate themselves on them *not by directly opposing positions but by varying emphases on a shared position*. It was this discovery by Robertson (1976), later extended and codified in the MRG procedures, which enabled the whole range of policy issues to be incorporated in Downsian style spaces.

Table 3.5. Theoretical assumptions of a confrontational approach to measuring party policy

---

1. Issues are generally confrontational and not valence in nature, i.e. parties take up a range of explicit positions on each issue, ranging from fully pro to fully con, without inherent constraints.

2. The party position on each issue can thus be measured separately and independently of its position on any other issue by the balance of 'pro' versus 'con' references to that issue proposal.

3. Hence party policy differences on individual issues are separate from and independent of relative emphases on them and must be measured from direct statements of support or opposition to specific policy proposals.

4. Relative emphases on issues only come into the measurement of party policy differences as weights attached to previously measured pro-con differences, when putting individual issues together to form a composite index or policy space.

To see how far confrontational approaches miss this point we need only consider their assumptions in a form analogous to that of the 'saliency and valency' approach in Table 3.3. The differences mostly go back to Assumption 1, about the ability and willingness of parties to take up opposing stands on individual issues in their manifestos. The presumption is that parties *will* take opposing stands on each issue (Laver and Hunt 1992: 124–5). If this is so then the party position on the issue is clearly defined regardless of what (or how much) it says about other issues (Table 3.5, Assumption 2 and 3). Relative saliency only enters at another level of measurement, when individual issue differences are aggregated to form a space or composite index, and may then be weighted by the relative attention paid to them in the manifestos.

A corollary of these assumptions which does not seem to have been explicitly considered so far in discussion is that it is electorally worthwhile for parties seeking votes to adopt minority stands on issues (in contrast to Assumption 1, Table 3.3). There will be a popular majority and minority on most issues, thus a confrontational stance will put at least one party in the minority position. What seem to be purely technical assumptions about measuring texts inevitably have substantive implications about the nature of party competition itself, when the text is such a central one as the party election programme.

If 'saliency and valency' ideas are correct, bringing saliency in only later gives a misleading impression of what party policy differences actually are. Either parties will be recorded as agreeing on some issues to which they give very varying emphases, or these varying emphases will actually do all the differentiation without being credited for it, as seems to have happened in Laver and Garry's (1998, 1999) computer analysis. Here text units *are* assigned to bipolar scales (e.g. extend/reduce State intervention)—but on the basis of parties' emphases on one-positional non-opposed terms. Words like (cutting) taxes and (increasing) assistance are central to the coding but do not themselves denote pro-con positions on the same issue. Cutting taxes does not imply cutting assistance either logically or empirically, since it can be paid for in many other ways (e.g. deficits, defence cuts, economic growth, EU subsidies, etc.). Party positions on the scales are thus defined by the relative saliency of certain themes just like the overall Left-Right scales in Figures 1.1–1.25 and our other policy scales. All computerized procedures based on word counts (c.f. Chapter 7 below) base themselves on the relative saliency of words and hence seem more naturally linked to saliency codings than to confrontational ones.

A LEVEL OF ANALYSIS PROBLEM: SPECIFIC ISSUES VERSUS OVERALL IDEOLOGICAL PRIORITIES

In part these differences in coding approaches may stem from misunderstandings about what constitutes a 'specific issue' as against a 'general' or 'ideological' party stand. Our Manifesto coding identifies specific issues with each of the coding categories in Table 3.2. It is within these that parties endorse only the one position, while the relative degree to which they emphasize one issue against the other is what really distinguishes them. It follows when a number of issues are combined in a Left-Right or other policy scale that the Manifesto approach clearly distinguishes between parties, as demonstrated time after time in Chapter 1.

Such scales seem to tap into the way a party defines its general position or ideology at a given point in time, rather than into any one concrete decision on, e.g. tax levels. Within our framework we certainly regard them in this way. They are about priorities over a range of specific issues rather than about policy on any one of them.

Confrontational codings on the other hand seem to conflate such general policy orientations with the specific issues under current political discussion (Laver and Hunt 1992; Harmel, Janda and Tan 1995; Laver and Garry 1998, 1999). Words like taxes or sentences like 'Increases in taxes are generally undesirable' are not taken as focussing on the one specific issue of whether to adopt 'Financial Orthodoxy' (to use our coding category). They are only to be used directly to place parties on a general scale of 'extend/reduce State intervention'.

If this is indeed the case, and our general policy scales are functionally equivalent to what these analysts regard as the 'issues', then we are not really coding party programmes in very different ways. We simply record party positions and emphases at a more specific level which can then be aggregated upwards to measure general policy orientations, whereas they only provide the latter.

One significant difference still remains however which as always derives from the underlying measurement theory we are operating on. The saliency approach recognizes that the general policy differences between parties which emerge from codings are about overall political priorities. Left-wing parties on this interpretation may well think tax cutting in itself is a good thing, but much less of a priority than extending social services. Right-wing parties put things the other way round. This is different in terms of general political consequences from counterposing 'tax cutting versus service extension', which implies that one necessarily excludes the other. This assumption was shown to be empirically wrong by the many governments of the eighties and early nineties who pursued both policies together by using the 'peace dividend', or EU subsidies, accelerating economic expansion, incurring massive debts and so on. By assuming a confrontational stance—'either increase taxes or reduce services'— one loses these subtler political possibilities.

At the measurement level operational differences remain because the view we take of parties at a general policy level as making a choice of priorities over the whole range of issues, contrasts with one which sees the party position as an aggregation of specific stands inside each policy area. Our view leads to us calculating the Left-Right scale for example as Right sentences minus Left sentences over the total number of sentences in the programme. As a result, parties may move closer in Left-Right terms simply because they choose to give more attention, relatively speaking, to new issues such as the environment.

From a saliency point of view this effect does indeed reflect party intentions in writing the Manifesto. By emphasizing 'green issues', for example, they do intend to de-emphasize older ones. One purpose may well be to come closer to other parties on Left-Right questions. Politicians do see the Manifesto as a whole and it is a conscious decision to de-emphasize some old issues by promoting new ones. We must realize, however, that this interdependency of categories may have hidden effects on statistical analyses of the data (c.f. Weber 1990: 70–1), to the extent they use most or all of the specific categories (e.g. Janda, Harmel *et al.*1995). Nevertheless the effects of interdependency are usually avoided because:

(a) interest focuses on one or few categories rather than all, e.g. emphases on 'freedom' or on 'groups'. In analyzing variation in such cases those categories which co-vary are not of interest and are omitted, so problems of interdependency do not arise.

(b) data reduction techniques and dimensional analyses are expressly designed to deal with a mass of separate indicators suspected of being interrelated. They have as their object the reduction these large numbers of indicators to a more limited number of (substantially) independent indicators. The scales and dimensions reported here are largely the result of such reduction techniques and are substantially independent of each other.

Most users of the Manifesto data have confined themselves to analyses of individual categories or 'reduced' indices and so have not been much affected by the interdependency of the percentage scores. This is in any case a fact of political life—of the actual approach of parties to writing their manifestos—which analysts have to live with.

The opposite tack is to assume that one policy area has nothing to do with the others, and standardize party differences by dividing by the total number of references to that area, rather than by the total number of references to all topics over the whole document (R–L/R+L). Substantively, this implies that the authors of a programme present policy in one area totally separately from policy in another area, never reviewing the balance of the document as a whole. This seems unrealistic from what we know of the writing of programmes, which are finely tuned and revised as a whole not once but many times.

The general point about which level of analysis we are operating on, and the need to distinguish between specific issues and overall ideologically based priorities, is one which we should bear in mind both in coding and analyzing the textual data. Realization of the differences between these levels of analysis reduces but does not eliminate the contrasts between saliency and confrontational approaches—to which Chapter 6 devotes some empirical analysis.

A GENERAL STANDARD FOR POLICY ESTIMATES

For the reasons given above we think the saliency codings are theoretically more justified and empirically better validated than any rival approach—quite apart from having produced the only detailed and comprehensive estimates in the field! This is an important conclusion because we clearly need a validated standard measure in the field of textual analysis to be sure that new techniques, and particularly computerized ones produce trustworthy results. The comprehensiveness of the Manifesto measures, the plausibility of their estimates, external and internal validation of assumptions and procedures—all designate them as a central point of reference for party policy estimation. Indeed if these data were ruled out, there is no standard that could replace them and we would have to rely on *ad hoc* comparisons of very disparate and problematic estimates (electoral perceptions and 'expert' judgements for example) which are in any case available only for limited time-points.

Using our data as a central standard means, where there are disagreements with other measures, that our estimates should be taken as the more authoritative ones. It is quite likely, of course, that better standards may be developed in the future. But they should be *shown* to be so through the same detailed evaluations already applied to these data, not simply *asserted* to be better. Otherwise we risk methodological anarchism, where every investigator has their own measure and there is no way of evaluating their substantive conclusions properly.

The question of authority is particularly relevant to computerized textual analysis. Clearly this offers the possibility of rapid, reliable coding with vast savings in cost and a consequent extension of quantitative research. However, we need to be able to test the computer estimates to know that they really are valid and useful. A comparison with MRG codings and Left-Right mappings of the documents is facilitated through the 'valency and saliency' assumptions underlying both the manual and the computer codings. However, only when the results of the latter match the former can we proceed to use them with any confidence (c.f. Chapter 7). Validating computerized coding in this way is a first necessity before proceeding to substitute it for manual procedures.

Of course, even an authoritative general coding scheme for party policy positions does not always serve more specialized concerns within the policy field. Debating whether a *general* coding of election programmes is best based on saliency assumptions is not the same thing as assuming that it can serve all purposes equally well. Specialized investigations may well need their own specialized codings. For overall comparability, however, we need a general cross-time, cross-national coding of all election programmes, focused on party policy positions, but able to serve other investigations when :-coding cannot be done. The central question is, therefore, what kind of general scheme best serves these purposes? In terms of the argument here, this is clearly our present codings and data.

These examples also help demonstrate what a standard is *not*. It is not a final, unsurpassable procedure set in stone. We have already demonstrated that the present coding has defects (e.g. overlapping of original codes and inserted bipolar check codes) to which others could be added (e.g. 'noise' particularly involving less populated categories (Laver and Budge (eds.) 1992, 23). However, this is no reason for abandoning it for, or substituting it by, more dubious alternatives. Indeed not only is the present scheme the best general measure of party policy positions we presently have, but it is likely to remain so until computerized text processing is fully validated.

When computerized coding *is* validated against the Manifesto scheme it may gradually substitute for it (though probably the two should run in parallel for a considerable period to make more extensive validation possible). Basing themselves on the same saliency assumptions about parties the computerized estimates should be entirely comparable with ours. However, the new coding could, prospectively, vastly improve the range and flexibility of existing categories. Setting a standard is thus very far from reifying existing measures. But it is to lay down a systematic way of developing new ones. The considerations laid out above show that the point of departure has to be the MRG data. Once this is accepted we can get on with the job of improving on them.

Part II
Measurement: Procedures and Checks

4

Quantifying the Election Programmes: Coding Procedures and Controls

Andrea Volkens

INTRODUCTION

This chapter introduces Part II of our text, which applies the general concerns of Part I to detailed questions of operationalization and measurement. We outline the procedures we have developed to co-ordinate and supervise the coding of post-war election programmes in more than 50 countries—a vast never-ending task, since elections recur every 3 to 5 years in general. These procedures are, as we shall argue, the real guarantees of the stability and quality of the estimates published on the accompanying CD-ROM. Although we report their performance mainly in relation to the 25 countries covered by this book, the discussion has a direct bearing for the entire set of countries to which they have now been applied. Clearly the ability of the coding frame to fit new national experiences beyond those covered originally is an important testimony to its generalizability and credibility.

A sound system of organization and documentation to co-ordinate and control the coding exercise over a more extended range of countries and languages also lends credence to the procedures applied to the 25 countries which we focus on in this volume. Its open-ended commitment to updating and maintaining the data-set distinguishes the Manifesto research from other content-analytic projects, which have generally addressed a.finite selection of texts, which they have moreover tended to sample rather than code as a whole. The open-ended nature of the research puts a premium on continuity of both personnel and organization. It is inevitable that individuals coding documents relating to different countries will change, though this natural turnover can be minimized so far as possible. The main factor in continuity nevertheless has to be the permanence of the central organization. Even if individuals change, extensive documentation and detailed records provide a collective memory of decisions and procedures, which is the major factor contributing to the stability and reliability of coding across time and place.

Clearly all users of the Manifesto data have to be sure that a similar unit of text written in Swedish in 1951 will be coded into the same category when written in Spanish in 1996. Reliability in this sense has to be a prime concern for all involved with the data. Equally, conventional tests such as two coders independently processing the same texts and assessing agreement of results (inter-coder reliability) are useful but insufficient to assess 'mega-reliability' across many different languages. The main emphasis in the 'quality control' of the data has therefore been on setting and enforcing central standards on coders—first by getting them to conform to a prescribed English-language standard and secondly by very close interaction between them and the central supervisor. Particularly in these days of instant electronic communication, difficult coding decisions can be discussed and taken jointly. Interaction, procedural stability, and detailed documentation—to the extent of recording each individual coding decision on a copy of the text—are the keys to reliability described below.

The reliability and validity checks applied to assess the success of the coding procedures also have to be holistic in nature. Checking the equivalence of individual coding categories within or across countries is all very well. But the main question—already addressed in part in Chapter 1—is how the whole data set across time and countries connects. It is for this reason that Chapter 5 correlates the data set collected up to 1983 and used in the first MRG analyses (Budge, Robertson and Hearl (eds.) 1987) with the full data set up to 1997 to see if there is a satisfactory overall concurrence between them. Similarly with regard to validity, Chapter 6 compares the main manifesto-based measures—Left-Right scales—with other estimates of party positions. This is a technical check of 'convergent' validity to supplement the investigation of 'face' and 'predictive' validity already reported in Chapters 1 and 2.

The chapters of Part II document the enormous attention devoted to the creation of the estimates reported below. This is made worthwhile by the absolutely unique status of party election programmes in the democratic process. Not only are they the only medium term programmes for general political, social and economic development prepared by parties—real 'Five Year Plans'. They also constitute the main policy-premises used by electors in choosing how to vote for parties in elections. The presumption is that the party or parties which win will then put these programmes into effect in government. If they do not there is no guarantee that popular wishes will shape government policy, which is after all the central premise of representative democracy itself.

Composed and adopted according to a set of legally prescribed rules, the election programme is the only statement of preferences made by a party as such. All other statements originate with individual members or leaders or factions or groups within a party. However influential or important, these cannot be taken as the party position. To estimate party preferences we therefore have to base ourselves on the only statements which have authoritative endorsement, that is the manifestos or platforms put forward in the election. These also have the advantage of recording changes in party policy from one election to another. Fortunately these documents are written to be comprehensible to—and even to appeal to—a mass audience. They therefore emphasize and repeat what they have to say, not once but many times. As their main purpose is to convince electors of the importance of one problem or priority relative to others they do not need to go into excessive detail about it. Emphasis and repetition are the hallmarks of their rhetoric, which makes coding them, even in different languages, reasonably straightforward. These characteristics ease the problems we face in quantifying these texts across time, space and language and certainly simplify questions associated with the reliability and validity of the coding procedures. We now turn to a description of these procedures.

HISTORICAL DEVELOPMENT OF THE MANIFESTO RESEARCH PROJECT

From 1979 to 1989 the Manifesto Research Group (MRG) collected and coded as many post-war election programmes as it could get hold of in 20 countries, with a view to estimating the policy preferences of their political parties and how they change over time. Detailed descriptions of this work and its results can be found in Budge, Robertson and Hearl (eds.) (1987), Laver and Budge (eds.) (1992), Klingemann, Hofferbert, Budge *et al.* (1994). During the first phase of the project, while the classification scheme was being developed, each group member was responsible for his or her own data collection, though Belgium, Luxembourg, Austria, Australia, New Zealand and the US were already co-ordinated by a research officer.

A second phase followed in 1989. In the context of its 'Comparative Manifestos Project' (CMP), the Social Science Research Centre in Berlin (WZB) provided resources for updating and expanding the MRG data set to cover 2347 programmes of 632 different parties in 52 countries.[1] Coders are now hired to do the content analysis according to procedures specified in a printed handbook. A reliability test associated with the handbook is used for training, close links are maintained between supervisors and coders, and all decisions are recorded for later review.

This chapter describes the basic classification scheme used for coding election programmes across all countries and time periods and details the procedures used in applying it, particularly those associated with quality control of coding decisions. We provide a short description of the initial phase of Manifesto Research and introduce the coding unit and the classification scheme developed there. Subsequently we discuss the quality control of data in the second (CMP) phase of the project. Finally we present statistics that cast some light on the results obtained from coding, opening the way for the assessments of their general reliability and validity made in the following chapters.

THE MRG:CODING UNITS, CLASSICIATION SCHEME AND PROCEDURES

The MRG originally set out to cover all significant parties in 19 democracies mainly in Europe and North America for the whole post-war era. The first published version of the Manifesto Data Set contained 1018 election programmes which were subjected to content analysis, 'a research technique for the objective, systematic and quantitative description of the manifest content of communication' (Berelson 1952: 18). In 1995, a second publication of data covering the 20 countries for the time period 1945 to 1988 was deposited at both the British and German National Data Archives. One country (Norway) had been added to this set before the CMP more than doubled the number of countries by expanding the collection to Eastern Europe and Latin America which are beyond the scope of this publication. Table 4.1 shows the numbers of elections, parties, and programmes for the 25 countries covered by the data set on the CD-ROM.

In order to embark on the content analysis of the party programmes, the group had to select a coding unit and devise a classification scheme. After considerable experimentation and discussion, it settled for the so-called 'quasi-sentence' as a general coding unit. A quasi-sentence is defined as an argument which is the verbal expression of one political idea or issue. In its simplest form, a sentence is the basic unit of meaning. Therefore, punctuation can be used as a guideline for identifying arguments. The starting point of coding is the sentence, but long sentences may contain more than one argument so that long sentences are broken up into 'quasi-sentences', usually contained by commas, semi-colons or colons.

The major task of the MRG was to develop a classification scheme that could accommodate the content of election programmes in a comparative as well as longitudinal perspective. The starting point for this were the 21 one-positional categories developed by David Robertson (1976: 73–5) for analysing modes of party competition in Britain (1922–74). Two considerations guided extensions to these categories. The wider country coverage meant that more topics were covered in the programmes—a concern driven particularly by the anxieties of specialists within the group that 'their' country was not being covered adequately. The other factor was the scepticism of some members about saliency theory and the consequent introduction of 'pro' and 'con' codings of what they felt were issues likeliest to encourage party confrontation (Chapter 3).

On the basis of these considerations the MRG devised a classification scheme with 54 broad categories grouped into seven policy domains. The categories, called the Standard Coding Frame, are listed in Table 3.2 and Appendix III. Each category is composed of a set of typical issues and political ideas (Budge, Robertson and Hearl (eds.) 1987: 459–65). The classification scheme comprises 24 bipolar positions, such as (504) 'Welfare State Expansion' as opposed to (505) 'Welfare State Limitation', and 30 unipolar positions (or valence issues) such as (501) 'Environmental Protection'. Each quasi-sentence is coded into one, and only one of the 54 categories.

Table 4.1. Elections, parties, and programmes for 24 OECD Countries and Israel (MRG and CMP Coding 1979–2000, excluding estimated cases)

Countries	Elections	No. of Elections	No. of Different Parties	No. of Programs
1. OECD				
Australia*	1946–1998	22	5	78
Austria*	1949–1995	15	5	50
Belgium*	1946–1995	17	17	109
Canada**	1945–1997	17	6	62
Denmark**	1945–1994	21	16	183
Finland	1945–1995	15	13	93
France**	1946–1997	14	15	66
Germany**	1949–1998	14	15	61
Greece	1974–1996	9	8	33
Iceland	1946–1995	16	10	68
Ireland*	1948–1997	16	9	62
Italy*	1946–1996	14	20	106
Japan*	1960–1996	13	12	70
Luxembourg*	1945–1994	12	8	49
Netherlands*	1946–1998	16	10	86
New Zealand*	1946–1996	18	5	52
Norway*	1945–1993	13	9	85
Portugal	1975–1995	9	14	59
Spain	1977–1993	6	14	45
Sweden*	1948–1998	17	8	93
Switzerland	1947–1995	13	9	63
Turkey	1950–1995	12	13	35
United Kingdom**	1945–1997	15	5	47
United States*	1948–1996	13	2	26
2. Other				
Israel**	1949–1996	14	40	121

*   coded by MRG member until the beginning of the 1980s
**   all documents coded by MRG member

However, Scandinavian specialists within the MRG were particularly concerned with characterising the rhetoric of Communist parties within their region. Because the original coding categories failed to recognise this rhetoric, 'Marxist Analysis' had been used as an additional category for Scandinavian countries. In addition, increasing environmentalist rhetoric in the 1980s also needed to be accommodated. As a result the categories (415) 'Marxist Analysis' and (416) 'Sustainable Development-Non Growth Economy' were added to the standard classification scheme in 1989. Test codings had shown that these categories would not have been relevant for platforms coded up to this juncture except for the Scandinavian Communist parties. Hence the continuity and comparability of the coding frame was safeguarded. Therefore, the number of general coding categories in the scheme is now 56 (Volkens 1992).

The creation of sub-categories to capture the particularities of national politics has always been allowed for, provided they can be recombined into a general category (Budge, Robertson and Hearl (eds.) 1987: 466–7). Due to limited entries and missing comparability between countries these have not been kept in the combined data set. However, sub-categories were created later for Eastern European and South American countries to capture the specific policy problems of transitional democracies. Indeed, with the extension of the data set to Eastern Europe in particular, more than 80 sub-categories have been created, but on average only 10 per cent of the quasi-sentences are devoted to these sub-categories which are hierarchically nested into the General Categories so that they can be easily aggregated up into one of these.

The classification scheme that has emerged from this development process discriminates well between parties (Chapter 1) but is at the same time reasonably parsimonious. It permits three types of comparison: a) comparisons of changes in policy positions over time within specific parties; b) differences in policy positions across parties even in different countries, and, c) differences across countries. The basic data used to support such comparisons are the percentages of total quasi-sentences devoted to each category. Thus, the MRG coding generally combines a (one-) positional with a saliency approach in one measure, as explained in Chapter 3.

The approach opened up many interesting research perspectives. Three books and numerous articles demonstrate its potential to locate political parties in a programmatic space. However, after many years of co-operative work it turned out that many MRG members had changed their research interests. Meanwhile, the manifesto data had become central to major projects of the Social Science Research Centre, Berlin. Thus, the Centre's research unit on 'Institutions and Social Change' decided to continue and broaden this data collection using its own resources.

QUALITY CONTROL WITHIN THE COMPARATIVE
MANIFESTOS PROJECT SINCE 1989

Since 1989, the CMP has more than doubled the number of parties and election programmes, mainly by expanding the collection to further OECD countries (Finland, Greece, Iceland, Mexico, Portugal, Spain and Turkey), Eastern European countries (Albania, Armenia, Azerbaijan, Belarus, Bosnia, Bulgaria, Croatia, Czech Republic, Estonia, German Democratic Republic, Georgia, Hungary, Latvia, Lithuania, Macedonia, Moldova, Montenegro, Poland, Romania, Russia, Serbia, Slovakia, Slovenia and Ukraine) and the two Western applicants for European Union membership (Cyprus and Malta).

To cover these additional countries and to replace MRG members who had left the group, coders have been recruited to carry out the content analysis. The central feature of training and control is a coding handbook (Volkens 1992), introduced in Appendix II and largely reproduced on the CD-ROM contained in this book. The handbook explains in detail how to identify quasi-sentences, how to choose the correct categories, and how to cope with difficult coding decisions. Specimen texts annotated with correct coding decisions serve as exercises in coding. After having studied the handbook, all new coders are requested to fill in a reliability test for training purposes. Production coding is only permitted after their performance in the test has been assessed, discussed in detail and approved. Finally, coders are required to fill in coding protocols for all country-specific peculiarities and code sheets for each party as given in the handbook.

The reliability test is used primarily to identify mistakes made by new coders after having studied the handbook. A sample election programme which is difficult to code correctly in terms both of coding units and categories has been selected as the reliability test and is reproduced in the CD-ROM. After having completed this task, in ignorance of what the correct decisions should be, all coders receive detailed replies and are informed about any deviations from the approach of the MRG/CMP. The more coders deviate from the approach, the more time is devoted to subsequent training and the more strongly coders are urged to contact the supervisor via email during the actual coding process.

Although the reliability test employed by CMP is not a final check but a device for training, standard inter-coder reliability measures can be computed to examine how well coders conform to the MRG/CMP approach after studying the handbook. A measure of reproducibility, 'the degree to which a process can be created under varying circumstances, at different locations, using different coders' (Krippendorf 1980: 131) can be computed by comparing the results of the reliability tests for all pairs of coders. A measure of accuracy shows whether data are reproducible by 'independent researchers, at different locations, and at different times, using the same instructions for coding the same set of data' (Krippendorf 1980: 132) and measures the degree to which the solution of a coder conforms to the 'correct' solution of a supervisor. Both measures yield similar results (Volkens 2001). With respect to the identification of quasi-sentences, coders deviate an average 10 percentage points from each other in terms of the number identified. They also deviate by this amount on average, from the 'correct' solution. With respect to placement of quasi-sentences in the 56 categories of the Standard Classification Scheme, the average Pearson correlation is above 0.7 between all pairs of coders taking the test and between individual coding decisions and the 'correct' solution. Given the difficulty of the test with respect to the identification of quasi-sentences and categories, this is quite an impressive result. It shows that most coders get a very good grasp of the procedures by simply studying the handbook.

An even stronger test than mere correlation might have been a measurement based on the sequence of categories coded for every quasi-sentence. However, such a comparison is very time-consuming and test measurements have shown that wrong codings tend not to cancel out. This emerges from the most common coding errors uncovered in these checks:

1. Quasi-sentences that should have been coded into a substantive category were treated as uncodable.

2. Category (408) 'General Economic Goals' was chosen instead of precise policy positions such as (410) 'Economic Growth'.

3. Coding for references to (703) 'Agriculture' in general was neglected in favour of more specific references such as (402) 'Incentives'.

4. Category (305) 'Political Authority', interpreted in the sense of the party's general competence to govern, was chosen instead of a more precise policy position.

5. Generally speaking, policy statements can express the meaning of the categories more or less strongly. Some coders tended to neglect weak expressions of arguments. A good example concerns weak expressions of (601) 'National Way of Life Positive' where a cultural response pattern emerged. Coders from long-term Western democracies tended to identify weak expressions of nationalism as such whereas coders from countries with a more recent experience of democracy tended to overlook them.

It follows from what has been said that assessments of the reliability and quality of the CMP data should be based on the procedural safeguards put in place rather than any finite test. The procedures define a continuing process rather than a completed project to which finite tests can be applied. A final point about the reliability figures is of course that they apply to the training programme of the CMP from 1989 over 52 countries, rather than to the coded documents supporting our estimates in this book which are drawn from 25 countries. These were mostly coded by country specialists (the original members of the group) who had themselves helped define the coding frame. On the face of it their decisions should show even more reliability than the CMP data. Many of these codings were checked out on an individual country basis with standard inter and intra coder reliability tests. In addition, the co-ordinator of the MRG from 1982 to 1987, coded and/or closely supervised codings for six countries (Australia, Austria, Belgium, Luxembourg, New Zealand and US) (Budge, Robertson and Hearl (eds.) 1987: 23–4). From an early stage therefore emphasis was put on the procedural contacts and checks which were later systematically developed by the CMP.

The somewhat differing basis of coding under the CMP and MRG, of course, opens up the possibility of systematic differences between pre-1989 data and data collected afterwards. This is the specific focus of Chapter 5 which checks at a holistic level if the early MRG data are distinguishable from the rest—and concludes not. This section of our discussion reinforces the basic point made in earlier chapters. Such a complex data set extending over many countries, periods and languages cannot be assessed in terms of any one or any simple test of reliability. Like the Universe, our expanding data-set is constantly changing and growing, reliability assessments at any one time point are provisional and render holistic approaches, such as those in Chapter 5, more appropriate (even if they will also be superceded in time by subsequent expansions of the data).

We must emphasize again, therefore, that none of the figures cited above can be used as summary measures of reliability for the Manifesto data as such. To do so is both mistaken and highly misleading for several reasons. Firstly, 'blind coding' is a diagnostic device for coder training, and is not a final figure for inter-coder reliability over all the data. In fact it does not relate directly to any of the actual data. Secondly, because the reliability exercise forms part of coder training, the results are rapidly overtaken by subsequent assessment, discussion and production—itself a constant learning process. Moreover, in the case of coders who do badly, the supervisor draws their attention to all deviations and re-discusses procedures with them. Naturally such coders are the ones on whom the supervisor keeps a closer eye. They themselves, however, also contact the supervisor most during the actual coding process to ask for coding solutions. They translate all sentences that are difficult for them to code into English and the coding decision is then taken by the supervisor. Therefore, the reliability figures given in this section actually underestimate the quality of our data because of the training and correction procedures that followed the tests.

GETTING ON TO VALIDITY

The validity of the data is more difficult to establish than their reliability. 'We speak of a measuring instrument as being valid if it measures what it is designed to measure, and we consider a content analysis valid to the extent its inferences are upheld in the face of independently obtained evidence' (Krippendorf 1980: 155). Of the many types of validation possible (see Krippendorf 1980: 155ff), the MRG/CMP has relied mostly on face and predictive validity (Weber, 1990: 18). The major check must be the extent to which the codings generate results that make sense within and across countries. Our individual chapters assess this in more detail, but 'their overall results suggest that the estimates of party and government policy generated by the coding scheme are quite plausible' (Laver and Budge (eds.) 1992: 22).

A number of independent researchers have also investigated the 'correctional validity' of these data (Krippendorf 1980: 164) by comparing positions of parties as measured by content-analyzing election programmes with positions of parties as measured by expert judgements or left-right placements of voters (Gabel and Huber 2000; Chapter 6 below). On the whole these results show the MRG data to have good validity, especially when comparing changes in policy positions over time (Chapter 1).

In this section we provide a background to the more detailed assessments of validity covered elsewhere in this book by assessing information which emerges directly from the coding procedures we have discussed. We also include information about countries not covered by the estimates on the CD-ROM for comparative purposes. Below in Table 4.2 we provide information on the mean (cross national and cross temporal) length of electoral programmes and distributions of references to categories of the coding frame. This reinforces some points made in the general discussion of Part I (about Saliency Theory for example) while also providing context for Chapters 5 to 8.

Table 4.2 Average number of quasi-sentences in election programmes over seven decades and four groups of countries

Decades	24 OECD Countries	Eastern Europe	South America	Other Countries	All Countries
1930s	237	–	–	60	145
1940s	160	–	94	68	151
1950s	171	–	225	104	165
1960s	260	–	265	73	237
1970s	333	–	335	122	321
1980s	561	–	510	36	509
1990s	649	221	886	26	388
1930s–1990s	384	221	508	69	333

The length of programmes has important consequences for measurement. The longer programmes are, the more detailed the information one can get from them about policy positions. With short programmes, the problem of 'structural zeros' arises. If a party does not mention a specific issue, one can assume the saliency of the issue to be low. But one cannot assume the party is totally side-stepping it to the extent it would be with a longer programme. Thus the information one can get by analysing short programmes may be best provided by aggregated policy dimensions. Table 4.2 shows the average number of quasi-sentences identified in 2326 programmes, broken up into seven decades and four groups of countries. The table demonstrates that parties nowadays compile much longer programmes than they did after World War II. Moreover, parties from older democracies tend to compile longer election programmes than parties in the newer Eastern European democracies. For all research questions that are longitudinal and include comparisons between Western and Eastern countries, a 56 category scheme such as that used in the MRG/CMP approach is sufficient, given the small number of policy statements in the older programmes and those of the newer democracies. However, for the more recent Western programmes, there is perhaps leeway for a more differentiated classification than that of the original MRG scheme, which could be provided by subdividing more populous categories.

Table 4.3 presents the mean percentages of references to the different policy areas over all manifestos, breaking this down to different groupings of countries. The first (OECD) and last (all country) columns are of particular interest here. The other country columns are also of interest for validation purposes, however, as they show how well the coding performs at a general level in very contrasting political contexts. We can see, for example, whether there is a reasonable spread of references over all areas or whether reference get pushed into one area in particular contexts, and how high the proportion of uncoded sentences is.

Uncoded sentences form only ten per cent of references at most, which does not seem an unduly high level. The exception in the table consists of one country (Mexico) and may be due to a dedicated investigator taking the general injunction to locate all sentences in a specific category very seriously indeed. The opposite case is Denmark with about 30 per cent of cases uncoded owing to the original MRG investigators not wishing to locate vague general statements in substantive categories. While both attitudes may be perfectly legitimate in individual national contexts they are potential sources of methodological rather than 'real' variation in the estimates. However, this is ameliorated by the fact that the tendency to code more or less references than usual seems not to affect one substantive category more than another in either case. Thus the overall spread of estimates over categories does not seem unduly affected.

The single most populous category over both the OECD and all countries turns out to be references to welfare expansion (over 6 per cent). Even this does not seem to constitute an undue concentration of references, given the importance of welfare in the domestic policies of all countries. It does give scope for a more refined analysis of the content of welfare references however. The same might be said of social justice, the next leading category, which has a different bearing than welfare references within the MRG scheme, with class, sexual and racial discrimination figuring large.

Table 4.3. Mean percentage distribution of programmatic (quasi-) sentences over 56 substantive policy categories plus uncoded sentences in various groupings of countries

Countries/ Category	24 OECD Countries	Eastern Europe	South America	Other Countries	All Countries
Foreign Special Relations +	1.079	0.564	0.106	1.996	1.031
Foreign Special Relations −	0.387	0.115	0.641	0.992	0.388
Anti-Imperialism	0.391	0.317	0.729	0.695	0.407
Military +	1.331	1.373	0.271	4.381	1.545
Military −	1.116	0.581	0.559	0.830	0.982
Peace	1.311	0.696	0.793	4.927	1.457
Internationalism +	2.355	1.923	2.736	2.484	2.293
European Community +	1.136	0.961	0.001	0.002	0.994
Internationalism −	0.481	0.510	1.451	0.445	0.505
European Community −	0.305	0.003	0	0	0.223
Freedom and Human Rights	2.670	4.442	3.794	3.578	3.092
Democracy	3.602	4.843	8.985	2.994	3.907
Constitutionalism +	0.809	1.807	1.889	1.471	1.068
Constitutionalism −	0.401	0.122	0.366	0.860	0.383
Dencentralization	2.202	2.471	2.880	0.571	2.145
Centralization	0.219	0.250	0.131	0.004	0.209
Gov-Admin Efficiency	2.904	1.185	2.376	2.000	2.505
Political Corruption	1.047	0.990	1.297	2.194	1.129
Political Authority	3.462	3.363	2.355	1.675	3.284
Free Enterprise	2.417	2.830	1.963	1.338	2.402
Incentives	2.516	2.132	1.779	1.568	2.357
Market Regulation	1.908	1.669	2.833	1.228	1.833
Economic Planning	1.303	0.376	1.139	0.712	1.083
Corporatism	0.342	0.133	0.002	0.140	0.280
Protectionism +	0.390	0.555	0.371	0.562	0.433
Protectionism −	0.274	0.413	0.237	0.007	0.284

Table 4.3. *(continued)*

Economic Goals	3.206	2.319	1.269	3.388	3.012
Keynesian Demand	0.325	0.313	0.005	0.239	0.310
Productivity	2.334	1.556	2.043	3.679	2.284
Infrastructure	3.889	2.912	3.674	1.767	3.542
Controlled Economy	1.021	0.578	0.436	0.523	0.888
Nationalization	0.521	0.289	1.097	0.154	0.463
Economic Orthodoxy	2.978	1.764	1.692	1.030	2.577
Marxist Analysis	0.008	0.317	0.381	0	0.125
Anti-Growth Economy	0.215	0.308	0.001	0.002	0.213
Environmental Protection	3.224	3.283	2.856	0.142	2.995
Culture	1.863	2.431	1.173	0.366	1.841
Social Justice	4.429	2.829	4.821	3.547	4.074
Welfare +	6.340	3.701	5.303	5.052	6.101
Welfare −	0.397	0.206	0.005	0.008	0.331
Education +	3.405	2.859	3.444	2.812	3.259
Education −	0.006	0.005	0.000	0.002	0.006
National Way of Life +	0.963	3.290	5.168	6.713	1.922
National Way of Life −	0.152	0.347	0	0.420	0.205
Traditional Morality +	1.712	2.210	1.648	7.613	2.247
Traditional Morality −	0.197	0.220	0.195	0.740	0.242
Law and Order	1.302	2.590	1.456	0.591	1.491
Social Harmony	1.721	2.125	1.392	1.654	1.784
Multiculturalism +	0.720	2.022	0.448	2.027	1.054
Multiculturalism −	0.196	0.131	0.000	1.319	0.264
Labour +	2.751	1.603	6.437	1.759	2.545
Labour −	0.191	0.001	0.443	0.303	0.172
Agriculture	3.784	4.632	7.621	1.539	3.858
Middle Class	1.201	0.424	1.080	0.598	1.009
Minority Groups	0.911	0.379	0.180	1.241	0.821
Non-economic Groups	4.187	1.951	3.429	2.867	3.655
Uncoded Sentences	8.618	3.637	.907	10.009	7.622

On the opposite side there are many categories with less than half a per cent of references. Many of these turn out to be the negative categories inserted as a check on whether it was sufficient in the original coding simply to record

Mapping Policy Preferences

Table 4.4. Mean percentage distribution of programmatic (quasi-) sentences over 56 substantive policy categories within various party families in 24 OECD countries

Party Families/ Categories	Communist/ Left Socialist	Labour/ Social Dem	Christian Democrat	Liberal Conservative
Foreign Special Relations +	0.984	1.020	1.295	1.609
Foreign Special Relations –	0.989	0.422	0.208	0.196
Anti-Imperialism	1.046	0.375	0.464	0.198
Military +	0.190	1.235	1.478	2.631
Military –	3.375	1.292	0.363	0.273
Peace	2.829	1.499	0.771	0.931
Internationalism +	1.819	2.868	2.439	2.089
European Community +	0.252	1.188	2.636	0.940
Internationalism –	0.890	0.321	0.194	0.402
European Community –	1.166	0.118	0.041	0.081
Freedom and Human Rights	2.184	2.275	3.049	2.614
Democracy	6.024	3.727	3.877	2.445
Constitutionalism +	0.821	0.752	1.275	0.758
Constitutionalism –	0.622	0.404	0.161	0.563
Dencentralization	1.153	1.617	3.071	1.978
Centralization	0.089	0.203	0.218	0.226
Gov-Admin Efficiency	1.292	2.794	3.704	3.583
Political Corruption	1.278	1.100	0.373	1.070
Political Authority	5.282	3.266	1.949	4.335
Free Enterprise	0.124	0.696	2.956	4.556
Incentives	0.953	2.034	3.157	3.911
Market Regulation	2.338	2.402	1.805	1.165
Economic Planning	1.758	1.760	0.975	0.987
Corporatism	0.201	0.439	0.588	0.261
Protectionism +	0.399	0.422	0.106	0.481
Protectionism –	0.092	0.197	0.122	0.458
Economic Goals	2.438	3.876	2.668	3.430
Keynesian Demand	0.230	0.369	0.307	0.296
Productivity	1.657	2.537	1.973	3.312
Infrastructure	2.206	4.432	4.821	4.691

Table 4.4. *(continued)*

Controlled Economy	2.169	1.532	0.513	0.410
Nationalization	1.894	0.825	0.101	0.096
Economic Orthodoxy	1.017	1.893	2.342	5.391
Marxist Analysis	0.523	0.071	0.001	0.009
Anti-Growth Economy	0.182	0.176	0.116	0.029
Environment	2.820	2.745	2.940	2.087
Culture	1.708	2.013	2.871	1.614
Social Justice	6.251	5.716	3.826	2.597
Welfare +	6.556	7.944	6.610	5.428
Welfare −	0.033	0.140	0.382	0.620
Education +	2.880	4.207	3.684	3.438
Education −	0.009	0.038	0.100	0.117
National Way of Life +	0.325	0.661	1.093	1.592
National Way of Life −	0.359	0.072	0.095	0.045
Traditional Morality +	0.330	0.628	4.221	1.454
Traditional Morality −	0.215	0.222	0.106	0.052
Law and Order	0.600	1.130	1.778	2.345
Social Harmony	1.119	1.845	2.105	1.838
Multiculturalism +	0.238	0.384	1.675	0.405
Multiculturalism −	0.075	0.194	0.067	0.133
Labour +	5.744	3.931	1.997	1.830
Labour −	0.058	0.083	0.070	0.472
Agriculture	1.970	3.658	3.396	4.003
Middle Class	0.762	1.102	1.492	1.911
Minority Groups	0.832	0.948	1.090	0.689
Non-economic Groups	3.454	4.244	4.617	3.753
N	182	441	159	249

Notes:

Communist/Left Socialist parties were drawn from Denmark, Finland, France, Germany, Greece, Iceland, Ireland, Italy, Luxembourg, Japan, Norway, Portugal, Spain and Sweden (14 counties)

Social Democratic parties were drawn from all OECD countries in the data set with the exception of the United States (23 countries)

Christian Democratic parties were drawn from Austria, Belgium, France, Germany, Italy, Luxembourg, Netherlands and Switzerland (8 countries)

Liberal Conservative parties were drawn from Australia, Canada, Denmark, Finland, France, Greece, Iceland, Ireland, Italy, Japan, New Zealand, Norway, Spain, Sweden, United Kingdom and United States (16 countries)

Liberal Conservative parties were drawn from Australia, Canada, Denmark, Finland, France, Greece, Iceland, Ireland, Italy, Japan, New Zealand, Norway, Spain, Sweden, United Kingdom and United States (16 countries)

emphases on a particular policy area (Chapter 3 and Table 3.5 above). Finding that they attract so few references supports the contention of Saliency Theory that parties emphasise different issues rather than confronting each other inside any one policy-area. The only exception to the general tendency for opposing positions not to be emphasised are references to military alliances and expenditures, where pro and con references are relatively evenly balanced among OECD countries, though less so among all countries.

The distributions between 'pro' and 'con' categories provide continuing evidence for the relevance of our saliency coding assumptions although the averaged figures do not provide a definitive check on assumptions, as they mask the extent to which the agreed position which parties emphasize or de-emphasize may vary from one national context to another. Thus foreign special relations with a particular country are generally viewed positively—but not in Mexico (South America) where they refer overwhelmingly to the United States.

On the other hand, these averages could certainly have disproved our assumptions if confrontations did occur in most policy areas, with pro and con categories equally populated. The validity of the coding framework can never be taken wholly for granted and thus must always be subject to a continuous process of testing at the individual country and party level as well as the aggregate one. While the chapters in this part of the book are primarily concerned with aggregate tests, Chapters 1 and 2 have reported results over individual countries where the coding assumptions have been applied with highly plausible results.

Always taking on board the caveats about aggregate testing, we can also check the overall references made by each party family to policy areas over the OECD countries (Table 4.4). If our reasoning is correct the references made by each should vary systematically, with Socialists and Christian Democrats emphasising welfare and social justice more than Market Liberals and Conservatives, for example, and the latters' references concentrating more on freedom, tradition, and financial orthodoxy.

Of course, we are not saying that any party can totally ignore the others' issues, since they are important topics on the political agenda. What saliency ideas do indicate, however, is that disadvantaged parties will stress such areas less while emphasising 'their' issues more and *vice versa*. Such expectations are richly upheld by Table 4.4, echoing earlier findings at lower levels of aggregation (e.g. Budge, Robertson and Hearl, (eds.) 1987: Table 3).

We are only setting out on the road to validation with Tables 4.2 to 4.4. However, they do provide a perspective for the more searching analyses of reliability and validity carried out in the next two chapters. Like all the checks to which the Manifesto data have been subjected they are positive but not definitive. Just as the process of collecting data is scheduled to go on, so is testing its reliability and validity.

CONCLUSIONS AND OVERVIEW

This is a conclusion which can be generalised to all the procedures and checks discussed in this chapter. They are ongoing. As the results of any one check must be provisional, guarantees of validity and reliability are primarily procedural. Does the underlying (saliency) theory seem plausible? It has been upheld so far. Are procedures in place for checking and stabilising coding decisions? We have described how they operate and how far they satisfy preliminary checks. Clearly the data-set is not without problems of compatibility especially across countries. Errors and coding variability do seem to be held within tolerable limits, however. In fact, the possibility of error has been checked and analysed more thoroughly for the Manifesto data than for any other set of policy estimates. Their extensions over so many time points opens them to more detailed checks, which on the whole they pass. Their transparency should not lead to their abandonment for cruder and less valid measures (following Kitschelt 1994: 139; c.f. Budge, 2000).

Transparency was a goal which guided the development of CMP coding procedures. In addition to clean copies of election programmes, coders have to deliver all copies with codes annotated in the margins. If there is any reason to suspect the reliability of results the annotated texts, held centrally, can always be re-coded independently.[2] This, incidentally, can also facilitate the development of computer coding decisions as they can help to provide instructions for content analysis programmes about how to apply coding categories automatically to text. With ever more parties advertising their election programmes on their home page in the world wide net, many texts are nowadays readily available for computerized analyses (See Chapter 7 below).

Compatibility across countries is still impeded by language differences but major steps to overcome this difficulty have been taken by the Vrije Universiteit Amsterdam where all election programmes for which we publish estimates with this book are currently scanned and translated into English. Availability of all programmes in the English language will also provide a basis for training teams of coders better and providing more direct checks on inter- and intra-coder reliability which we could not use in our ongoing project now covering more than 50 countries. In Chapter 5 we proceed to a more holistic test of the reliability of the data followed in Chapter 6 by checks on their validity. These leave the data among the most thoroughly investigated and positively tested in modern social science.

---

1 Figures for 52 countries given in this chapter are correct as of Spring 1999.
2 A complete recoding has actually been carried through for Germany, under even tighter supervision than normal. However, even this total recoding has rendered only marginal deviations.

5

Checking the Party Policy Estimates: Reliability

Derek J. Hearl

INTRODUCTION

The previous chapter has emphasized procedural continuity and control as the key guarantors of the stability and reliability of the estimates reported here. It is hard to quarrel with this, particularly as this assertion could be generalized to all content analyses and indeed all coding exercises of whatever kind. It is just that in the context of collecting and coding manifestos indefinitely into the future, over such an extended range of countries and time points, procedures assume even more prominence than they do in more limited one-shot analyses.

Even though the procedural continuity which has been achieved provides a good guarantee of the ¬quivalence of coding categories across space and time (and language), we still want to check on how well it is succeeding. For this we need to run tests on t⁻⁻ estimates themselves. Given the cross national, over time nature of the estimates, the comparability of which constitute their chief appeal, the main checks have to be holistic in nature, dealing with the data-set as a whole across time and space.

Saying this is not to denigrate the usefulness either of single country time series, which can greatly enrich studies of national politics (Evans and Norris (eds.) 1999), or of conventional tests of intra- or inter-coder reliability within one country. Clearly these are important and have been carried out at various times for different countries and elections in the MRG data set (Budge, Robertson and Hearl (eds.) 1987; Laver and Budge (eds.) 1992).

In addition, however, comparative checks need to be carried out on this highly comparative data-set. As it is open-ended and growing, no test, not even mega tests such as the ones reported below, can be definitive. But they can give some assurance that the estimates reported here not only yield plausible results (Chapters 1, 2 and 4 above) but also pass direct assessments of their stability and comparability at different time points.

THE MRG AND CMP DATA SETS

If there is any one major source of potential non comparability and instability in the coding of our election programmes, it is that deriving from the coding handover from the MRG to the CMP, which has been referred to in Chapter 4.

Table 5.1. CMP additions to MRG data set as at September 1997: original
countries: new elections

Country (and dates of first and last elections in MRG data set)	No. of elections included in MRG data set	New elections added by CMP	No. of elections added by CMP
Australia		1983, 1984, 1987, 1990,	
(1946–1980)	15	1993, 1996	6
Austria			
(1949–1979)	10	1983, 1986, 1990	3
Belgium			
(1946–1981)	13	1985, 1987	2
Canada			
(1945–1980)	13	1984, 1988, 1993	3
Denmark		1984, 1987, 1988, 1990,	
(1945–1981)	16	1994	5
Germany			
(1949–1980)	9	1983, 1987, 1990, 1994	4
France			
(1946–1981)	7	1986, 1988, 1993	3
Ireland		1982 (Feb), 1982 (Nov),	
(1948–1981)	10	1987, 1989, 1992	5
Israel			
(1949–1981)	10	1984, 1988, 1992, 1996	4
Italy			
(1946–1983)	10	1987, 1992, 1994	3
Japan			
(1960–1980)	8	none	none
Luxembourg			
(1945–1979)	9	1984, 1989	2
Netherlands			
(1946–1981)	11	1982, 1986, 1989, 1994	4
New Zealand		1984, 1987, 1990, 1993,	
(1946–1981)	13	1996	5
Sweden			
(1944–1982)	12	1985, 1988, 1991, 1994	4
United Kingdom			
(1945–1983)	2	1987, 1992	2
United States*			
(1948–1980)	9	1984, 1988, 1992, 1996	4
Northern Ireland			
(1921–1973)	13	none	none
Sri Lanka			
(1947–1977)	7	none	none
Total of elections in MRG data set	187	Total of new elections added by CMP	59

* Presidential election years only

The collection and coding of election programmes was begun by a group of academics (the Manifesto Research Group—MRG) who by and large worked on election programmes emanating from the countries which interested them and of which they had some knowledge (including linguistic knowledge). The codings they produced were utilized in the first publication of the Group (Budge, Robertson and Hearl (eds.) 1987), and generally went up to 1983 (Table 5.1).

When the Comparative Manifestos Project took over in 1989, many elections of the mid and late 1980s had been left uncovered as members left. A first updating of the set was therefore to arrange for coding of all programmes for the 1980s. While some of the original investigators collaborated in this, others had to be replaced and central procedures and controls brought to bear, as outlined in Chapter 4.

Table 5.2. CMP additions to MRG data set as at September 1997: new countries

Country (and dates of first and last elections in CMP data set)	No. of new elections added by CMP
Finland (1945–1991)	14
Greece (1974–1990)	8
Iceland (1946–1987)	14
Norway (1945–1993)	13
Portugal (1975–1987)	7
Spain (1977–1993)	6
Switzerland (1947–1995)	13
Turkey (1950–1995)	12
Total of new elections	87

The great break point in the collection of data as between the MRG and CMP is therefore 1983. Up to then programmes had been collected and coded by the original investigators. After that, they largely dropped out and new personnel and procedures were substituted. The same coding frame, as developed by the MRG, was of course used. However, if there is any likely point at which purely methodological variation (technical error) could affect the Manifesto estimates, it is before and after 1983. Table 5.1 gives a more exact specification of the change between MRG and CMP and of how this appears within each of the original countries. About a quarter of the total set of estimates had been added by the CMP in the case of the countries originally covered.

However this is not the only change involved in the hand-over of coding responsibility, and which affects our set of estimates. The CMP also added new countries to those originally collected and studied in the first book. These include countries, such as Norway and Finland, in our data-set here. The new countries and elections thus added to the main collection of programmes are shown in Table 5.2

The overall size of the main data-set (exclusive of Eastern Europe and South America) has increased by the addition of new elections and new countries by some 57 per cent over the MRG version. If procedures have changed or control slackened-tightened, therefore, there is ample opportunity to investigate the effects by making comparisons between the original and enlarged sets. This is, of course, an important substantive question too. Most of the MRG analyses have depended wholly or in part on through-time and/or cross-national comparisons. To what extent will the availability of new data for more recent elections, and especially of course from additional countries, force us to re-assess these early findings and analyses? Any significant change in the 'base' lines used to measure these things might potentially be important. From the point of view of reassessing what we think we know it would certainly be important in terms of the trust we put in the estimates.

One obvious check that can be run at this stage is to replicate at least some of the original MRG analyses but with the addition of the new CMP data both for the new countries and for new elections in the old ones. This will show if significant changes follow in the overall data-analytic structures which emerge. If they do it implies that the original findings were largely determined by accident and should therefore be regarded as inherently unstable. Much, if not all, of the earlier work that has been done using this data would be highly suspect or simply wrong.

A slight qualification to this follows from the success of the CMP in adding additional parties in a number of the original countries, i.e. parties which for one reason or another had been left out of the first stage of the project. The subsequent inclusion of such parties could make a difference to data-structures for understandable reasons (e.g. they represent a new line of political division not represented in the data before). From a broader perspective however we would wish the estimates based on the existing data to remain stable even with the entry of new parties. The general issue is whether we can use them with confidence or not, and this implies that they do not have to be revised every time new data is entered. For this, a comparison of results obtained from using the original and the enlarged data sets is wholly appropriate and is accordingly made in the next section.

COMPARING OVERALL RESULTS BEFORE AND AFTER 1983:
A HOLISTIC CHECK

A first simple check on the comparability of the data can be made by examining the overall means and their associated standard deviations for each of the 54 coding categories which the two data sets have in common together with the absolute differences in these means. With the exception of 'Political Authority' and 'Environmental Protection' the differences are all extremely small. None, indeed, are greater than 1.0 while 47 of the 54 differences do not exceed 0.2%. On this evidence at least we may conclude that the overall salience of the various coding categories relative to each other has been very little affected by the CMP extensions to the MRG data. In turn, this supports the inference that the meanings given to the categories and their operationalization in terms of coding decisions have not changed very much either.

Nonetheless, simple comparisons of this kind, although encouraging, cannot tell us very much about any changes that there may have been in the patterns of intercorrelations between the different coding categories. This would affect the overall data-structure on which most previous analysis have relied or which they have sought to explain. Consequently three simple factor analyses have been carried out on three separate sets of data. The results are summarized in Table 5.3. The first test was carried out using the original 19-country MRG data set and the original 54 variables and consisted of a Principal Components analysis. Nineteen Components having Eigenvalues greater than 1.0 were produced and the factor loadings are shown for the first two (unrotated). Components are shown as 'Factor I' and 'Factor II' under 'Analysis 1' in the Table.

The second test repeated the process for the same 19 countries but with the addition of the data for subsequent elections held between 1983 or so and 1997; the results are reported in the second column ('Analysis 2'). The third test consisted of another repeat of the operation but this time using data for the eight additional countries as well, these results being summarized in the third column (Analysis 3).

By and large, the results are very similar, particularly when it is remembered that the Table only shows those variables which 'load' in excess of 0.3 (or less than –0.3) on one of the six factors. There are 29 of these which means that none of the other 15 loaded at this level on either of the first two factors in any of the analyses. The structures for each of the three tests are of course far from being identical but the broad patterns are very much the same. A general left-right interpretation could be applied to all of them, though sometimes 'left' and 'right' get reversed. The dominance of this division of course mirrors the original MRG findings of 1987 (Budge, Robertson and Hearl (eds.). It is likely that the rotated solutions might show even more similarities to each other. However since the purpose of the present operation is only to gain some idea of overall stability as between the MRG and CMP versions of the data rotation is not really necessary.

Table 5.3. Comparing overall mean scores by variable and differences

	All CMP cases			All MRG cases			Difference in means
	N	Mean	SD	N	Mean	SD	
Foreign special relationships +	1662	1.1	2.0	947	1.3	2.3	-0.3
Foreign special relationships −	1662	0.4	1.4	947	0.6	1.8	-0.2
Anti-imperialism	1662	0.4	1.3	947	0.4	1.3	0.0
Military +	1662	1.7	3.5	947	1.8	3.6	-0.1
Military −	1662	1.1	2.5	947	1.0	2.6	0.0
Peace	1662	1.7	3.6	947	2.0	4.1	-0.2
Internationalism +	1662	2.3	3.0	947	2.2	2.8	0.1
European Community +	1662	1.0	2.1	947	0.9	1.7	0.2
Internationalism −	1662	0.5	1.9	947	0.3	1.9	0.2
European Community −	1662	0.3	1.1	947	0.2	1.1	0.0
Freedom and human rights	1662	2.8	3.7	947	2.8	3.7	0.0
Democracy	1662	3.5	4.7	947	3.3	4.0	0.2
Constitutionalism +	1662	0.8	2.1	947	0.8	1.9	0.0
Constitutionalism −	1662	0.4	2.1	947	0.3	1.1	0.1
Decentralization	1662	2.0	3.1	947	1.9	3.0	0.1
Centralization	1662	0.2	0.9	947	0.3	1.1	-0.1
Governmental and administrative efficiency	1662	2.6	3.6	947	2.1	3.0	0.5
Political corruption	1662	0.8	2.4	947	0.8	2.5	0.0
Political authority	1662	3.3	7.6	947	1.5	4.4	1.8
Free enterprise	1662	2.4	4.0	947	2.5	4.2	-0.1
Incentives	1662	2.5	3.4	947	2.4	3.5	0.0

Market regulation	1662	1.9	2.6	947	2.0	2.7	-0.1
Economic planning	1662	1.3	3.5	947	1.4	3.7	-0.1
Corporatism	1662	0.3	1.0	947	0.3	1.1	0.0
Protectionism +	1662	0.4	1.2	947	0.4	1.5	-0.1
Protectionism –	1662	0.3	0.8	947	0.3	0.8	0.0
Economic goals	1662	3.1	4.0	947	3.0	4.0	0.0
Keynesian demand management	1662	0.3	1.0	947	0.4	1.1	-0.1
Productivity	1662	2.4	3.5	947	2.7	4.1	-0.4
Infrastructure	1662	3.7	4.3	947	3.5	4.4	0.2
Controlled economy	1662	1.0	2.2	947	1.0	2.1	0.0
Nationalization	1662	0.5	1.4	947	0.6	1.7	-0.1
Economic orthodoxy	1662	2.9	5.0	947	3.1	5.7	-0.2
Marxist analysis	1662	0.1	0.8	947	0.0	0.0	0.1
No-growth economy	1662	0.2	1.2	947	0.0	0.0	0.2
Environmental protection	1662	2.9	4.8	947	1.6	2.8	1.3
Culture	1662	1.8	2.6	947	1.6	2.7	0.1
Social justice	1662	4.4	4.4	947	4.2	4.3	0.2
Welfare +	1662	6.2	5.9	947	6.0	5.7	0.2
Welfare –	1662	0.4	1.3	947	0.3	1.4	0.0
Education +	1662	3.3	3.4	947	3.2	3.4	0.2
Education –	1662	0.1	0.5	947	0.1	0.6	0.0
National way of life +	1662	1.5	3.8	947	1.6	4.0	-0.1
National way of life –	1662	0.2	1.2	947	0.2	1.3	0.0
Traditional morality +	1662	2.4	6.7	947	2.4	6.9	0.0
Traditional morality –	1662	0.3	1.1	947	0.2	0.8	0.1
Law and order	1662	1.2	2.2	947	0.8	1.6	0.4
Social harmony	1662	1.7	3.7	947	1.4	2.9	0.3
Multiculturalism +	1662	0.9	2.3	947	0.8	1.7	0.1
Multiculturalism –	1662	0.3	1.5	947	0.3	1.1	0.0
Labour groups +	1662	2.7	3.7	947	2.6	3.8	0.1
Labour groups –	1662	0.2	1.0	947	0.2	0.7	0.0

Table 5.3. (*continued*)

	All CMP cases			All MRG cases			Difference in means
	N	Mean	SD	N	Mean	SD	
Farmers and agriculture	1662	3.6	5.9	947	3.8	6.7	-0.2
Middle class and professional groups	1662	1.2	3.0	947	1.6	3.0	-0.4
Minority groups	1662	0.9	1.7	947	0.8	1.7	0.1
Non-economic groups	1662	4.3	5.0	947	4.7	5.4	-0.4
Uncoded	1662	8.8	14.2	947	11.8	16.9	-3.0
Total quasi-sentences	1662	341.5	465.1	947	266.9	318.5	74.6
Total manifestos	1662			947			715

Table 5.4. Principal components factor analyses for the different manifesto data sets

Variables	Analysis 1 Original MRG		Analysis 2 Original MRG plus additional elections		Analysis 3 All CMP cases	
	Factor I	Factor II	Factor I	Factor II	Factor I	Factor II
Foreign special relationships: negative	−.45		.32		.32	
Anti-imperialism					.32	
Military: positive		−.30		−.35		
Military: negative	−.54		.55		.52	
Peace	−.48		.39	−.34	.42	
Democracy			.35		.38	
Decentralization	.37			.35		.33
Governmental and admin efficiency					−.33	
Political corruption	−.31					
Political authority						−.31
Free enterprise	.33	−.32	−.45		−.44	
Incentives	.33		−.34		−.39	
Market regulation	−.33	.31	.37			
Infrastructure				.44	−.30	.41
Controlled economy				.38	.31	
Nationalization				.40	.37	
Economic orthodoxy		−.55	−.41		−.36	−.32
Environmental protection		.44		.45		.48
Culture	.30	.39		.55		.55
Social justice	−.41		.52		.44	
Welfare: positive		.35		.44		.42
Education expansion				.39		.44
National way of life: positive		−.35		−.49		−.46
Law and order					−.34	
Social harmony	.37					
Labour groups: positive					.37	
Minority groups		.33				.30
Non-economic groups	.34	.36		.43		.38

Note:
1. Analysis 1 = Original MRG cases only
2. Analysis 2 = Original MRG cases plus additional elections
3. Analysis 3 = All CMP cases 1946–97 (but MRG variables only)
4. Only variables loadings of >.30 or <.30 on at least one of the six factors are shown

Nor are we trying hard to interpret the factors in terms of substantive meanings. This is in part because of questions that have been raised about the general use of factor analysis to produce policy scales or dimensions (Van der Brug 1999) and about the tests necessary to be confident about results from a pooled data-set such as the one involved here. Since our purpose is purely to check the stability of the results between the different data-sets, Table 5.4 seems adequate to the purpose. But it should not be over-interpreted.

One other question which arises with regard to the table is how far the overall results fit individual country cases. Short of reporting all of these there is no definitive way of demonstrating the fit. We have satisfied ourselves that the overall means are reasonably representative and the estimates are available here for anyone who would like to check this on their own. We can, however, pick out one individual case on 'holistic' criteria. If additions to the data set through the occurrence of new elections 'upset' patterns at the level of individual countries, then the one where most elections have been added is at the greatest risk of instability. We supplement our aggregate analysis with this single-country case in the next section.

A 'GREATEST RISK' ANALYSIS OF STABILITY: AUSTRALIA

As will be seen from Table 5.1, Australia is the country which has had more elections added by the CMP Project than any other. If instability is going to occur anywhere, other things being equal, this is probably the most likely place to find it. In addition, Australia has the merit of not only having a relatively simple party system but, crucially, one that has not undergone any significant changes since 1980, the last year covered by the MRG analysis. This source of possible change is therefore controlled. It is therefore one of the obvious candidates to look at first, in terms of single countries, in order to check the stability of estimates and results.

One of the simplest and yet most effective analyses carried in the original Budge, Robertson and Hearl (eds.) volume, were the so-called 'Top Ten Tables' in which the most emphasized categories were tabulated by party. The resulting party 'profiles' were often extremely informative showing mainly those issues which distinguish between them. If there have been any major changes to the overall structure of the Australian data as the result of the addition of new elections, party profiles of this kind should be sensitive to it. The original 'Top Ten' Frequencies analyses for the three main Australian parties appear in Table 5.5. This shows how the rankings have changed as a result of the addition of the new data. Again we can see that although there have been some changes they are rather minor.

Finally, Table 5.6 shows the differences between the original Two-Stage Factor Analysis of the Australian data conducted by Robertson (Chapter three

Table 5.5. 'Top Ten' frequencies analysis for Australia: original ranking and rankings for CMP data set

		MRG	CMP	New ranking
	Liberal Party of Australia			
1.	Economic orthodoxy	14.45	12.05	1
2.	Labour groups: positive	9.44	7.16	2
3.	Military: positive	6.24	5.52	4
4.	Farmers and agriculture	6.12	5.28	7
5.	Political authority	5.88	5.40	6
6.	Non-economic groups	4.93	5.73	5
7.	Free enterprise	4.84	4.52	8
8.	Social harmony	4.63	3.87	9
9.	Infrastructure	4.25	4.01	
10.	Welfare expansion	3.75		
	Incentives		4.14	10
	Australian Labor Party			
1.	Labour groups: positive	15.53	10.96	1
2.	Economic goals	7.36	6.27	4
3.	Welfare: expansion	7.35	8.07	2
4.	Farmers and agriculture	6.23	4.83	7
5.	Incentives	5.57	6.38	3
6.	Non-economic groups	4.95	5.82	5
7.	Political authority	4.89	4.46	9
8.	Education expansion	4.55	4.42	10
9.	Social harmony	3.71	4.82	8
10.	Market regulation	3.48	3.53	
	Infrastructure		5.10	6
	National (formerly Country) Party			
1.	Farmers and agriculture	29.23	24.40	1
2.	Economic orthodoxy	18.88	14.93	2
3.	Infrastructure	6.18	5.90	3
4.	Social harmony	5.63	4.80	5
5.	Political authority	3.62	4.84	4
6.	Democracy	3.58	2.68	8
7.	Protectionism	3.46	2.92	6
8.	Free enterprise	2.46	2.88	7
9.	Economic goals	2.05	1.79	
10.	Labour groups: positive	1.94	1.50	
	Productivity		2.77	9
	Incentives		2.74	10

Note:
Source for original rankings (left hand side) is Budge, Robertson and Hearl (eds.) 1987: Chapter 3.

Table 5.6. Comparing Robertson's 1945–1980 analysis for Australia with replication for 1946–1996, based on CMP data set

First Stage:

Domain	Robertson (1946–1980)			Replication (1946–1996)		
	Qualifying variables	No. of factors	Interpretation	Qualifying variables	No. of Factors	Interpretation
1.	Foreign spl relations + Military Internationalism +	1	F11 Internationalism vs. Isolation	Same	1	Same
2.	Freedom & human rights Democracy	–	2 vars. Only; Not Factored	Same	–	–
3.	Decentralization + Govt & Admin Efficiency Political authority	2	F31 Efficiency vs. Authority; F32 Federal vs. States Power	Same	1	Essentially same as F31
4.	Free enterprise Incentives Market regulation Economic planning Economic goals Productivity Infrastructure Economic orthodoxy	4	F41 Ec. Orthodoxy vs. Goals and Regulation; F42 Productivity	Same except not economic planning	3	Same as F41–F42
5.	Environmental Protection Welfare + Education +	2	F51 Education & Social Services F52 Environment vs. Social Services	Same plus culture social justice	1	Same (with extra vars. Loading positively on same uni-polar factor)
6.	National effort	–	1 var. only; Not factored	Same plus National Way of Life +; Traditional Morality	1	National Way of Life + and Traditional Morality vs. Social Harmony
7.	Labour groups + Farmers and Agriculture Non-economic Groups	1	F71 Labour Groups vs. Farmers and Agriculture	Same plus Labour Groups -	2	Same as F71 (with labour Groups–loading negatively)

Second Stage:

	Robertson (1946–1980)		Replication (1946–1996)	
	First Order Factors/Variables (Loading >.3 or <.3)	Interpretation	First Order Factors/Variables (Loading >.3 or <.3)	Interpretation
Factor I	F11, F41, F51, F71	Left-Right	F11, F41, F51, F71, (plus VAR201, F31, F42)	Left-Right
Factor II	F52, VAR606	Discipline vs. Free Pursuit of Goals	F52 plus F32	Discipline vs. Free Pursuit of Goals

Notes:
Variables not scoring an overall average of at least 1% references overall or at lest 3% for any one party are omitted.
Factors are only reported if their Eigenvalue $\geq$ 1.0.
The original analysis is reported in Budge, Robertson and Hearl (eds.) 1987: 51–60, 70.

of the original 1987 volume), and a replication done on the expanded CMP data. The results together with those from the re-analysis are summarized in Table 5.6. Again, any methodological doubts about the general role of factor analysis in the policy area should not affect this tightly focussed examination of the comparability of results.

As will be seen from the Table, the general structure obtained by factor-analyzing each of the seven domains separately (variables not scoring an overall average of at least 1% overall or at least 3% for any one party were excluded) is very similar whichever of the two data sets is used. It is not altogether surprising therefore that the second stage analysis too shows a very similar pattern to Robertson's. Indeed the only real difference is that a number of First Stage Factors and Variables which just failed to load in excess of 0.3 (or less than − 0.3) in Robertson's analysis do just manage to do so when the extended data set is used. However, this does not affect interpretation. The first Second Stage Factor is still a very clear left-right one while the second is equally clearly what Robertson describes as 'Discipline vs Free Pursuit of Goals' but which might be better labelled a 'Social (as opposed to Economic) Policy dimension.'

On this evidence at least, the addition of some 24 new manifestos from six new elections does not particularly affect the overall structure of the Australian data at all. Pending more sophisticated tests, therefore, readers can proceed to the analysis of our estimates with reasonable confidence in their stability and reliability. Findings here support the general credibility of the Manifesto Group's earlier research on which we can now build with at least some measure of confidence.

OVERVIEW AND CONCLUSIONS

In this chapter we have singled out the most obvious 'fault line' in the Manifesto data—that between the original data collected and coded by the MRG up to 1983, and the estimates subsequently added by the Comparative Manifestos Project based on the Wissenshaftzentrum Berlin. This is not to deny, of course, that there are other places where contrasts might appear as a result of methodological error rather than truly substantive differences. However, 1983 is the most obvious break-point at which a change in management and procedures might make a difference.

Our analyses show that whatever the potential for methodological error roundabout 1983, it has not actually materialized. Comparable analyses still produce the same results whether using the original data pre-1983, or the expanded data sets covering 1946–1997 inclusive.

The positive findings reported here stem, of course, from only one of the possible checks on the reliability of our estimates. Others might investigate cross linguistic as opposed to cross country variation. The effects of applying the coding instructions to different languages might indeed be to produce purely methodological variation. It is here that holistic tests covering all the estimates, rather than conventional checks on inter and intra coder reliability inside any one language, appear most appropriate in assessing reliability.

Indirect checks on purely linguistic versus ideological sources of variation in the data base have already been carried through. For example, Budge and Robertson found that parties grouped with the appropriate ideological 'family' rather than falling into national/language groups (however, only with the pre-1983 MRG data) (Budge, Robertson and Hearl (eds.) 1987: 399–414).

Obviously, there are almost an infinite series of checks that could be applied to our estimates. So one can never be entirely conclusive in assessments of their standing. What we can say is that they have passed all the checks applied up to now with quite impressive credibility. Computerized textual analyses have an inbuilt reliability which manual coding can never emulate. It seems, however, that the estimates presented here have few problems to the extent we have tested them and may well have advantages in terms of their underlying validity. It is to an assessment of this that we turn in the next chapter.

6

Checking the Party Policy Estimates: Convergent Validity

Michael D. McDonald and Silvia M. Mendes

INTRODUCTION

In a sense most of this book has been concerned with the validity of the Manifesto data and the estimates derived from them. Chapter 1 has matched the major Left-Right indicator with the historical record (predictive validity); Chapter 2 has reported their use in research (hypothesis validity); Chapters 3 and 4 have gone into the plausibility of the underlying Saliency Theory and the match between the coding distributions and its expectations (face validity). What this chapter deals with in particular is construct validity—whether the codings correlate with other measures of the same conceptual construct (Weber 1990: 18).

The construct in question is the Left-Right scale which has been central to most chapters of the book and used in most applied research. It also, as noted in Chapter 1, bases itself on all the variables of the coding frame either directly or indirectly. As argued above, there are merits in a holistic approach to checking such a large and open ended data-set. We want to know if it generally gets things right when used in a comparative over time context rather than evaluating the details of particular coding decisions.

There is also a practical reason for concentrating on the Left-Right scale rather than on the other policy estimates given below or on particular categories of the coding frame. It is the only measure based on the data where there are enough alternative indicators to support an investigation of construct validity. While the same approach could be applied in principle to the other policy scales, the empirical basis is lacking. They must therefore rely for the time being on the other forms of validation discussed above—though, like the rest of the data, their standing will be enhanced if the general Left-Right measure comes successfully through the checks imposed here.

We do include a number of other Left-Right scales derived from Manifesto data in the comparisons. These are derived from suggestions made by other investigators as to how the coding categories might be combined in this context. As they draw on a somewhat different range of categories and combinations to the MRG scale, their collective performance can be taken as a more generalized check on the validity of the entire data-set, rather than of one particular measure derived from it.

One difficulty with comparing measures however is that not all of them have equal standing. The 'expert judgements' of parties' Left-Right positions (Castles and Mair 1984; Laver and Hunt 1992; Huber and Inglehart 1995) against which we validate the Manifesto-based scales have been severely criticised for mixing up declared party policy with their actual behaviour (fatal if one wants to explain behaviour by party positioning) and being imprecise about the time period and criteria involved in the judgements, among other things (Budge 2000). The other Left-Right scales derived from the Manifesto data, which we also use in comparisons, are generally exploratory attempts at measuring party positions on inductive factor-analyses of the data as it then was (Budge and Robertson 1987; Bartolini and Mair 1990). Given the problems involved with the other measures, the 'saliency' measure employed here could well be accepted as a superior standard by which the others should be judged, rather than using *them* to judge *it*, which is what we propose to do here.

The general status of the measures is not a question to argue about at this point. In order to set up the test we will simply assume that expert judgements directly reflect the 'real' positions of the political parties and see how far the saliency-based scale measures up to them. To put it in context we will also include the other left-right measures based on the Manifesto data, regardless of their general standing. Shaping our research design in this way makes our test of convergent validation a harder one for the main Left-Right scale to pass. If it does, it should gain greater credibility than if it had been accorded a more privileged status.

RELATING THE EXPERT PARTY POLICY SCALES TO EACH OTHER

Following this reasoning we are going to accept the Left-Right party positioning on expert scales as the meaning of Left-Right that we intend to measure. That simplifies the question; so that we ask: Can the CMP data be used to measure the Left-Right positions of parties as those Left-Right positions are understood by experts? Of course, taking the expert scales as the standard for evaluation without knowing much about their reliability and validity runs the risk of inferring that any mismatch between the expert and the CMP scales results from problems with the CMP data. It might well be the case that different expert scales measure Left-Right positions differently, contain a good deal of random noise, or both. That would force the unrealistic requirement that the CMP scales match moving targets. Therefore, we begin by exploring the reliability and validity of three expert scales.

Since 1980 Frank Castles and Peter Mair (1984), Michael Laver and W. Ben Hunt (1992), and John Huber and Ronald Inglehart (1995) have produced expert scales of party positions. They provide a common coverage of 84 parties in 16 Western countries operating as democracies throughout the post-war period. The

Castles-Mair and Huber-Inglehart scales expressly focus on the Left-Right location of parties. Laver and Hunt asked their experts to place the parties along eight dimensions. They suppose that their public ownership dimension is the most indicative of the usual conception of Left-Right (Laver and Hunt 1992: 122). Relating their public ownership, social issues, and taxes-versus-spending dimensions to the other scales through regression analysis confirms this idea, though all three dimensions have some relationship to the overall Left-Right indices casting some doubt incidentally on whether experts can distinguish between the separate policy dimensions well enough to place parties quite independently on them.

To bring the Laver-Hunt measures into line with the Left-Right content of Castles-Mair and Huber-Inglehart, we calculated a weighted average of the public ownership/social value/tax-service scales in order to generate a general Left-Right scale. The public ownership and tax/spending scales have a weight of 1.5 and the social scale has a weight of 1.0. That gives three times as much weight to economic as to social issues, a fact that accords with the coefficient weights found in the two regression equations.

Correlations between the three expert indices are:

C–M/H–I	0.93
C–M/L–H	0.94
H–I/L–H	0.94

To assess the reliability and stability of these measures we can apply the Heise (1969) measurement model, which distinguishes between the two. This model assumes a Markovian process, in which a party's change from today's position to tomorrow's will be unaffected by its position yesterday. As each of the expert scales can be associated with a different time period prior to its date of publication, we can check change over time (begging the question of whether or not all the experts focused on the whole of the post-war period).

The Heise measurement model produces stability and reliability estimates of:

Reliability	=	0.947
Stability, early 80s to late 80s'	=	0.988
Stability, later 80s to early 90s'	=	0.994
Stability, early 80s, to early 90s	=	0.982

The measurements are highly reliable; 94.7 per cent of the variation is systematic and just over 5 per cent is random. Once the modest unreliability is taken into account, the positioning of the parties is almost perfectly stable. This can be taken as both good news and bad news. To the good, there is very little randomness in the experts' placements of the parties. The bad news is that a problem would arise if one were to attempt to use the expert scales as a basis for analyzing party strategic movements. There are essentially no observable movements other than those due to a small amount of measurement error. Across a decade's time, the experts saw the parties in essentially the same relative locations. Perhaps the parties never moved, or perhaps the experts are reporting an over-time general statement about party locations in the post-war period.

THE MANIFESTO LEFT-RIGHT SCALES

Various scales have emerged from factor-analytic and theoretically based explorations of the Manifesto data conducted at various time points and with different concerns. For reasons explained in previous chapters the theoretically driven but inductively informed measure developed in Laver and Budge (eds.) (1992) has developed as the leading one. The coding categories included in it and the other Left-Right scales are shown in Table 6.1.

What is interesting is that each of the scales grouped rather different combinations of coding categories, drawing in almost the whole range of Manifesto variables into one or other of them. This makes an assessment of their overall validity in some sense a check on the validity of the Manifesto data-set as a whole, even if our main interest focuses on the first scale.

The Manifesto Research Group (MRG) appear to have created a global form of a Left-Right scale, inasmuch as they include coding categories from all seven policy domains of the data-set. Budge and Robertson, whose analysis actually identifies a left-wing isolationism position and a capitalist traditionalist position (1987: 404), are nearly as catholic. The Left versus Capitalist positions cover all but the welfare domain. Bartolini and Mair's (1990) Left-Right measure decidedly focuses on economic matters. Coding categories from the economic domain alone are included in their Left-Right scale. Finally, Laver and Garry propose that Left-Right party positions are best described in terms of concerns for state intervention versus capitalist economics plus negative mentions of welfare. They alternatively treat concerns over social and cultural values as a separate liberal versus conservative aspect of Left-Right politics.

The scales we check out in this chapter take the combinations of variables proposed by the various authors in Table 6.1, but score them in the subtractive way originally suggested by Laver and Budge (1992: 25–30). They identified 26 coding categories that go into their measurement definition of Left-Right. They add 13 Left items and subtract from this quantity the sum of 13 Right items. A party that makes 200 total statements with 100 (or 50 per cent) of them about Left items and 40 (or 20 per cent) about the Right items receives a score of +30 (i.e. 50 minus 20).

This difference or subtractive measure is consistent with saliency theory. Of all the statements the party made, on balance, 30 more units were devoted to Left matters than to Right matters. Imagine that at the next election this party says exactly the same things it had said last time but adds 200 new statements about an issue that is not of concern to the Left-Right scale (e.g. favourable statements about protecting the environment). Now the party is making 400 total statements, and relative to that total they are making only half as many Left statements (25 per cent) and half as many Right statements (10 per cent) as they did for the first election. The party's Left-Right position is recorded as moving from +30 to +15. That is, the party is scored as considerably less left-leaning at the second election compared to the first. It has moved toward the centre by virtue of devoting attention to policy matters that are not within the categories relevant to the Left-Right scale.

This is clearly not the only way categories could be aggregated. For one thing they could be weighted by their factor loadings rather than treated equivalently, as the original investigators in fact scored them. In this analysis however we treat them all in a subtractive form, with equal weighting of categories, which makes them more equivalent for later comparison.

THE MANIFESTO SCALES: VALIDITY

In order to evaluate and reliability of the scales constructed from the CMP data, we use the five Left-Right scales described in Table 6.1. We have created scores for each of the five scales by, first, summing the Right items and the Left items and then calculating a subtractive measure (Left-Right). Because the expert scales show no sign of change in the party positions, as if the experts have summarized the typical positions of the parties, we use each party's 1972–92 period average over the Manifesto scales for testing their scale validities. Requiring a party to have a Manifesto throughout this 20-year period reduces the number of parties we analyse from 84 to 66. Once we know something about validity, we turn back to the Heise reliability and stability test and apply it to the five scales under consideration.

Figure 6.1 illustrates the factor loadings (principal axis with varimax rotation) of all five Manifesto scales. The analysis includes the three expert Left-Right scales and, in order to help define the factor space, the Laver and Hunt (1992) public ownership and social ratings.

For ease of exposition at this point, the two factors can be discussed as 'pure' indicators of an economic dimension (the horizontal axis) and a social dimension (the vertical axis). In that view, the expert scales appear to be a mix of those two dimensions, with slightly more weight attributable to the economic as compared to the social. Relative to the expert scales, the CMP scales are more economic-laden. Indeed, they are even closer to the horizontal axis than is the Laver-Hunt public ownership expert scale.

Given that we are accepting the expert scales as the meaning of Left-Right, the Manifesto scales are slightly off the mark on the validity question. To determine by how much they miss the mark of the expert scales, we follow Guildford and Hoepfner's (1969) advice and rotate the horizontal dimension so that it goes directly through the centroid formed by the three expert scales. The rotation substitutes the criterion of defining a dimension by how well it hits a theoretical mark as opposed to how well it accounts for particular types of

Table 6.1. CMP Coding categories included in Left-Right scales across four studies

CMP Var No.	Domain	MRG	Budge & Robertson	Bartolini & Mair	Laver & Garry Economic	Laver & Garry Social
102	Foreign		Foreign special relations, con			
103	Foreign	Decolonization	Decolonization			
105	Foreign	Military, con				
106	Foreign	Peace				
107	Foreign	Internationalism, pro				
110	Foreign		European Community, con			
202	Freedom	Democracy				
204	Freedom					
304	Govt					Constitutionalism, con
403	Economic	Regulation of capitalism	Regulation of capitalism	Regulation of capitalism	Regulation of capitalism	Government corruption
404	Economic	Economic planning		Economic planning	Economic planning	
406	Economic	Protectionism, pro		Protectionism, pro	Protectionism, pro	

Left

Items

				Economic goals		
408	Economic					
409	Economic			Keynesian economics		
410	Economic			Productivity		
411	Economic			Tech & infrastructure		
412	Economic	Controlled economy		Controlled Economy	Controlled Economy	
413	Economic	Nationalization	Nationalization	Nationalization	Nationalization	
504	Welfare	Welfare, pro				
506	Welfare	Education, pro				
602	Fabric		Nat'l way of life, con			Nat'l way of life, con
604	Fabric		Traditional morality, con			Traditional morality, con
701	Groups	Labour groups, pro	Labour groups, pro			
104	Foreign	Military, pro				
108	Foreign		European Community, pro			
203	Freedom	Constitutionalism, pro				Constitutionalism, pro
201	Freedom	Freedom & human rights	Freedom & human rights			
301	Govt		Decentralization			

Table 6.1. *(continued)*

	CMP Var No.	Domain	MRG	Budge & Robertson	Bartolini & Mair	Laver & Garry Economic	Laver & Garry Social
	303	Govt		Government efficiency			
	304	Govt		Government corruption			
Right	305	Govt	Government authority	Government authority			Government authority
Items	401	Economic	Free enterprise	Free enterprise	Free enterprise	Free enterprise	
	402	Economic	Incentives	Incentives	Incentives	Incentives	
	407	Economic	Protectionism, con		Protectionism, con	Protectionism, con	
	414	Economic	Economic orthodoxy	Economic orthodoxy	Economic orthodoxy	Economic orthodoxy	
	505	Welfare	Welfare, con			Welfare, con	
	601	Fabric	Nat'l way of life, pro				Nat'l way of life, pro
	603	Fabric	Traditional morality, pro	Traditional morality, pro			Traditional morality, pro
	605	Fabric	Law & order				Law & order
	606	Fabric	Social harmony	Social harmony			Social harmony
	607	Fabric		Multiculturalism, pro			

variance (where the varimax criterion is maximizing the squared factor loadings).

The expert scales are quite well defined by the Left-Right axis. They load highly on it and near zero on an orthogonal axis. This corroborates the inferences that they are highly reliable (communalties>.9) and valid (nearly pure measures) of what we take to be Left-Right party positioning. The loadings of the CMP scales show them to be measuring something similar but slightly angular. In that sense, none of them are precisely valid measures of Left-Right. They have, it would appear, too much economic content and/or too little social content to match what the experts have in mind for Left-Right.

This conclusion should not be overdrawn. The Manifesto measures, especially those of Budge-Robertson and the MRG scale, are close approximations to the Left-Right party positions given by the expert scales. The Bartolini-Mair and Laver-Garry Manifesto scales were designed to measure principally the economic or the social positioning of parties, and they do.

We want to press on, however, and see whether the Manifesto data can be used to produce an even more valid Left-Right measure, with validity still defined in terms of the expert scales. The prime candidates for adjustment are the Budge-Robertson and MRG scales. The intuitively appealing way to move their outcomes closer to the expert scales is to add social items, remove economic items, or both. Those sorts of additions and deletions should move the locations up along the social dimension and therefore closer to the positions of the expert scales. We made several adjustments on this sort, and they sometimes moved the factor analysis position closer to the Left-Right dimension that passes through the expert scales' centroid. However, none of those efforts resulted in the Manifesto scale being as close to the Left-Right dimension as any one of the three expert scales themselves.

A residual analysis revealed that for both scales, and for virtually all the adjustments we made to them, five parties were being scored consistently differently by the experts and CMP scores. The Italian Communists (PCI) and Danish Centre Democrats (CD) were scored as considerably farther Left by the experts than by the CMP scores. The experts placed the Italian PCI as nearly as far Left as the French PCF; the CMP scales have the PCI decidedly more toward the centre. The Danish CD are seen by the experts as a centrist party, similar to the Norwegian SP and the Swedish CP, but the CMP scales score them as right of centre, as far right as, say, the Danish KF and FRP. The conservative Italian MSI are about as Right-leaning as a party gets, according to the experts. The CMP scales place the MSI to the right of centre but not at the extreme right. Finally, the Finnish KESK and Norwegian Høyre are each scored as right of centre by the experts, whereas the CMP scales have both parties as Centre-Left. (c.f. Gabel and Huber (2000) for similar discrepancies).

After removing the five parties that mismatch on the expert versus Manifesto scales, factor analysis of the subtractive CMP scales reported in Figure 6.1

Factor loadings of expert scales and CMP subtractive scales

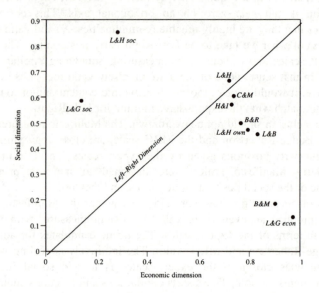

CMP Subtractive scales numerical value of factor loadings

Scale	Varimax rotation		Rotation to expert scales centroid	
Castles-Mair	.731	.610	.952	-.013
Laver-Hunt	.713	.670	.977	.044
Huber-Inglehart	.723	.577	.924	-.033
Budge-Robertson	.759	.505	.905	-.111
MRG	.825	.462	.927	-.186
Bartolini-Mair	.895	.192	.804	-.437
Laver-Garry econ	.965	.141	.824	-.521
Laver-Garry social	.133	.592	.486	.363
Laver-Hunt own	.787	.479	.909	-.149
Laver-Hunt social	.275	.858	.767	.472

Figure 6.1. Factor analysis results for expert and manifesto scales

Factor loading plot

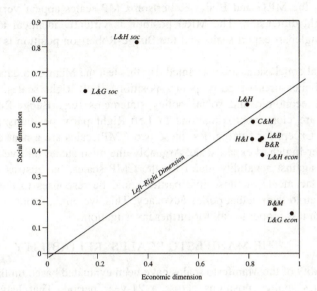

Numerical values of factor loadings

Scale	Varimax rotation		Rotation to expert scales centroid	
Castles-Mair	.809	.515	.959	.002
Laver-Hunt	.787	.581	.976	.070
Huber-Inglehart	.836	.444	.944	-.072
Budge-Robertson	.806	.448	.921	-.053
MRG	.845	.451	.955	-.071
Bartolini-Mair	.896	.176	.851	-.331
Laver-Garry econ	.963	.160	.899	-.380
Laver-Garry social	.145	.633	.461	.457
Laver-Hunt own	.846	.387	.922	-.126
Laver-Hunt social	.349	.822	.735	.508

Note
The five excluded parties are: Danish CD, Finnish KESK, Italian PCI, Italian MSI and Norwegian Høyre.

Figure 6.2. Two-dimensional factor analysis results for expert and manifesto scales (excluding five parties)

produces the results reported in Figure 6.2. Without those five parties in the analysis, the MRG and Budge-Robertson CMP scales appear very near to the Left-Right dimension. The MRG position is virtually identical to that of the Huber-Inglehart expert scale, and the Budge-Robertson position is quite near to them.

Several conclusions are warranted. By this test the Manifesto data can be used as valid measures of party policy positions. Left-Right scales, designed to combine economic and social policy statements (e.g. Budge-Robertson and MRG), are close approximations to Left-Right party positions produced by experts. Except for five parties, these two CMP scales are a near equivalent of the Huber-Inglehart expert scale. Arguably, the mismatches on five parties could be held against a validity claim for the CMP scales, but just as arguably the expert placements of those five parties could be responses to their reputation rather than to their actual policy advocacy. This, we think, is one of those issues for which it is proper to call for further investigation.

THE MANIFESTO SCALES: RELIABILITY

The validity of the Manifesto scales have been evaluated based on the average of the parties' policy positions across a 21-year period. That leaves open the question of whether the CMP data can be used for single time points. Application to shorter time frames would make it possible for researchers to use the Manifesto to analyze movements as parties adopt various mixes of strategic and sincere positions from one election to the next. This is not possible with the expert scales, for we have already seen that experts place the parties in almost completely stable locations. If, however, the Manifesto scales cannot be applied to single elections, then they can be deemed no more nor less useful than the expert surveys. Either the expert or the Manifesto scales can be used to locate the parties, but neither data source would allow investigation of the dynamics of party movements. In other words, we need to know two additional facts about the Manifesto scales with respect to single elections: (1) Are they reliable measures of the party positions? (2) If they are reliable, do the parties move around or stay at fixed positions in the policy space?

We evaluate reliability through the same Heise measurement model we earlier applied to the expert scales. The time points are, as nearly as practicable, the most recent election prior to each expert survey—Castles-Mair prior to 1983, Laver-Hunt prior to 1990; and Huber-Inglehart prior to 1993. In countries that held no election between 1990 and 1993, the time-3 point is the last election in the CMP94 data set (Volkens 1994), and the time-2 election is the one preceding that. With these data, we generated the correlation matrix reported in Table 6.2. In turn, from the threefold sets of correlations for each scale we

Table 6.2. Correlations, reliability and stability of Left-Right party positions for each of five manifesto scales, based on a three-wave panel for 66 parties

Scale	Correlations			Reliability	Stability		
	Time 1	Time 2	Time 3		T1–T2	T2–T3	T1–T3
Budge and Robertson				.889	.480	.831	.399
Time 1	1.00						
Time 2	.427	1.00					
Time 3	.355	.739	1.00				
MRG				.942	.786	.845	.664
Time 1	1.00						
Time 2	.741	1.00					
Time 3	.626	.796	1.00				
Bartolini and Mair				.654	.938	1.016	.953
Time 1	1.00						
Time 2	.614	1.00					
Time 3	.624	.665	1.00				
Laver and Garry Economic				.874	.891	.920	.820
Time 1	1.00						
Time 2	.778	1.00					
Time 3	.716	.804	1.00				
Laver & Garry Social				.069	–	–	–
Time 1	1.00						
Time 2	.039	1.00					
Time 3	.202	.350	1.00				

NOTE. The time points are defined by a nation's prior election closest to 1983, 1990 and 1995. In countries that held no election between 1990 and 1993, time 3 point is the last election in the CMP94 data set (Volkens, 1994), and the time 2 election is the one preceding that. The reliability and stability estimates are calculated by the measurement model formulae developed by Heise (1969).

estimate the reliability of the measure and the stability of the positions using the Heise model.

The MRG scale—that is the one used elsewhere in this book—is just as highly reliable as the expert scales. The Budge-Robertson scale and the Laver-Garry economic scale are also reasonably reliable. The Bartolini-Mair scale falls below most conventions for acceptable reliability, with less than two-thirds of its variation being systematic. The Laver-Garry social policy scale, with a reliability of only .069, is mostly noise.

There are likely to be several reasons for these varying reliabilities. First, scales formed with a large number of items, such as Budge-Robertson and MRG, tend to produce higher reliabilities compared to those with fewer items. This is true in conventional testing, and it appears to be true for the Manifesto data. Second, it may well be that the Bartolini-Mair scale really requires that different items have different weights. Third, reliability could be sensitive to the inclusion of certain items. In particular, the welfare items, excluded from the Bartolini-Mair scale but included in Budge-Robertson, MRG and Laver-Garry economic scales, are likely to add systematic variation to the party positions.

The stability estimates are as heartening for analysts as the reliability estimates are for those who have used or want to use the Manifesto scales. As measured by the Budge-Robertson and MRG scales, the parties are not completely stable. Parties do offer different positions from one time to another. This, as we have been suggesting, opens the door to the possibility of using the CMP scales to analyse party movements, particularly strategic movements. We know from other analyses (Budge, Robertson and Hearl (eds.) 1987; Budge and Laver (eds.) 1992; Klingemann, Hofferbert and Budge 1994) that over the long run parties do not stray too much from their usual ideological, Left-Right location. It is rare to see one party 'leapfrog' another. We see from Table 6.2, however, that the party positions are changeable in the short run. Together these sets of findings mean that the parties do not wander so far from their ideological base as to alienate their core constituents, but they do take up different positions at different times.

CONCLUSION

The main message to draw from the analyses presented here is that the Manifesto data can be and have been used to provide valid and reliable measurements of party policy positions. Accepting the problematic claim of expert assessments of party policy positions as the standard for what it means for a party to be on the Left, on the Right, or in the Centre, we have shown that the Budge and Robertson as well as the MRG measure of Left-Right party locations are quite similar to what the experts say. And, once we take account of the expert versus CMP differences with respect to five parties—the Danish CD, Finnish KESK, Italian PCI and MSI, and Norwegian Høyre—these two CMP measures place the parties in essentially the same way on the Left-Right positions. On the question of reliability, we demonstrate that the three expert surveys are highly reliable measurements of party Left-Right positions, with reliabilities close to 95 per cent. We also show that the MRG Left-Right 'Saliency' scale is just as reliable. With respect to validity and reliability there is little that distinguishes the results of expert surveys from, at least, that scaling of parties. The evidence here tells us that to the extent one has confidence in the party positioning from expert surveys there is every reason to have just as much confidence in party positioning based on the Manifesto data.

Validity and reliability are necessary measurement conditions. Our analysis strongly suggests that expert surveys are deficient and the Manifesto measures are useful on two important and additional concerns involved in measuring party policy positions. The experts place the parties in such stable locations that there is little hope of using expert surveys to investigate party policy dynamics. The CMP is probably the only viable data source for observing such dynamics and analyzing the party movements predicted by various theoretical propositions.

Furthermore, there is also a strong indication that expert surveys may produce suspect results about where the parties stand on different dimensions of politics and policy. The Laver and Hunt (1992) survey was expressly and carefully designed to elicit expert responses to party policy positions along several seemingly distinct policy dimensions. Our results indicate some reasons to doubt whether expert respondents actually can and do make clear and sharp distinctions between these.

All-in-all, the Manifesto data and scales offer analysts everything that can be offered by expert surveys. But that is not all. On the matter of party policy dynamics the CMP data are all we have, and they are good—valid and reliable.

7

Using Manifesto Estimates to Validate Computerized Analyses

Judith Bara

INTRODUCTION

Since the inception of the MRG in the late nineteen seventies, many scholars have taken advantage of the vast repository of data, which has been produced by the continuous review and updating of the material. At the same time, content analysis as a general method of enquiry for researchers has become increasingly popular and has been harnessed to serve the needs of projects as diverse as identifying a 'New Labour' vocabulary (Fairclough 2000) to aiding research in nursing studies (Wilde Kelly and Sine 1990) or historiography (Sedelow and Sedelow 1978). In addition to the greater usage of content analytic tools, the method has become progressively more quantitative in orientation. Indeed, it may be seen as a useful technique for bridging the gap between the qualitative and quantitative traditions in research, a process that has given greater rigour to scientific analysis and enriched scholarly collaboration and debate.

In order to develop the use of content analysis further, advantage needs to be taken of new technological advances and, in particular, of opportunities provided by computerized analysis.[1] This is especially appropriate for the large-scale study of documents, which is able to provide a rich source for political research. The amount of documentation within the political arena, much of it available on the World Wide Web, has increased exponentially. This repository of course includes political programmes such as manifestos, platforms and long-term political party plans. The justification for using these documents is widely accepted. Despite debate and some disagreement as to the precise methods to be used in their analysis it is agreed by all concerned that 'manifestos (and platforms) are a core source of information about party policy positions' (Laver and Garry 2001). Such election programmes also form a vital link in helping to establish government accountability and obviously provide an opportunity for the construction of estimates of political preferences (Budge, Tanenbaum and Bara 1999). This is especially relevant in terms of links between the issues perceived to be important by the public, political parties and government.

However, to apply content analytic techniques in the same ways as those developed by the MRG in the early nineteen eighties is costly and resource-intensive. The original MRG project took a relatively large group of researchers more than a decade and is in constant need of updating. It is necessary to seek cheaper means of engaging in this very labour-intensive analysis while still producing reliable and accurate results.

New technology now makes possible the computer analysis of huge volumes of political text This is of course not a new idea. Stone et al undertook pioneering work in the 1960s, exemplified by the publication of *The General Inquirer* in 1966. Despite valiant efforts to develop software more appropriate to processing a broader range of data than that susceptible to analysis by *The General Inquirer*, including early versions of the content analysis program TEXTPACK, results were somewhat inconclusive (Klingemann 1983). Today, however, better computers and software, combined with the widespread availability of machine-readable text, suggest that there are virtually unlimited possibilities for the coding and analysis of politically relevant material. Although manual coding will probably never be dispensed with completely, it will be used at a much lower level of coverage, for micro-analysis and checking the validity of computer techniques (Zuell *et al.* 1996; Alexa, 1997; Bara, 1998; 2000). While computerized coding is certainly not trouble-free, it has vast potential for further applications to the content analysis of documents (Laver, 2000), as well as being completely reliable (i.e. the same procedure applied to the same document will always give the same results). Kleinnijenhuis, Pennings and colleagues at the Vrije Universiteit Amsterdam have recently embarked on research involving widespread computerization of both content analysis and linguistic translation which develops further work already carried out in the field (Kleinnijenhuis and Pennings 2000).

There are many other advantages in using computerized coding. Given the centrality of documents to the operation of the democratic process, many alternative categorizations can be used to develop estimates and indices of preferences and outputs (see, *inter alia*, Riffe, Fico and Lacy, 1998, Roberts, 1997). Party manifestos and platforms represent only one data source for this type of analysis. Others include throne speeches, 'State of the Union' addresses, parliamentary reports such as Hansard, etc.

The pioneering work of the Manifesto Research Group in the 1980s demonstrated that content analysis could be extended across a broad range of political and governmental activity (see, *inter alia*, Budge, Robertson and Hearl (eds.) 1987; Laver and Budge, (eds.) 1992, Klingemann, Hofferbert and Budge et al, 1994). To do so on the basis of traditional manual coding procedures would be extremely time-consuming, however. It would also be expensive and less reliable, though no less valid, than computerized techniques. Where manual coding will always have a role is in validating the computerized results, since major doubts arise about the possibility that they may not be measuring what we think they measure.

This chapter discusses ongoing work in developing new, computerized coding and shows how the well-established estimates produced by the MRG, and contained in the CD-ROM accompanying this volume can be used to validate them. In a sense this chapter takes up the point made in Chapter 3 about the need for a general standard for evaluation and the ability of the Manifesto estimates and scales to supply this—especially evident after the checks on their own reliability and validity carried out above.

ESTABLISHING THE BASIS FOR COMPARISON

In order to validate computer-derived estimates as fully as possible against manual ones, it is important to establish a firm basis for comparison. We need to be able to demonstrate that, all things being equal, we are indeed comparing like with like. Hence, we need as far as possible to work with the same units of analysis. The computer estimates discussed below code (quasi) sentences on the basis of the words and phrases they contain. The quasi-sentences quite closely replicate the analytic units used in the Manifesto data.

The original MRG study (Budge, Robertson and Hearl (eds.) 1987) found that a strict grammatical definition of the sentence as the unit of analysis proved to be a dubious basis for quantification. This was because many statements, rather than representing specific declarations of intent, were actually strings of assertions separated by semi-colons or bullet points and often laid down very different priorities. Since each assertion is only coded once, treating each of these strings as a single sentence would mean that large amounts of relevant data would be lost and the analysis might be skewed. Thus the unit of analysis used in the Manifesto data is the 'quasi-sentence'—a cogent statement possibly separated by grammatical symbols other than a full stop or period. This simple procedure provides a good indication of party concerns and also represents a reliable focus for the application of computerized coding

Although textual data can easily be divided into these analytic units before being fed into the analysis, it is important to check that computerized techniques are also able to produce—as near as possible—identical analytic units. Thus the same punctuation marks need to be used within the election programme to create chunks of text which can be coded electronically. This however is only part of the problem of producing comparable results from the manual and computerized analysis and can be overcome relatively easily. It is far more difficult to replicate the manual 'codebook' as a computer 'dictionary'.

For the first of the analyses below, *a priori* categories constructed for MRG manual coding were also used as the basis for a computer dictionary. For ease of working the categories were not the standard 54 (Table 3.2) but a condensed set of twenty, suggested in Laver and Budge (eds.) (1992: 24 ff). Each category in this scheme was used to create a computerized coding category, augmented by additional words, word strings and alternative signifiers to aid in contextualization. Hence, for example, 'armed services' was used to distinguish the use of the term 'services' from 'social services' or 'educational services'.

Similar distinctions were made in terms of 'rights'—'welfare rights', 'human rights', 'civil rights' etc. Such phrases may not come into play as often as single words, but the greater degree of accuracy and correspondence with human coders' contextual skills makes this worthwhile in order to produce results which are as valid as possible.

The fully computerized dictionary was applied using TEXTPACK 7.0 software in order to generate a computer-coded data set. Although other packages were assessed, it was felt that TEXTPACK was especially suited to this application as it provides for construction of dedicated dictionaries, 'key word in context' checks and interfaces with readily available statistical packages such as SPSS. It also allows for construction of a similar basic unit of analysis to that employed in the manual coding procedure.[2]

The *a priori* computer dictionary includes synonyms, alternative words that produce the same meaning and even American spellings to maximize the use of contextual signifiers. Sources for the various additions were the documents themselves and other coding schemes (for example that developed in an ESRC-sponsored project using different coding schemes and extensive use of thesauri (Budge, Tanenbaum and Bara 1999). The *a priori* dictionary was refined several times in this way and the primary version used in this study consists of about 900 entries representing single words, word strings, word stems and common abbreviations.

The ultimate payoff from applying computers to coding may well be the complete computerization of the process, always depending on what investigators want of course. The most likely point at which they will want to intervene and retain control is in the compilation of the dictionary which represents the coding frame and which specifies the words and phrases the program will count in the text. But there is an alternative to this. A dictionary could also be left to the computer on the basis of most repeated words/phrases (for example all those appearing three or more times, excluding articles, pronouns and connectives). The validation of estimates produced by such a process against those derived from manual schemes is more difficult, however, since the categories which emerge will be far less comparable with the manual ones than where these were used as the starting point for the *a priori* dictionary.

However it is illuminating to see how well a totally automated inductive procedure works compared to a *a priori* one. Hence a 'Computer Derived Policy Analysis Dictionary' was constructed for this analysis. It consists of inductive categories built on the basis of words / phrases which occurred more than twice in any single document within a large sample (49 per cent) of all British manifestos covering the three main parties throughout the entire post war period. These words were then grouped into 25 clusters representing concepts/policy, which formed the basis for twenty-five coding categories. The latter were then applied directly to all the documents by computer, again on the basis of units of analysis   constructed   as   far   as   possible   to   replicate   those   used

Table 7.1. Categories of the three dictionaries used in the textual analysis of British manifestos 1945–1997

MRG manual 20 categories	*A priori* computer 20 categories	Computer derived 25 categories
State Intervention	State Intervention	Foreign
Quality of Life	Quality of Life	International
Peace & Co-operation	Peace & Co-operation	Defence
Anti-Establishment	Anti-Establishment	Environment
Capitalist Economics	Capitalist Economics	Agriculture
Social Conservatism	Social Conservatism	Education
Productivity & Technology	Productivity & Technology	Heritage
Military Positive	Military Positive	Regions
European Union Positive	European Union Positive	Government
European Union Negative	European Union Negative	Freedom / Democracy
Freedom	Freedom	Health
Democracy	Democracy	Welfare
Decentralization Positive	Decentralization Positive	Social Justice
Government Efficiency	Government Efficiency	Social Policy
Social Justice	Social Justice	Demographic Groups
Social Services Positive	Social Services Positive	Finance & Tax
Education Positive	Education Positive	Trade & Industry
Labour Groups Positive	Labour Groups Positive	Professional & Tech
Agriculture & Farmers	Agriculture & Farmers	Energy / Utilities
Minorities	Minorities	Transport & Comm
		Employment / Labour
		Market Economy
		State Control
		Pro-Change
		Consumption

originally by the MRG. This dictionary has fewer entries than the *a priori* one (approximately five hundred).

The main difference in the construction of these two computer dictionaries is that in the case of the automatically derived one there is very little human intervention in terms of deciding which words are included. Thus the categories are much less prone to any built-in bias or ethnocentrism. A small amount of intervention was considered necessary in order to allow for idiosyncrasies of political vocabulary, for example the inclusion of some word strings such as 'proportional representation', 'Northern Ireland' or 'local government'. By the same token, there is no direct attempt to improve contextualization or the number of hits by the use of synonyms and therefore the most that such a dictionary can really hope to achieve is provision of a basic, accurate measure of saliency based on the most frequently appearing categories over time.

The great advantage of computerization is reliability. Given the same instructions and the same document, computers will always make the same decision—not something which can necessarily be said of human coders! As between different documents there is always a guarantee that the instructions (dictionary) are being applied in the same way.

The negative side of using computers in this way is that there is no sensitivity in the process nor querying of instructions which might produce nonsensical results. Computers moreover so far are able only to count words and phrases whereas in most languages the 'real' grammatical unit, which provides meaning and context, is the sentence. It is crucial therefore to engage in a rigorous validation exercise in order to demonstrate clearly that the results of computerized coding are just as meaningful as those derived from manual coding.

VALIDATING THE RESULTS OBTAINED FROM A PRIORI COMPUTERIZED CODING AGAINST THE MRG STANDARD

Validation must therefore be regarded as the nub if we are going to make greater research use of computerized coding. We are sure computer programs such as TEXTPACK can be used to analyze and summarize texts. The question is whether this is sufficient. Are the computerized category counts really giving as adequate and realistic a representation of the documents as a human coder might?

To answer this question we need to apply checks. The usual mechanical tests applied to manual coding—checking the inter-coder correspondence for generally high coincidence between decisions made by different coders confronting the same documents and using the same instructions—mean that we have confidence that the same standards of rigour apply. These are not relevant in the case of computer programs since we know they do this. More emphasis must therefore be placed on plausibility and face validity.

In this context the possession of a previously validated standard in the shape of the original MRG manual codings is very important. This we have in the form of the Left-Right scale evolved from these estimates—which enables graphical representations of Left-Right movements to be made over time (Klingemann, Hofferbert, Budge *et al.* 1994: 40; Laver and Budge (eds.) 1992: 22–7). Graphs of Left-Right party locations in most countries are extraordinarily convincing when set against the historical record—as may be seen from the representations in Chapter 1. One can accordingly test the validity of the related computerized word-count by seeing how far the Left-Right scale it generates resembles the original MRG one. To the extent it does can be regarded as validated. Inferentially the success of the computerized count in matching the original Left-Right scale can be generalized to the other computerized codings of documents for which no direct comparison is possible. To the extent one set of results can be taken as externally validated, all can, if the same procedure is applied. It is especially convincing to use an aggregate measure as a tool for validation since this allows for comparison of overall results rather than individual coding decisions and it is the accuracy of results that we are mainly interested in.

A validation check was therefore effected on the basis of the Left-Right measure familiar from earlier chapters. This was then applied to the manifestos of the UK Labour and Conservative parties and results of the analysis of the different computer codings were compared with those obtained from analysis based on manual coding. It should be noted that because this measure is obtained from subtracting the sum of scores for each party along the categories designated as 'left' from those designated as 'right', the term 'Left-Right' is applied to the figures. The more negative the score, the more left-orientated the party. The results of the first, *a priori* computerized analysis compared with the estimates derived from the MRG estimates are displayed in Figures 7.1 and 7.2 below.

There are three criteria we can use to decide on the validity of the computerized representations. First, are the parties placed broadly in their appropriate ideological location—left for Labour and right for the Conservatives? Secondly, does the computerized map produce reasonable movement? (After all, the object is to trace policy change over time, so perfectly stable estimates are inappropriate.) Thirdly, how far do movements correspond to those of the MRG standard?

On the question of broad location, we can see immediately that Labour is placed appropriately to the left of the computer version, but the Conservatives are placed inappropriately there as well! This would seem to indicate that the words and phrases the computer is picking up, even from Conservative manifestos, are too 'Leftist' in orientation. We shall return to this point below.

Both Labour and Conservative Figures show considerable movement from election to election, thus meeting our second criterion. The correlations between the computer and MRG maps are shown in Table 7.2 under 'First *a priori*

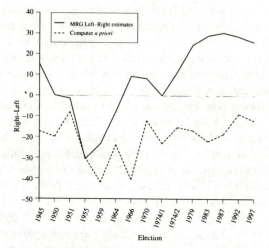

Figure 7.1. UK Conservative 1945-1997: Comparison between
Computer *a priori* and MRG estimates

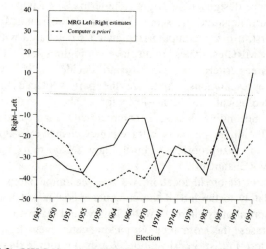

Figure 7.2. UK Labour 1945-1997: Comparison between Computer
a priori and MRG estimates

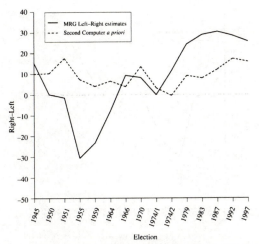

Figure 7.3. UK Conservative 1945-1997: Comparison between Second
Computer *a priori* and MRG estimates

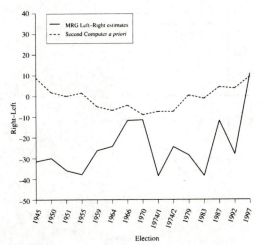

Figure 7.4. UK Labour 1945-1997: Comparison between Second
Computer *a priori* and MRG estimates

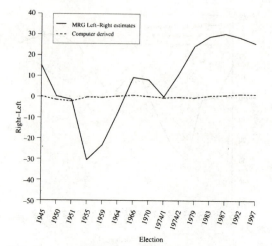

Figure 7.5. UK Conservative 1945-1997: Comparison between Computer Derived and MRG estimates

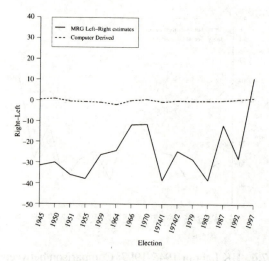

Figure 7.6. UK Labour 1945-1997: Comparison between Computer Derived and MRG estimates

dictionary'. These are surprisingly high, especially for the later post-war period. Over all the time points and for both parties, roughly one half of the movements are plotted similarly (r=.55),whereas for the period 1974–97 this rises to over eighty per cent (r=.84). This is a pattern which also appears for the parties individually, though correlations are lower and less significant owing to the fewer cases involved.

These encouraging results prompted us to try to improve both the fit and the plausibility of the Conservative location in the space. Adding words and phrases to the dictionary made little difference, however. A more analytic strategy was to work out what caused the problem of the Conservative mislocation. Here our earlier diagnosis of a leftward bias in the British political vocabulary proved useful as a way of getting a more plausible representation in terms of all three criteria sketched out above.

Our reasoning was that since both parties were shown as more 'Left' than they should have been, the selection of words and phrases in the computer dictionary was biased in this direction. A possible enhancement therefore might be produced by omitting the main elements which on *a priori* grounds were regarded as the core 'proprietal' issues of the Left. Specifically these related to word/phrase entries signifying categories for (103) anti-imperialism, (105) military negative, (504) welfare positive and (505) welfare negative as included in the relevant categories of the collapsed scheme first used in Laver and Budge (1992)

This version—designated as 'Second Computer *a priori* Dictionary'— produced the representations shown in Figures 7.3 and 7.4. These are much more plausible in positioning the Conservatives to the Right, while still allowing for reasonable policy movement between elections in both cases. Labour is of course positioned more to the Right than seems realistic but the parties are still distinguished from each other with no leapfrogging. The main advantage is that the representation is clearly less distorted for the Conservatives than it was in Figure 7.1.

Table 7.2 (under 'second *a priori* dictionary') gives correlations between the new computer representations and the MRG standard. They are either comparable with those for the first representation or somewhat better. So, over all criteria the second representation seems more accurate than the first. Again this conclusion applies particularly to the later post-war period. Whether computerizing the *a priori* categories has the same effect of picking out Leftist more than Rightist themes in other countries is an interesting question to which we will devote further research.

The Computer-Derived Content Analysis dictionary could not be validated in exactly the same way as the *a priori* ones because the categories produced on the basis of word counts were not totally compatible with the general Left-Right scale. Given the centrality of economic measures to any discussion of Left-Right differentiation, a general comparison of a simplified measure was undertaken.

Table 7.2. Correlations between computerized *a priori* and MRG estimates of Right-Left positions for British parties 1945–1997 and 1974–1997

		First *a priori* dictionary			Second *a priori* dictionary		
	n	R	Sig.	Level	R	Sig.	Level
Both Parties							
1945–1997	30	.55	.002	.001	.64	.000	.01
1974–1997	14	.84	.000	.01	.83	.000	.01
Conservative							
1945–1997	15	.55	.032	.05	.37	.171	ns
1974–1997	7	.68	.092	ns	.75	.054	ns
Labour							
1945–1997	15	.12	.675	ns	.21	.450	ns
1974–1997	7	.65	.119	ns	.76	.050	Ns

Table 7.3. Correlations between computer derived and MRG estimates of market economy vs state control positions for British parties 1945–1997 and 1974–1997

	Computer derived dictionary			
	n	R	Sig.	Level
Both Parties				
1945–1997	30	.39	.032	.05
1974–1997	14	.56	.028	.05
Conservative				
1945–1997	15	.52	.049	.05
1974–1997	7	.70	.080	ns
Labour				
1945–1997	15	.45	.090	ns
1974–1997	7	.80	.030	.05

This examined the percentage difference between the categories of Market Economy and State Control, both of which represented several combinations of the original MRG categories.

An examination of the Figures for both the Conservative and Labour parties (Figures 7.5 and 7.6) shows that the estimates obtained on the basis of the Computer-Derived dictionary are very flat and neutral. They also fail to distinguish between the parties, even though the results for the Conservatives are statistically significant (Table 7.3). This suggests that the automatic dictionary, based essentially on word counts, is not suitable for dealing with analytic units constructed on a more complex basis.

It is also clear from Figures 7.1 and 7.2 that despite differences in scores for the parties on the general Left-Right index, there are some encouraging signs for the eventual success of the computerized *a priori* coding scheme. The similarity in directional change for the Conservative scores—indeed for both parties after 1970—is discernible. The figures in Tables 7.2 and 7.3 show that half of the relationships between the MRG and computerized *a priori* positions are statistically significant—despite the fact that some of the calculations are based on very small numbers of cases.

CONCLUSIONS

Even though there may be payoffs from working on the *a priori* computerized scheme, perhaps by using more sophisticated programming, and by extending it to other countries to see if we get the same results, it is clear that we will hardly be able to dispense with the manually-coded Manifesto data yet awhile. For substantive applications the manual estimates remain far and away the most credible. So far as we know the computerized representations of Left-Right movements shown above are the most extensively checked and tested of those available up to now. Their failure to match up adequately to the manual codings leaves the latter unchallenged at the moment for use in actual political research. This failure, however, is not complete and there is a clear way forward for developing further research on this method.

What this chapter was also designed to demonstrate was the indispensable role of the Manifesto data in validating computerized representations. We clearly need a standard to decide whether these are performing well or badly. Matching maps of party movement, particularly on the Left-Right dimensions, provides a basis for validation of the computerized estimates, which we need to have before we can proceed to apply them with any confidence.

The MRG-CMP data are the only over-time indicators of policy movement which exist. So if we are to get more than spotty comparisons with one or two static indicators, we must bring them into the validation process. The results reported in this Chapter also suggest that the most successful computer representations are likely to take off from Saliency theory and the derived MRG coding frame, rather than from purely inductive categorizations of the documents.

1 I should like to thank Ian Budge and Eric Tanenbaum for their continuing support, advice and encouragement and Ekkehart Mochmann and Bruno Hopp of the ZA-EUROLAB, Universiteit Koln, for their invaluable help and guidance through the labyrinth of computerized textual analysis techniques.
2 More recent versions of The General Inquirer allow for dedicated dictionaries to be inserted, but at the time the project was undertaken, this was not available for use with Windows-based software. Now this is available it is anticipated that we will run a parallel analysis using The General Inquirer.

8

Extending Party Estimates to Governments and Electors

Hee-Min Kim and Richard C. Fording

INTRODUCTION

Previous chapters have concentrated strictly on the Manifesto estimates as such, giving a direct insight into party policy preferences. Similar coding procedures have been applied to the policy declarations of coalition governments, taken as a measure of at least promised outputs. The estimates generated from this supplementary content analysis also appear on the CD-ROM and are used in the analyses below.

The Manifesto data, however, are also capable of supporting indirect estimates of voter and government preferences, discussed in this chapter in regard to their Left-Right ideology. This constitutes a dramatic extension of the range of the data-set, of use for many purposes not previously envisaged by either the Manifesto Research Group or other investigators working with the data (Chapter 2).

Because of their many analytic uses estimates of median voter position are provided in the CD-ROM not only for the Left-Right scale but for other central policy scales such as Market Reliance, Planning, Welfare and Peace. To illustrate the mode of estimation and some applications of the estimates, our discussion is, however, focused in this chapter on ideology, in the sense of placements on the Left-Right scale introduced in Chapter 1 and employed in most previous chapters.

The term 'ideology' has been used in the social science literature for some time. In part, this is due to the fact that many political events are either known or assumed to have been driven by ideological differences between groups, political parties, or even countries. As a result, many political scientists have tried to describe the ideological tendencies of political parties, governments, or the electorate within countries during various historical periods.

Since it is ideological differences that seem to drive many political phenomena, political scientists often want to compare ideological positions among different political parties, governments, or voters. Too often, however, we are forced to do so in a more or less subjective fashion. (For a review of the existing measures of government ideology and the problems associated with them, see Kim and Fording (2000a). For a similar review of the existing measures of voter ideology and their problems, see Kim and Fording (1998).)

Ironically, given the importance of ideology in our theories of political behavior and change, there has been little systematic effort put forth to construct a measure of ideology that is comparable both across time and across countries. In this chapter, we introduce measures of voter ideology and government ideology developed elsewhere, building on the estimates provided by the Manifesto data which we feel allow meaningful comparisons across different countries as well as across different time periods. In the first section, we briefly review the measure of Left-Right party ideology used elsewhere in this book, particularly in Chapter 1, which becomes an integral part of our measures of voter and government ideology. In the following section, we describe how we operationalize the concept of voter ideology and present cross-national and cross-time comparisons of voter ideology in 25 Western democracies. In the third section, we describe how we operationalize the concept of government ideology and present cross-national and cross-time comparisons of government ideology in 14 selected countries. We summarize our findings in the conclusions.

PARTY IDEOLOGY

As we describe below, our measures of voter ideology and government ideology use party ideological scores as their component. Therefore, it is necessary to develop a reliable, interval-level measure of party ideology that is comparable across countries and time. Here we use the measure of party ideology based on manifesto data, first developed by Laver and Budge (1993) and described in Chapter 1. This builds on a priori ideas about Left and Right but also on an analysis of 20 countries over the entire period in the manifesto data set to create a Left-Right scale. Thirteen categories were identified as comprising left ideology and another 13 as comprising right ideology. These ideological categories consistently loaded together in a series of factor analyses (1993: 24–7) and formed the basis for Laver and Budge's measure of party ideology.[1]

The data in the manifesto set are collected such that statements in each of these 26 categories demonstrate either pro-left or pro-right tendencies. Based on these 26 categories, Laver and Budge developed separate measures of left and right ideology for each party in each election for these countries in the following manner:

$$IDLeft = \Sigma \text{ Pro-Left Categories}$$
$$IDRight = \Sigma \text{ Pro-Right Categories}$$

In other words, IDLeft represents the percentage of all party statements that advocate left-wing positions, and IDRight represents the corresponding percentage of all party statements that represent right-wing positions. They then computed their measure of party ideology (IDParty) as follows:

$$IDParty = IDRight–IDLeft$$

They assume that voters evaluate parties on their net ideological position (scores) with respect to the left-right dimension. The measure is thus computed by subtracting the leftist score from the rightist score (%rightist statements–%leftist statements). This procedure yields a measure of party ideology that ranges from −100 to 100 where the larger score indicates greater support for rightist policies.[2]

VOTER IDEOLOGY

Since it is not feasible to describe the exact shape of the voter distribution on an ideological dimension in all Western democracies, we estimate the *median* voter position in these countries as our indicator of voter ideology. The choice of the median voter position is well justified not only because it indicates the central tendency among voters, but also due to the amount of attention paid to the median voter in the (formal) theoretic literature.

Our measure of voter ideology rests on three basic assumptions about how voters think and behave when making voting decisions. First, we assume that a left-right ideological dimension can be found in most industrialized democracies. Survey research has repeatedly shown that the majority of voters in most (if not all) Western democracies conceive of politics in such a fashion, and can readily place themselves on some type of left-right scale (e.g. Inglehart and Klingemann 1976). Even in the United States, where early research seemed to demonstrate an absence of ideological thinking, more recent research has found ideology to be an important organizing framework for political attitudes for a significant portion of the electorate (Achen 1975; Jacoby 1995; Nie, Verba and Petrocik 1976).

A second assumption inherent in our approach is that left-right ideology is an important, and often primary determinant of vote choice in Western democracies, and that it has been so for the entire post-war period. Few would dispute the importance of the left-right dimension in influencing vote choice in these countries.[3] There is the perception, however, that the salience of this ideological cleavage has diminished over time, and particularly since WWII. Such a view is fueled by evidence of the diminishing importance of social class in predicting vote choice (e.g, Franklin 1985). It does not necessarily follow, however, that the importance of left-right ideology has diminished thereby. Indeed, recent evidence suggests that although ideological cleavages are not as strongly related to class position as they once were, the left-right dimension remains a most significant, if not dominant cleavage in Western democracies (Blais, Blake and Dion 1993; Budge and Robertson 1987; Knutsen 1988; Lijphart 1984; Morgan 1976; Warwick 1992).[4]

Finally, we assume that the left-right dimension is comparable across countries. Though little direct evidence exists to evaluate this claim, there is reason to believe this assumption is more or less plausible. Over the years, a large literature has developed which confirms that there is a common ideological dimension with which one can compare *party ideology* across different countries (Browne, Gleiber and Mashoba 1984; Budge and Robertson 1987; Castles and

Mair 1984; Cusack and Garrett 1993; Dodd 1976; Gross and Sigelman 1984; Janda 1980; Laver and Budge 1993; Laver and Schofield 1990: 248; Morgan 1976; Warwick 1992). From these results, along with the common perception that in many countries, left-right ideological orientations serve as a basic reference point for voters' choices of candidates/parties (Fuchs and Klingemann 1990; Inglehart and Klingemann 1976; Lancaster and Lewis-Beck 1986; Langford 1991; Laponce 1981; Lewis-Beck 1988; Percheron and Jennings 1981), it logically follows that there is a common ideological dimension with which one can compare *voter ideology* across different countries.

Assuming the comparability, continuity, and relevance of the left-right dimension, it is then possible to develop a measure of the ideological position of a particular electorate that is comparable across countries and across time. To do so, one must first begin to conceive of elections as large-scale opinion polls. In this sense one might think of ballots as questionnaires which instruct the 'respondent' to choose the party that is closest to him or her on a left-right ideological scale. Assuming we have accurate, comparable, interval-scale measures of party ideology for each party in an election, we can then treat election results, along with the corresponding measures of party ideology, as a grouped frequency distribution and calculate fairly reliable estimates of measures of central tendency such as the median and the mean. In other words, we infer ideological tendencies based on the rational choices of ideological voters.

MEASURING VOTER IDEOLOGY

In this section, we describe how we estimate the median ideological position within the electorate of each country, at each election. We proceed in a series of three steps. First, for each election, we obtain ideology scores for each party in that election using the Laver-Budge formula above and place the parties on an ideological dimension by their score.[5]

Second, for each party, we find an interval on this dimension where its supporters are located. This was done in the following manner: for each party we calculate the midpoint between this party and the one immediately left of it and another midpoint between this party and the one immediately right of it. We assume that those who vote for this party fall into this interval between these two midpoints on the left-right ideological dimension. In other words, this is a simple application of the Euclidean preference relations: simply put, voters choose the candidates/parties that are closest to them. Voters beyond the left side of this interval will vote for the party on the left of this party and the ones beyond the right side will vote for the party on the right of it.[6]

Third, for each election, we find the percentage of the vote received by each party. At this point, we now have the percentage of the electorate that fall into each interval that we have created. Having now transformed the data to a

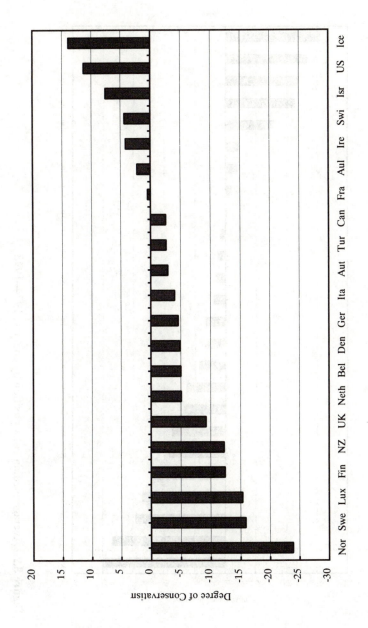

Figure 8.1. Average median voter position by country, 1945–1998

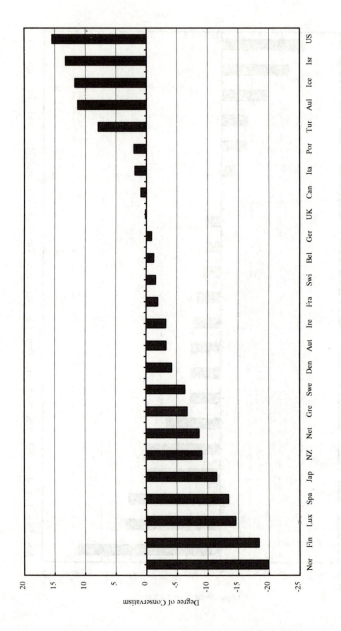

Figure 8.2. Average median voter position by country, 1974–1998

grouped frequency distribution, we estimate the median position by using a formula outlined in almost any introductory statistics text (we use Bohrnstedt and Knoke 1988: 52). The particular variant of this formula that we use is as follows.

$$M = L + \{(50–C) / F)\} * W$$

Where:

M = Median voter position (ideological score)

L = The lower end (ideological score) of the interval containing the median.

C = The cumulative frequency (vote share) up to but not including the interval containing the median.

F = The frequency (vote share) in the interval containing the median.

W = The width of the interval containing the median.

Having created a measure of voter ideology for each country for each election month, we then compute a monthly series of voter ideology scores within each country. We estimate values for missing (non-election) months by using linear interpolation, which assumes steady change in ideology between elections. While we realize that ideology is not likely to change this steadily in every case, we feel that in general this approach is reasonable since it is likely that ideology is relatively stable in the short run. More importantly, estimation of missing years facilitates comparisons across countries, which would otherwise be biased due to the irregularity of the timing of elections across countries. Finally, we create a yearly series of voter ideology scores by computing the average monthly voter ideology score for each year.[7]

VOTER IDEOLOGY: CROSS-NATIONAL AND CROSS-TIME COMPARISONS

In Figure 8.1 we present a cross-national comparison of the average ideological scores of 21 Western democracies during the entire period of 1945–98.[8] In short, Figure 8.1 presents a snap-shot describing the entire period of analysis. During this period, it is clear that Norway, Sweden, and Luxembourg have been the most left-leaning states, while Iceland, the U.S.A., and Israel have been at the opposite end of the ideological spectrum of Western democracies.

There are four countries in the manifesto data set for which the data are available for shorter time periods (Greece, Spain, Japan, and Portugal). To take advantage of all of the information in the data set, we present a cross-national comparison of the average ideological scores of 25 Western democracies during the period of 1974–98. During this period, we see roughly the same set of most left-leaning and right-leaning states, with the exception of Finland replacing Sweden as one of the most left-leaning countries.

Next, we examine *aggregate* movement in ideology among our panel of countries during the years 1950–94. The results of this analysis can be found in Figure 8.3, which displays ideology scores averaged across 21 countries in

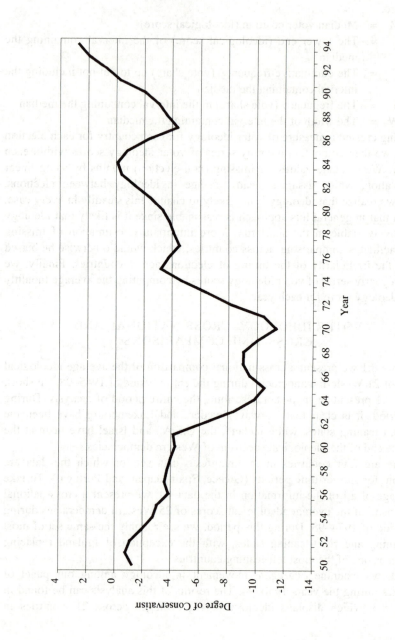

Figure 8.3. Average median voter position by year, 1950–1994

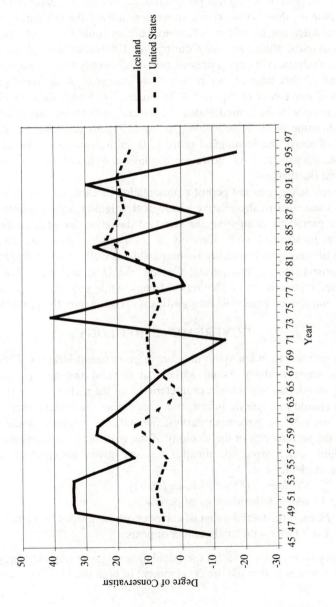

Figure 8.4. Examples of ideological volatility and stability

Figure 8.1.[9] Consistent with conventional wisdom, Figure 8.3 indicates that the period of the 1960s and early 1970s was indeed a relatively left-leaning period followed by shifts to the right in the late 1970s and 1980s among these democracies.

Though Figure 8.3 displays ideological movement among most countries in our sample, there is no reason to believe that all of these countries have followed this identical pattern during this period. Indeed, though the majority of countries we examine do show some type of movement toward the left during the 1960s, in general there are significant differences across countries in the magnitude of such ideological shifts, not only during the 1960s, but throughout the entire period of analysis. Although a presentation of all twenty five countries is beyond the scope of this chapter, we present two examples of different patterns of ideological movement in Figure 8.4. In Figure 8.4, which displays ideological movement in both the United States and Iceland, we can see that although there have been some shifts, voter ideology in the U.S. has been relatively stable, as it has stayed above the ideological score of 0 throughout the period of analysis. Voter ideology in Iceland, however, displays a different pattern with greater short-term fluctuations.

Although space does not permit a presentation of each individual country, we can get some idea of the relative ideological volatility across countries during this time period by computing the standard deviation for each country series. Since our measure of voter ideology is comparable across countries, such a measure of ideological volatility is comparable as well. Figure 8.5 presents such a comparison. During this period, Canada, the U.S., and New Zealand have maintained relatively stable ideological trends, while voter ideology in Sweden, Iceland, and Ireland has exhibited significant variation over the years 1945–98.[10]

GOVERNMENT IDEOLOGY

Now we turn our attention to our measure of government ideology. Conceptually speaking, most analysts would agree that a valid measure of government ideology should tap two distinct characteristics of the parties in power. First, the measure should incorporate information concerning the relative share of power held by each of the governing parties. Second, the measure should take into account the preferences, or the ideology of the governing parties as measured on a left-right scale. More specifically, for any given government we define government ideology as:

$$\sum \{Ideology_i * (\#Posts_i / Total\ Posts)\}$$

where: $Ideology_i$ = the ideology of party i

$Posts_i$ = the total number of cabinet posts controlled by party i

$Total\ Posts$ = the total number of posts

Recently both components for the calculation of government ideology have become available through the development of both the Manifesto data set and

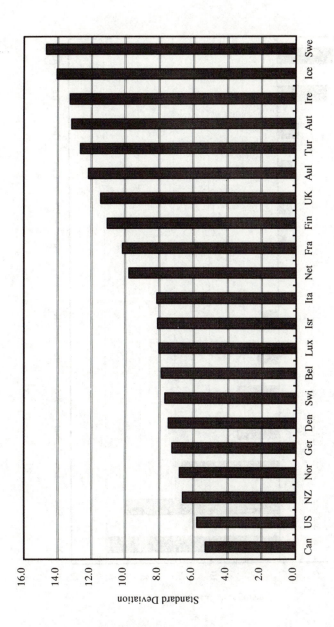

Figure 8.5. Ideological volatility, 1945–1998

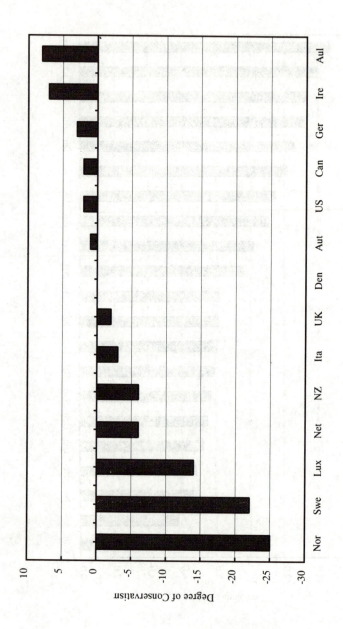

Figure 8.6. Average government ideology score by country, 1945–1997

one on the composition of governments and distribution of portfolios in a number of countries (Woldendorp, Keman, and Budge 1993). We take advantage of both to build our measure of government ideology.

MEASURING GOVERNMENT IDEOLOGY

We build a continuous measure of government ideology for Western democracies as follows. We first compute a yearly series of party ideology scores within each country using the Laver-Budge measure of party ideology. We estimate missing (non-election) years using linear interpolation, which assumes a steady change in ideology between elections. While ideology is not likely to change this steadily in every case, in general this approach is reasonable since it is likely that ideology is relatively stable in the short run. More importantly, estimation of missing years facilitates comparisons across countries, which would otherwise be biased due to the irregularity of the timing of elections across countries.

We then collect yearly data for the number of cabinet portfolios for each party in each country in our sample, for the entire postwar period through 1997.[11] Finally, for each year, we combine this information with the party ideology scores by taking a weighted average of party ideology scores, where the weights are the proportion of total cabinet portfolios held by each party (as in the equation above). Thus for some countries where unified control of government occurs on a regular basis, the government ideology score reduces to the party ideology score for the party in power. For multi-party governments, however, the measure takes advantage of the information we have about the varying ideologies of the parties and their relative shares of power.

We built this new measure of government ideology for 14 countries for most of the postwar period.[12] Since the measure of party ideology is a continuous measure of conservatism taking on a possible range of −100 to 100, our measure of government ideology also becomes a measure of relative conservatism and takes on a possible range of −100 to 100.[13]

GOVERNMENT IDEOLOGY: CROSS-NATIONAL AND CROSS-TIME COMPARISONS

In Figure 8.6, we present average government ideology scores for each of the countries, averaged over the period 1945–97.[14] As we would expect, Norway and Sweden, on the average, have had the most left-leaning governments during this period, while Australia and Ireland have had the most conservative ones. Since Figure 8.6 presents a snap-shot describing the entire period of analysis, different trends may surface if we look at a shorter time period. To examine that possibility, we present a cross-national comparison of the average ideological scores during the period of 1974–97 (the post-oil shock period) in Figure 8.7. Although similar trends exist during this period, now the U.S. and the U.K.

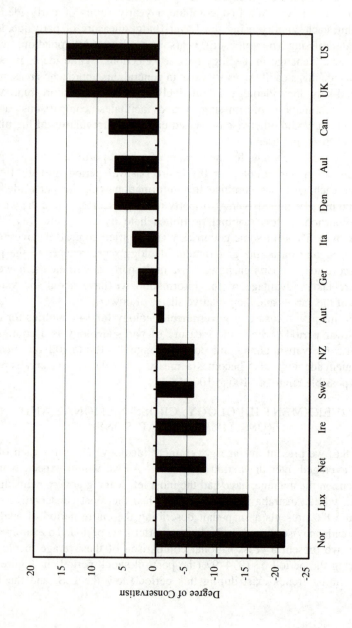

Figure 8.7. Average government ideology score by country, 1974–1997

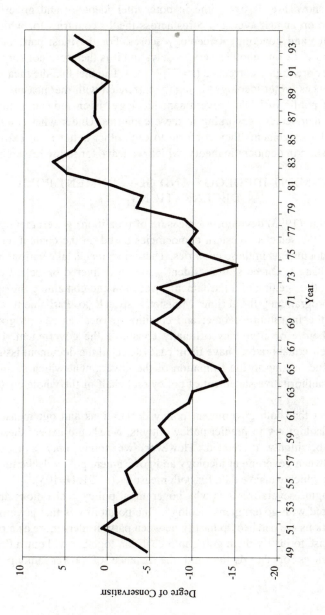

Figure 8.8. Average government ideology score by year, 1949–1994

reflecting the Reagan-Thatcher governments have moved to the extreme right.

Trends over time are consistent with expectations as well. In Figure 8.8, we present government ideology scores across time for the 1949–94 period, where the score for each year is the average across all 14 countries in this analysis.[15] As the figure shows, generally speaking, the 1960s and 1970's was a period marked by a shift to the left, while the 1980's witnessed an increasing shift to the right.

Figure 8.9 shows trends over time in both voter ideology and government ideology based on annual average scores across the 14 countries for which we have both voter and government ideology scores. For the most part, the two series appear to track one another very closely, and it is therefore not surprising to find that they are highly correlated (r=.77; N=45). The fact that the measure of citizen preferences (voter ideology) is highly correlated with the measure of the preferences of public officials (government ideology) is an indication that the representative democracy is working in these countries. Under what conditions or institutional arrangements they conform to each other better is an extremely important question in democratic theory, which we leave for future research.

GOVERNMENT IDEOLOGY AND GOVERNMENT POLICY DECLARATIONS

Laver and Budge (1993) developed a measure of (coalition) government policy declarations in the selected Western democracies based on the content analysis of key policy documents in these countries. These documents take various forms including the King's, Queen's or President's speech delivered on behalf of the Government at the opening of a Parliamentary session and containing the agreed government programme; the Prime Minister's speech to Parliament at the beginning of the Investiture debate; and coalition parties' agreed programme issued either before or after they officially constitute the government. Laver, Budge, and their collaborators 'have in all cases selected the document issued as close as possible in time to the formation of the government which seemed to give the most authoritative statement of policy on behalf of the whole coalition' (1992:19).

To the extent that both government policy declarations and our measure of government ideology try to predict policy outputs, we should expect these two measures to be highly correlated. However, we found only a moderate correlation between government ideology and government policy declarations in 8 countries for which we have data for both measures (r=.51, N=105).[16]

We can imagine several reasons why government policy declarations are not highly correlated with government ideology. One possibility is that government policy declarations are patched up hastily between party leaders more as a public relations exercise to justify them going into coalition together without reflecting policy preferences of the parties and the balance of power among them (Luebbert 1986).

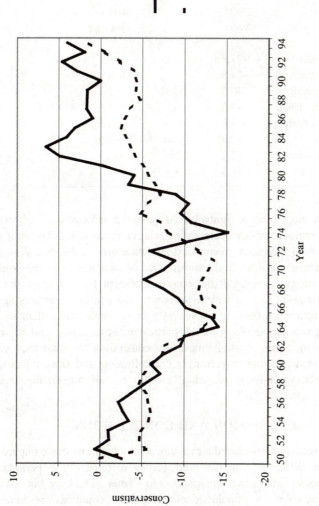

Figure 8.9. Average voter and government ideology scores by year, 1950–1994

Another possibility is that government ideology and government policy declarations may be highly correlated in some countries while not in others for country-specific reasons. We explore this possibility by looking at the correlation between the two measures in individual countries. Indeed, we find a high correlation between the two in the Netherlands and Ireland (r>.9) but a negligible correlation in Norway, Italy, and Germany (r<.2).

Table 8.1. Government ideology and policy declarations

Country	Government ideology	Government policy declarations
	Average	Average
Sweden	−21.5	−9.1
Norway	−24.8	−21.1
Denmark	−0.3	2.0
Netherlands	−5.5	5.5
Luxembourg	−13.8	−2.5
Italy	−2.9	−1.6
Germany	3.2	12.3
Ireland	7.3	−14.3

Finally, there might be a rightward or leftward tendency of government ideology or government policy declarations relative to the other. To see if this is the case, we compare country means of these measures. Table 8.1 shows that, indeed, government policy declarations are consistently on the right of government ideology scores. All the countries except Ireland show the same tendency. At this point, it is not clear to us why the coalition partners agree to government programmes that are consistently more conservative than what we would expect given the ideology of the parties in the coalition and the power distribution among them. Possibly there are constraints on what they can do deriving both from previous government commitments and from bureaucracy. Obviously unveiling this relationship would be an interesting research endeavour.

DISCUSSION AND CONCLUSIONS

In this chapter, we have introduced a measure with which one can compare voter ideology across different countries and across different time periods. Our measure provides interesting insights into voter ideology in Western democracies. The trends in popular ideology in these countries are themselves important. But there are many other ways to use this measure either to study political phenomena in ways which were previously not feasible, or to improve (or revitalize) existing research in comparative politics. The estimates presented in this chapter and in the CD-ROM should therefore be considered as the starting point for research into the origins of voter ideology, its impact on government and public policy, and general theories of democracy.[17] We have also introduced a continuous measure of government ideology, which allows meaningful comparisons across countries and across time. To the extent that our measure is an improvement over existing ones, we believe that comparativists need to exercise caution in interpreting and evaluating the findings of past empirical studies of the role of government partisanship in policy outcomes and government performance.[18]

Acknowledgements: Part of our earlier research on voter ideology was published in *European Journal of Political Research* in 1998. We thank William Berry, Ian Budge, William Clagget, Mike Lusztig, Erik Plutzer, Evan Ringquist, and Duane Swank for their valuable comments at various stages of our voter ideology project. We also benefited from the suggestions and information provided by Shaun Bowler, Russ Dalton, Neal Jesse, George Tsebelis, and Guy Whitten. We thank William Berry and Ian Budge for their valuable comments on our government ideology project. Jun Young Choi and Carl Dasse provided research assistance.

1 For a review of the existing measures of government ideology and the problems associated with them, see Kim and Fording 2000a. For a similar review of the existing measures of voter ideology and their problems, see Kim and Fording 1998.

2 For various validity tests of the measure of party ideology, see Kim and Fording 1998, 2000a. In our earlier work, we constructed our measure of party ideology somewhat differently, although we used the same manifesto categories as Laver and Budge (see Kim and Fording 1998). Our measure is the difference of IDLeft and IDRight as a percentage of the total left and right statements. The Laver-Budge measure is equivalent to the numerator of our measure, or in other words, the difference of IDLeft and IDRight as a percentage of all statements in the document. In a recent conference paper, McDonald and Mendes (1999: 4–5) call the Laver-Budge measure a 'subtractive measure' and our original measure (as well as the Laver-Garry measure (1998), which employs the same formula as ours) a 'ratio measure'. There are some philosophical differences between these two measures, and as McDonald and Mendes (1999: 5) correctly point out, 'validity depends on what the researcher intends to measure. If one's intention is to locate a party in a space defined by its emphases on Left versus Right values relative to all values (thereby stressing the overall saliency of Left and Right values), then the subtractive measure is preferred. If, on the contrary, one's intention is to locate the party along the Left-Right dimension as such, then the ratio is preferred'. Regardless of this difference in the two measures, the two are nearly identical in empirical terms as they are correlated at .95.

3   While the role of ideology has often been ignored in the American voting literature, both experimental (e.g., McKelvey and Ordeshook 1990) and survey-based studies (e.g., Levitan and Miller 1979) find ideology to be an important determinant of vote choice in the United States.

4   Using party manifesto data, Laver and Budge (1993) convincingly show that the left-right dimension not only exists but is essential in the party programs in Western democracies.

5   One objection to using manifesto statements to construct a measure of party ideology is likely to be that voters rarely, if ever, read them. Although this is undoubtedly true, this does not necessarily mean that manifesto statements are poor *indicators* of ideology if manifestos are representative of party behavior that *is* observable to voters. Recent evidence concerning this question indicates that this may indeed be the case. Contrary to the expectations of many political scientists, evidence from the United States, Great Britain and former West Germany indicates that parties do indeed fulfill the vast majority of their pledges (Budge and Hofferbert (1990); also see Robertson (1987) for a review of research in this area). As a result, though manifesto statements may not affect voter perceptions of parties in any direct way, a measure of party ideology based on manifesto statements is likely to be highly correlated with voter perceptions due to their common relationship with party ideology.

6   We assume sincere voting by assuming that voters choose the candidates/parties that are closest to them. We minimize the potential impact of tactical/strategic voting by using appropriate election data in countries with ordinal ballot structures where vote transfer is possible (Ireland and the Australian House) and in Germany with a mixed electoral system. See Kim and Fording 1998 for details. For insignificant impact of tactical voting on the estimate of the median voter position in countries with a multi-party system whose electoral system is characterized by single-member district plurality rule (Canada, New Zealand (until recently), and the United Kingdom), see Kim and Fording (2000b; 2001).

7   For various validity tests of the measure of voter ideology, see Kim and Fording (1998).

8   The average scores reported in Figure 8.1, as well as the subsequent analyses, are based on observed *and* interpolated scores for each country. Because of the irregularity of the timing of elections across countries, the first and last years for which we have manifesto data vary somewhat across countries. The first election year for which data are available among the countries in Figure 8.1 ranges from 1945 to 1950, while the last year for which data exist varies from 1994 to 1998.

9   The 1950-94 time period reflects the set of common years for which ideology scores are available for all 21 countries in our analysis.

10 One needs to be cautious about interpreting the analysis in Figure 8.5, since the standard deviation analysis captures different types of ideological volatility. For example, some countries exhibit an ideological pattern with continued short-term fluctuations (e.g., Iceland and Ireland). Some other countries have experienced just a few periods of marked ideological shifts (e.g., Sweden in the 1990s and Austria in the 1970s and the1990s). Still others have shown gradual, but significant, change (e.g.,

the U.K.). Counties with all of these types of ideological change scored high on the volatility analysis in Figure 8.5.

11 We use cabinet composition data contained in Woldendorp, Keman, and Budge (1993; 1998).

12 Out of 21 countries for which manifesto data exist for the entire postwar period, we calculated government ideology scores for 14 countries. These are the countries for which, we are certain, we have reliable yearly series of cabinet portfolio data at the time this chapter was written. We will add the remaining countries in the future as we develop reliable yearly data on the cabinet composition.

13 For various validity tests of our measure of government ideology, see Kim and Fording (2000a).

14 As was the case with our estimates of voter ideology, the first and last years for which government ideology scores can be computed varies slightly across countries. The first year of available data ranges from 1945-49, while the last year of available data varies from 1994-97.

15 The 1949-94 time period reflects the set of common years for which ideology scores are available for all 14 countries in our analysis of government ideology.

16 They are Sweden, Norway, Denmark, Netherlands, Luxembourg, Italy, Germany, and Ireland.

17 See Kim and Fording (1998) for a list of potential avenues of future research in comparative politics utilizing our measure of voter ideology.

18 See Kim and Fording (2000a) for an in-depth discussion of the existing measures of government partisanship, a comparison of our measure and the existing measures, and our replications of past studies of the role of government partisanship in Western democracies.

9

Approaching the Data

Eric Tanenbaum

OVERVIEW

In this final chapter we move to a discussion of the material contained in the CD-ROM and demonstrate some of the ways in which this may be utilized and extended. The CD-ROM contains the data described in the earlier chapters of this book, organized to ease the execution of further analyses suggested in those chapters. This chapter begins by describing that organization. It continues with suggestions about how the data could be used to answer questions about party policy positions within and among the 24 OECD countries (and Israel) discussed in the text. It concludes with suggested procedures for incorporating new party manifestos in the MRG context.

The Files

The disk holds four types of files. *Documentation* files describe the procedures used to create the policy indicators from the original party platforms and manifestos. These are in Adobe pdf format which can be accessed with the Acrobat 4 reader supplied on the CD-ROM. *Data* files hold the policy preference indicators. These appear in three formats: (i) Comma delimited text; (ii) Excel spreadsheets; and (iii) SPSS[1] portable files. *Text* files include samples of the original material used by the MRG to produce the substantive policy codes underlying the analyses reported earlier in this book. *Utility* files include two programs designed to facilitate use of the documentation and data files by readers without computer programs that can access these files. Each set of files will now be described in turn.

Data Files

These data files cover four topics related to the broad theme of policy preferences: (i) Government Declarations, (ii) Median Voters, (iii) Party Policy Positions, and (iv) Party Mean Scores on Four Policy Positions.

Three data formats are used for each topic area to enhance the material's accessibility by different computer programs. Files with an '**.xls**' extension are designed for the Microsoft Excel spreadsheet programs and are compatible with releases 5 onwards of that program.[2] As the Excel format is becoming a *de facto* data transfer standard, users of other analysis programs will likely find that their programs will easily convert this format of file. Files with a '**.por**' extension are

USING THE CD-ROM: SYSTEM REQUIREMENTS

The CD-ROM included with the book is compatible with both MAC OS and Windows 95 (and above) computer systems.

Instructions for using the CD-ROM appear on the disk label.

WINDOWS

The CD-ROM will start automatically when inserted in a PC operating under Windows. To enter the disk's contents, click on Start.

MAC OS

A CD-ROM icon will appear when the disk is inderted. Click on the icon.

OTHER

The files described in Chapter 9 are stored in subdirectories on the CD-ROM. Subdirectory names are described in 'The Files' on page 179. Individual file names are intuitively meaningful --- it will be clear what each topic designates.

Figure 9.1 Instructions for accessing the data

designed for the SPSS analysis system, popular with many social scientists. Indeed, it is so commonly available, that files formatted for SPSS are often directly usable by other statistical analysis programs. Finally, files with a '.csv' extension are stored as text files in which each unit of information is set off (or delimited) by a comma. Files in this format should be accessible to any programs used to manipulate structured data.

The information is presented in a further two ways. Information for all the countries can be accessed simultaneously or the data for individual countries can be accessed. Individual country data are presented in straight character ('ASCII') format with the separate fields delimited by commas. These files are provided for readers who cannot use the '.xls' or '.por' files. Because these readers may have difficulty categorizing the observations by countries, separate country files were created.

PARTY POLICY POSITIONS

As Table 9.1 shows, this file contains the major country-by-country across-party across-time manifesto policy codes. These form the basis of all the analyses reported in the earlier chapters and lend themselves to further analyses.

Table 9.1. Party policy positions

Field name	Meaning
COUNTRY	country code
COUNTRY NAME	name of country
EDATE	day-month-year of election
PARTY	Party identification number—these are structured to identify party type. See Appendix 2 on the disk
PARTYNAME	Full party name
VOTEEST	original or estimated figure for votes: (0)_original (1)_estimated
PRESVOTE	percentage of votes in presidential elections
ABSSEAT	Absolute number of seats
TOTSEATS	total number of seats in parliament
PROGTYPE	type of programme data
DOMAIN 1	EXTERNAL RELATONS
PER101	Foreign Special Relationships: Positive[3]
PER102	Foreign Special Relationships: Negative
PER103	Anti-Imperialism

Table 9.1 *(continued)*

PER104	Military: Positive
PER105	Military: Negative
PER106	Peace
PER107	Internationalism: Positive
PER108	European Community: Positive
PER109	Internationalism: Negative
PER110	European Community: Negative
DOMAIN 2	FREEDOM AND DEMOCRACY
PER201	Freedom and Human Rights
PER202	Democracy
PER203	Constitutionalism: Positive
PER204	Constitutionalism: Negative
DOMAIN 3	POLITICAL SYSTEM
PER301	Decentralisation
PER302	Centralisation
PER303	Government and Administrative Efficiency
PER304	Political Corruption
PER305	Political Authority
DOMAIN 4	ECONOMY
PER401	Free Enterprise
PER402	Incentives
PER403	Market Regulation
PER404	Economic Planning
PER405	Corporatism
PER406	Protectionism: Positive
PER407	Protectionism: Negative
PER408	Economic Goals
PER409	Keynesian Demand Management
PER410	Productivity
PER411	Technology and Infrastructure
PER412	Controlled Economy
PER413	Nationalization
PER414	Economic Orthodoxy
PER415	Marxist Analysis
PER416	Anti-Growth Economy

DOMAIN 5	WELFARE AND QUALITY OF LIFE
PER501	Environmental Protection
PER502	Culture
PER503	Social Justice
PER504	Welfare State Expansion
PER505	Welfare State Limitation
PER506	Education Expansion
PER507	Education Limitation
DOMAIN 6	FABRIC OF SOCIETY
PER601	National Way of Life: Positive
PER602	National Way of Life: Negative
PER603	Traditional Morality: Positive
PER604	Traditional Morality: Negative
PER605	Law and Order
PER606	Social Harmony
PER607	Multiculturalism: Positive
PER608	Multiculturalism: Negative
DOMAIN 7	SOCIAL GROUPS
PER701	Labour Groups: Positive
PER702	Labour Groups: Negative
PER703	Agriculture and Farmers
PER704	Middle Class and Professional Groups
PER705	Underprivileged Minority Groups
PER706	Non-economic Demographic Groups
ADDITIONAL STATISTICS	INFORMATION ABOUT CODING UNITS
PERUNCOD	Uncoded quasi-sentences
TOTAL	Absolute number of quasi-sentences
SUMMARY POLICY INDICATORS	SUMMARY PARTY POLICY STANDS
RIGHTLEFT	Left-Right Index
PLANECO	Planned Economy
MARKECO	Market Economy
WELFARE	Welfare references
INTPEACE	International Peace

Table 9.1 shows the layout of the material in the file. Information is included for the 24 OECD countries and Israel that were the subject of the MRG's attention. The file has the percentage of (quasi-)sentences[4] on each specific policy area in each party's manifesto for elections occurring between 1945 and 1998. Besides these specific policy preferences, individual party scores are given on the four general policy stands (market economy, planned economy, welfare provision, and international peace) as well as the party's general Left-Right stance. This information is combined with details of each party's electoral success as indicated by the percentage of votes and seats gained in the election.

MEDIAN VOTER

These files contain the result of Hee-Min Kim and Richard C. Fording's use of the policy estimates, which describe party positions, to allow inferences to be made about the voters' positions. Because their approach is fully described in the previous chapter, there is no need to review their procedures. However it is worth emphasizing that their work exemplifies how the basic policy estimates can be extended to new areas. Table 9.2 describes the file contents.

Table 9.2. Median voter file structure

Field name	Meaning
COUNTRY	Country Numeric Code
COUNTRY NAME	Country Name
ELECYR	Election Year
EDATE	Year-Month of Election
PEACEMED	Voter Position on Peace (calculation: per102+per105+per106)
WELFMED	Voter Position on Welfare (calculation: per503+per504)
MARKMED	Voter Position on Market Economy (calculation: per401+per414)
PLANMED	Voter Position on Planned Economy (calculation: per403+per404+per412)
RIGHTLEFT	Voter Position on Left-Right spectrum (code: left(−100) <---> right(+100))

Two other aspects of their work can be mentioned under the broad heading of extensions. Firstly, Table 9.2 reinforces the notion of combining policy estimates to create new composite indicators. Secondly, they have calculated median positions for Sri Lanka, a country which is not part of the data sets discussed in this volume. Again, this is an example of how the work on the policy estimates can be geographically broadened by including other countries under the common headings provided by the project.

GOVERNMENT DECLARATIONS

Table 9.3. Government declarations

Field name	Meaning
COUNTRY	country number
COUNTRY NAME	
GOVID	Government ID after Woldendorp, Kenam and Budge 2000.
INAUGDAT	day-month of government's inauguration
PER101–PER706	As in Table 9.1

The data for the government declarations relates to a subset of countries covered by the party policy estimates data set and relates only to the period 1945–88.This was the data set created for the second major MRG study which compared the content of coalition government declarations with original party policy estimates (Laver and Budge eds. 1992) and established a means of gauging the likely membership of coalitions. The government declaration data used for this study was not extended to take account of governments formed in the relevant countries in the 1990s.

The precise aggregations of variables which are used to create these policy stands are provided in Appendix V. They are useful as indicators of major policy priorities—and indeed of differences between parties—which relate to standard left-right measures without involving large aggregations or negative readings. Thus parties of the right, for example, would be expected to manifest high scores on the market economy stand and low scores on the planned economy stand, whereas we would expect parties of the left to present the opposite profile. The arithmetic means provided for parties enable simple testing of preliminary hypotheses across a range of issues. Obviously, other descriptive statistics, such as the standard deviation, can be calculated for these policy stands using the full party policy positions data set.

PARTY MEAN SCORES ON FOUR POLICY STANDS

Table 9.4. Party mean scores on four policy stands

Field name	Meaning
Country	Country Name
Party	Name
Time Period[5]	Period for which estimates have been calculated
Planned Economy	Arithmetic mean
Market Economy	Arithmetic mean
Welfare	Arithmetic mean
International Peace	Arithmetic mean

Text Files

The data files described above are based on substantive codes assigned to party manifestos by members of the MRG working to a common coding scheme. Inter-coder consistency was achieved by asking new coders to work on a sample manifesto with known substantive content. The new coder's work could then be compared to this standard. Sample Manifesto Text Files are included on the disk to allow the reader to replicate this training, either because he or she wants reassurance about the procedure or, as is more likely, because the reader wants to add and treat additional new manifestos similarly.

The files contain extracts from two manifestos: (a) Great Britain's Liberal/SDP Alliance Party 1983 document 'Working Together for Britain'; and (b) New Zealand's National Party 1972 document 'A Guide to What the Next National Government Will Do for New Zealand.' **Original Documents**[6] holds the text as it originally appeared. **Quasi Sentences** breaks this material into coding units, in preparation for the reader's own application of the coding rules. Appendix 2: Manifesto Coding Instructions on this disk has the details. **Coded Sentences** contains the codes assigned by the MRG which can be used to verify the reader's codes.

Documentation Files

Documentation files contain supporting material for the analyses reported here and elsewhere. Moreover, they provide essential background for the further use of the Data files on the CD-ROM. The files and their contents are:

Appendix I Political Parties in the Data Set

   lists all the parties included in the Manifesto Data Set from 1945 through 1998. For each party information is included on: (a) party name and acronym

(b) elections in which the party was active (c) Manifesto Data Set identifier which is a unique code structured to identify the party's main policy interest focus

Appendix II Manifesto Coding Instructions

describes the MRG's coding procedure. It begins by describing how it developed over-time and then shows how it can be applied to a sample manifesto (contained on the CD-ROM in Original Documents). The file contains extensive definitions of the separate coding categories

Appendix III Description of Manifesto Data Set

lists the contents of Policy Positions with more extensive detail about each indicator than is provided in Table 9.1 above.

Appendix IV Missing Party Documents

lists the active parties in the period 1945–98 for which no party platforms are available. Consequently, these parties are excluded from the summary data sets on the CD-ROM.

Appendix V Mean Percentage for Parties on Four Policy Stands

gives the mean scores for parties in 18 countries on (a) planned economy, (b) market economy, (c) welfare and (d) international peace. These have been calculated for two time periods, 1945–98 and 1972–98.

Appendix VI Description of Government Declaration Data

lists the Government Declarations with more extensive detail about each indicator then is provided in Table 9.3 above.

Appendix VII Party Programme Titles and Sources

lists the party manifesto titles within countries by year.

Utility Files

Two program files will install utilities that allow browsing of the **.xls** data files and the **.pdf** documentation files

Adobe Acrobat Reader 4.0

To install 'Acrobat 4.0' click on **Acrobat** Then follow the instructions that appear on the screen.

Excel 97 Viewer (Not for MAC OS)

To install the 'Microsoft Excel 97 Viewer' under the Windows 95/98/ME operating system click on **MS Excel Viewer**. Then follow the instructions that appear on the screen.

SUGGESTIONS FOR FURTHER RESEARCH

Several questions were explicitly suggested in the earlier chapters but it is expected that many more will have occurred to the reader. Indeed, to reiterate what was said in the opening chapter, the motive for including the CD-ROM in this text, reflected in the choice of its contents, is to stimulate a continuation of the work begun by the original MRG in 1979.

The text itself synthesizes the work done to date with these data. The original MRG and its successor, the Comparative Manifestos Project, provide a launch pad for subsequent analyses which advance our understanding of the policy process by replication and extension. To continue the analogy, the CD-ROM can fuel further exploratory trips through the data.

This chapter concludes with suggestions about two types of extension. The summary data held in the files can be analyzed further. Several possible analyses are described. However, these freeze the world, and thus constrain descriptions of the policy process, to the 26 party systems operating between 1945 and 1998. Consequently researchers might wish to develop the basic themes by adding new party systems and/or new time periods to those provided on the disk. As this entails coding new party manifestos, we also describe how the researcher can build on the material provided on the disk.

Further Analyses

The data in the Party Policy Position file can be the basis for many further investigations. Several examples of these will be suggested:

*   Excel[7] users can use the <u>correl</u> function to assess the extent to which particular policy stances move together within parties. For example, positive correlations among **per607: Multiculturalism-Positive** and **per705: Minority Groups** and **per606: Social Harmony** may reveal attitude structures underlying policy-makers' assessment of this area. The inter-relationship between policy indicators can be visualized by using several of the multi-indicator charts provided by Excel.

    Here the emphasis is on the policy areas themselves—the parties are simple vehicles for these policy characteristics. However, within-country and/or within-time evaluation of the relationship among policy areas, showing the differences that time and place can make, are also feasible with these data, as the next example suggests.

*   Showing time and place differences in relationships requires the judicious sorting of the individual observations (or parties) into either country groups or time periods or into within-time and country groups together. Multiple rearrangements of data are a particular strength of spreadsheet programs like Excel. The analyses can then be conducted on the data constrained within these groupings.

- The impact of policy stances on electoral success can be gauged by regressing either the proportion of votes earned or the number of seats won onto one or more policy estimates. This can be done with Excel's <u>Regression analysis tool</u> (part of the analysis toolpack) or with Quattro Pro's @Regression function.

- Researchers interested in party strategy can also use these data and their program's regression functions, in conjunction with these programs' data transformation routines, to evaluate the success of different vote attraction strategies. For example, an analyst interested in the impact of a changing emphasis on minorities, could score each party on how its emphasis on per705: Minority Groups changed between elections. Similarly, their changed success, say as measured by a new variable created by scoring inter-election changes on either presvote or abseats ÷ totseats could be regressed on the 'change in per705' indicator.

- Profiles of any country's policy agenda for a particular year can be established by calculating the within-year policy scores. This will provide a description of the policy market-place available to that country's electorate— not every party has to offer Protectionism (per406: Protectionism Positive-per407: Protectionism Negative) but the elector interested in it should have at least one party purveying it in return for her vote. Changed emphases across time can then be plotted using one of the charting functions.

Adding Observations

The data in the Party Policy Position file also provide the basis for contextual analyses. Several authors, in works cited in this text's bibliographies, began with the MRG's policy estimates to establish similar ratings for parties operating in other countries and/or in other time periods. Indeed, Kim and Fording's, and McDonald and Mendes' contributions to this volume exemplify how the original estimates can be extended by adding new types of data. Adding new party systems to the data set requires a different approach for the appropriate party documents have to be transformed to a MRG compatible form before they can be analyzed. In other words, each new party document must be coded by applying the MRG coding frame *in the same way* that a member of the MRG would. Deviation in procedures would introduce incompatibilities which would bar subsequent comparisons.

Adding new parties is a two-stage process. Firstly, the researcher must become operationally conversant with MRG procedures. Secondly, these procedures must be applied. Each stage will be discussed in turn.

Learning to Code

File **Appendix II Manifesto Coding Instructions** on the CD-ROM is the best starting point for the training process. This material, in conjunction with Chapter 4 in this volume[8], establishes the MRG's guiding ethos.

Having read the material, we suggest that the sample manifesto material, extracts from the 1983 British Liberal-Social Democratic Alliance and the 1972 New Zealand National Party programmes, be coded using the MRG procedures. This will require, first, that the text be edited into quasi-sentences, the basic MRG coding unit. The MRG coding framework, presented in file 'Appendix II Manifesto Coding Instructions', can then be applied. Finally, the results of the reader's own coding can be compared to the MRG-applied codes. Any deviations can be reasoned through by looking at the MRG procedures for further guidance.

Three files on the disk support this training exercise. As mentioned earlier, **Original Documents** holds the extracts in their published formats, **Quasi Sentences** shows what the document looks like after the MRG rules have been applied to produce the coding units and **Coded Sentences** shows the grouping of sentences into the MRG topic codes.

The structure of these three files lead to our recommendation about how the second stage of the addition of new parties should be organised. Budge, Tanenbaum and Bara (1999) found that the spreadsheet format eased the coding of new party documents, reduced clerical errors and facilitated the analysis of the coded material. It also facilitated comparisons between manual and computerized coding, such as that discussed in Chapter 7.

Clearly, using this approach requires that the party documents be in computer-readable format. While this may entail scanning printed documents, our experience is that recent party documents are available on the World Wide Web sites maintained by many parties. Consequently they can be 'downloaded' as electronic files.

They may, however, have embedded formatting instructions. These will be immediately recognizable when the document file is opened with a word-processor and can therefore be easily removed with the word-processor's 'find and replace' function. The word-processor can also be used to transform the original document into the quasi-sentences demanded by the MRG's coding procedure. Essentially this just means inserting a physical line break by doing a 'carriage return'[9] at the appropriate point in the text. If the resulting file is saved as a text file, it will be straightforward to input it to a spreadsheet program.

SUMMARY

When the MRG began its work in the 1970s, they could not have imagined that their work would launch such an extensive, open-ended investigation into a major part of the policy-making process. This book is evidence that it has.

This chapter has shown how this interest in extending their research might be developed even more. Its discussion of the nature of the CD-ROM resource included as an intrinsic part of the book shows how a number of possible substantive developments might be achieved using the procedures suggested for activating further potential applications. Our readers will undoubtedly have even more ideas of their own which will enable the data to be extended even further.

1. Statistical Package for the Social Sciences
2. These files can also be viewed, but not manipulated, with the XLViewer programs supplied on the disk.
3. Extended field definitions are given in Appendix 3 Description of Indicators in Policy Preferences File
4. The Manifesto Research Group's coding procedures are described in Chapter 4.
5. In several cases, two estimates for the same party are provided. This reflects the party's behaviour for the different time periods identified in the 'Time Period' field.
6. Files with a '**.csv**' extension hold the information as comma-delimited character text.
7. Although comments are directed to Microsoft Excel users, the functions that are described are generic and will have equivalent implementations in *any* spreadsheet programs. The suggestions have been tested with Quattro Pro 9 and Lotus 1-2-3.
8. Andrea Volkens 'Quantifying the election programmes: coding procedures and controls'
9. On some keyboards, this key is labeled **Enter**; on others it is called **Return**

Appendix I

Political Parties included in the Data Set

Appendix I lists all parties in the Manifesto Data Set 1945 to 1998 in alphabetical order by country. For each party in the 25 countries, the following information is provided:

1. Parties	1.1	Acronyms as usually used in original language; except Japan: acronyms of English names.
	1.2	Names of parties in original language as given in Arthur S. Banks (ed.): *Political Handbook of the World,* Binghamton: CSA Publications/New York: Mc Graw-Hill (various editions).
	1.3	Name of party in English (if original is not English).
	1.4	Changes in names of parties. In all appended data and documentation, the latest name of a party is used.
2. Elections	2.1	First and last election of time period covered.
	2.2	Number of elections in time period covered. This number equals the number of cases for each party, including its coded platforms, joint platforms and estimated cases.
3. MDS-ID		Identification number in Manifesto Data Set MDS-ID 11110 to ID 74715. The party identification code consist of five digits. The first two digits repeat the country code (see Appendix 1a). The third and fourth digits reflect a tentative grouping of political parties and alliances into the following party families but do not reflect changes in policy positions:

100	ECO	Ecology Parties
200	COM	(Former) Communist Parties
300	SOC	Social Democratic Parties
400	LIB	Liberal Parties
500	CHR	Christian Democratic/religious Parties
600	CON	Conservative Parties
700	NAT	National Parties
800	AGR	Agrarian Parties
901	ETH	Ethnic and Regional Parties
951	SIN	Special Interest Parties

If more than one political party of a specific party family is represented in a particular country, this fact is reflected in the fifth digit of the party code.

1. Australian Parties Covered

Parties		Elections		MDS-ID
		first-last	no	
ALP	Australian Labour Party	1946–1998	22	**63320**
AD	Australian Democrats	1990–1998	3	**63321**
DLP	Democratic Labour Party	1955–1977	10	**63330**
LPA	Liberal Party of Australia	1946–1998	22	**63620**
CP	Country Party	1946–1998	22	**63810**
NCP	**renamed:** National Country Party	in 1975		
NPA	**renamed:** National Party of Australia	in 1982		
Total number of cases			79	

2. Austrian Parties Covered

Parties		Elections		MDS-ID
		first-last	no	
GA	Die Grüne Alternative (Green Alternative)	1986–1995	4	**42110**
SPÖ	Sozialdemokratische Partei Österreichs (Austrian Social Democratic Party)	1949–1995	15	**42320**
VdU	Verband der Unabhängigen (League of Independents)	1949–1995	15	**42420**
FPÖ	**renamed:** Freiheitliche Partei Österreichs (Austrian Freedom Party)	in 1956		
	renamed: Die Freiheitlichen (Freedom Movement)	in 1995		
LF	Liberales Forum (Liberal Forum)	1994+1995	2	**42421**
ÖVP	Österreichische Volkspartei (Austrian People's Party)	1949–1995	15	**42520**
Total number of cases			51	

3. Belgian Parties Covered

Parties		Elections		MDS-ID
		first-last	no	
ECOLO	Écologistes Confédérés pour l'Organisation de Luttes Originales (Francophone Ecologists)	1981–1995	5	**21111**
AGALEV	Anders Gaan Leven (Live Differently—Flemish-speaking Ecologists)	1981–1995	5	**21112**

BSP/PSB	Belgische Socialistische Partij/ Parti Socialiste Belge (Belgian Socialist Party)	1946–1977 11	**21320**
BSP	Belgische Socialistische Partij (Flemish Socialist Party)	1978–1995 6	**21321**
SP	**renamed**: Socialistische Partij (Flemish Socialist Party)	in 1980	
PS	Parti Socialiste (Francophone Socialist Party)	1978–1995 6	**21322**
LP/PL	Liberale Partij/Parti libéral (Liberal Party)	1946–1968 8	**21420**
PVV/PLP	**renamed**: Partij voor Vrijheid en Vooruitgang/ Parti de la Liberté et du Progrès (Party of Liberty and Progress)	in 1961	
PVV	Partij voor Vrijheid en Vooruitgang (Party of Liberty and Progress)	1971–1995 9	**21421**
VLD	**renamed**: Vlaamse Liberalen en Demokraten (Flemish Liberals and Democrats)	in 1992	
PLP	Parti de la Liberté et du Progrès (Party of Liberty and Progress)	1971–1991 8 1991	**21422**
PRLW	**renamed**: Parti des Réformes et de la Liberté de Wallonie (Francophone Liberals)	in 1976	
PRL	**renamed**: Parti Réformateur Libéral (Francophone Liberals)	in 1979	
PRL-FDF	Parti Réformateur Libéral— Front Démocratique des Francophones (Liberal Reformation Party— Francophone Democratic Front)	1995 1	**21423**
PL	Parti Libéral (Brussels Liberal Party)	1971–1978 4	**21424**
PLDP	**renamed**: Parti Libéral Démocrate et Pluraliste (Liberal Democratic and Pluralist Party)	in 1974	
PSC/CVP	Parti Social Chrétien/Christelijke Volkspartij (Francophone Christian Social Party and Flemish Christian People's Party)	1946–1965 7	**21520**
CVP	Christelijke Volkspartij (Christian People's Party)	1968–1995 10	**21521**
PSC	Parti Social Chrétien (Christian Social Party)	1968–1995 10	**21522**
RW	Rassemblement Wallon (Walloon Rally)	1968–1981 6	**21911**

FDF	Front Démocratique des Bruxellois Francophones (Francophone Democratic Front)	1965–1991	10	**21912**
	Frontpartij (Front Party)	1954–1995	14	**21913**
VNV	**renamed**: Vlaamsch Nationaal Verbond (Flemish National League)	in 1936		
	renamed: Vlaamsch Concentratie (Flemish Concentration)	in 1949		
	renamed: Christelijke Vlaamse Volksunie (Flemish Christian Peoples' Union)	1954–1987		
VU	**renamed**: De Volksunie (Peoples' Union)	in 1954		
VB	Vlaams Blok (Flemish Block)	1978–1995	6	**21914**

Total number of cases   126

4. Canadian Parties Covered

Parties		Elections		MDS-ID
		first-last	no	
CCF	Co-operative Commonwealth Federation	1945–1997	17	**62320**
NDP	**renamed:** New Democratic Party	in 1961		
LP	Liberal Party of Canada	1945–1997	17	**62420**
PCP	Progressive Conservative Party	1945–1997	17	**62620**
RPC	Reform Party of Canada	1993+1997	2	**62621**
BQ	Bloc Québécois	1993+1997	2	**62901**
Socred	Social Credit	1945–1974	11	**62951**

Total number of cases   66

5. Danish Parties Covered

Parties		Elections		MDS-ID
		first-last	no	
VS	Venstresocialisterne (Left Socialist Party)	1968–1984	8	**13210**
DKP	Danmarks Kommunistiske Parti (Danish Communist Party)	1945–1984	17	**13220**
FK	Fælles Kurs (Common Course)	1987	1	**13221**
EL	Enhedslisten-De Rød-Grønne (Red-Green Unity List) Valforbund Enhedslisten: De Grønne, Solidarisk Alternativ, Invendrerlisten,	1994+1998	2	**13229**

Christianialisten, Arbeidsløshedsparteit,
Kærlighedspartiet, Miljøparti

SF	Socialistisk Folkeparti (Socialist People's Party)	1960–1998 16	**13230**
SD	Socialdemokratiet (Social Democratic Party)	1945–1998 22	**13320**
CD	Centrum-Demokraterne (Centre Democrats)	1973–1998 11	**13330**
RV	Det Radikale Venstre (Radical Party)	1945–1998 22	**13410**
V	Venstre (Liberals)	1945–1998 22	**13420**
DU	De Uafhængige (Independents' Party)	1953–1968 6	**13421**
LC	Liberalt Centrum (Liberal Centre)	1966+1968 2	**13422**
KrF	Kristeligt Folkeparti (Christian People's Party)	1971–1998 12	**13520**
KF	Konservative Folkeparti (Conservative People's Party)	1945–1998 22	**13620**
FP	Fremkridtspartiet (Progress Party)	1973–1998 11	**13951**
RF	Retsforbund (Justice Party)	1945–1984 17	**13952**
DS	Dansk Samling (Danish Union)	1945 1	**13953**

Total number of cases   192

6. Finnish Parties Covered

Parties		Elections		MDS-ID
		first-last	no	
VL	Vihreä Liitto (Green Union)	1983–1995	4	**14110**
SKDL	Suomen Kansan Demokraattinen Liitto (Finnish People's Democratic Union)	1945–1987	13	**14221**
DEVA	Demokraattinen Vaihtoehto (Democratic Alternative)	1987	1	**14222**
VL	Vasemmistoliitto (Left Wing Alliance)	1991+1995	2	**14223**
TPSL	Tyäväen ja Pienviljelijäin Sosialdemokraattinen Liitto (Social Democratic League of Workers and Smallholders)	1958–1966	3	**14310**
SSDP	Suomen Sosialidemokraattinen Puolue (Finnish Social Democrats)	1945–1995	15	**14320**
	Kansallinen Edistyspuolue (National Progressive Party) **renamed**: Suomen Kansanpuolue	1945–1991 in 1951	12	**14420**

	(Finnish People's Party)			
LKP	**renamed**: Liberaalinen Kansanpuolue	in 1966		
	(Liberal People's Party)			
NSP	Nuorsuomalainen Puolue	1995	1	**14430**
	(Progressive Finnish Party, also known as Young Finns)			
SKL	Suomen Kristillinen Liitto	1970–1995	8	**14520**
	(Finnish Christian Union)			
KK	Kansallinen Kokoomus (National Coalition)	1945–1995	15	**14620**
	Maalaisliitto (Agrarian Union);	1945–1995	15	**14810**
	renamed: Keskustapuolue (Centre Party);	in 1965		
SK	**renamed:** Suomen Keskusta (Finnish Centre)	in 1988		
	Suomen Pientalonpoiken Puolue	1966–1995	9	**14820**
	(Finnish Smallholder' Party)			
SMP	**renamed**: Soumen Maaseudun Puolue	in 1966		
	(Finnish Rural Party)			
RKP/SFP	Ruotsalainen Kansanpuolue/	1945–1995	15	**14901**
	Svenska Folkpartiet (Swedish People's Party)			

Total number of cases   113

7. French Parties Covered

Parties		Elections		MDS-ID
		first-last	no	
	Écologistes (Greens)	1993+1997	2	**31110**
	in 1997: Les Verts			
GE	Generation Écologie (Ecology Generation)	1997	1	**31111**
PCF	Parti Communiste Français	1946–1997	14	**31220**
	(French Communist Party)			
SIFO	Section Française de l'Internationale Ouvriére	1946–1997	14	**31320**
	(Socialist Party)			
PS	**renamed:** Parti Socialiste (Socialist Party)	in 1969		
RRRS	Parti Répulicain Radical et Radical	1946–1968	7	**31421**
	Socialiste (Radical Socialist Party)			
MRP	Mouvement Républicain Populaire	1946–1962	5	**31521**
	(Popular Republican Movement)			
CD	Centre Démocrat (Democratic Centre)	1967+1968	2	**31522**
	renamed: Centre du Progrès et de la	in 1968		
	Démocratie Moderne (Democratic Centre)			
CDP	Centre Démocratie et Progrés	1973	1	**31523**
	(Centre Democracy and Progress)			

MR	Mouvement Réformateur (Reformers' Movement)	1973	1	**31529**
	Gaullists **includes:** UNR Union Pour la Nouvelle République UDT Union Démocratique du Travail RPR Rassemblement pour la République	1946–1988	12	**31621**
	Conservatives **includes:** Parti Républicain de la Liberté Independants Républicains Parti Paysan CNIP Centre National des Indépendants et Paysans Action Répubilcaine et Sociale Centre Républicain Centre National des Indépendants	1946–1988	12	**31622**
	Poujadists	1956	1	**31623**
UDF	Union pour la Démocratie Française (Union for French Democracy)	1978–1997	6	**31624**
RPR	Rassemblement pour la République (Rally for the Republic)	1993+1997	2	**31625**
FN	Front National (National Front)	1986–1997	4	**31720**

Total number of cases   84

8. German Parties Covered

Parties		Elections		MDS-ID
		first-last	no	
	Die Grünen (The Greens)	1983+1987	2	**41111**
Greens-90	Grüne/Bündnis'90 (Greens/Alliance'90)	1990	1	**41112**
90-Greens	Bündnis'90/Die Grünen (Alliance'90/Greens)	1994+1998	2	**41113**
KPD	Kommunistische Partei Deutschlands (Communist Party of Germany)	1949	1	**41220**
PDS	Partei des Demokratischen Sozialismus (Party of Democratic Socialism)	1990–1998	3	**41221**
SPD	Sozialdemokratische Partei Deutschlands (Social Democratic Party of Germany)	1949–1998	14	**41320**
FDP	Freie Demokratische Partei (Free Democratic Party)	1949–1998	14	**41420**

CDU/CSU	Christlich-Demokratische Union/ Christlich-Soziale Union (Christian Democratic Union/Christian Social Union)	1949–1998 14	**41521**
DZ	Deutsche Zentrumspartei (Centre Party)	1949+1953 2	**41522**
DP	Deutsche Partei (German Party)	1949–1957 3	**41620**
WAV	Wirtschaftliche Aufbauvereinigung (Economic Reconstruction League)	1949 1	**41711**
DRP	Deutsche Reichspartei (German Reich Party)	1949 1	**41712**
BP	Bayernpartei (Bavarian Party)	1949 1	**41911**
SSW	Südschleswigscher Wählerverband- Sydslesvigsk Vaelgerforening (South Schleswig Voters' Union)	1949 1	**41912**
GB/BHE	Gesamtdeutscher Block/ Bund der Heimatvertriebenen und Entrechteten (Refugee Party)	1953 1	**41951**
Total number of cases		61	

9. Greek Parties Covered

	Parties	Elections		MDS-ID
		first-last	no	
KKE	Kommounistiko Komma Elladas (Communist Party of Greece)	1974–1985, 1993+1996	6	**34210**
SAP	Synaspismos tis Aristeras kai tis Proodou (Progressive Left Coalition)	1989–1996	4	**34211**
PASOK	Panhellinio Socialistiko Kinema (Panhellenic Socialist Movement)	1974–1996	9	**34313**
DIKKI	Dimokratiki Kinoniki Kinema (Democratic Social Movement)	1996	1	**34314**
EDIK	Enosis Kentrou (Centre Union) renamed: Enosi Dimokratikou Kentrou (Union of the Democratic Centre)	1974+1977 in 1977:	2	**34510**
ND	Nea Dimokratia (New Democracy)	1974–1996	9	**34511**
Pola	Politiki Anixi (Political Spring)	1993+1996	2	**34512**
EP	Ethniki Parataxis (National Alignment)	1977	1	**34610**
Total number of cases			34	

10. Icelandic Parties Covered

	Parties	Elections		MDS-ID
		first-last	no	
Ab	Sósíalistaflokkurinn (United Socialist Party) renamed: Alþhýðubandalagid (People's Alliance)	1946–1995 in 1956	16	**15220**
A	Alþhýðuflokkurinn (Social Democratic Party)	1946–1995	16	**15320**
BJ	Bandalag Jafnaðarmanna (Social Democratic Federation)	1983	1	**15321**
SFVM	Samtök Frjálslyndra og Vinstri Manna (Union of Liberals and Leftists)	1967–1974	3	**15322**
	þjóðvaki (Awakening of the Nation)	1995	1	**15323**
Sj	Sjálfstaedisflokkurinn (Independence Party)	1946–1995	16	**15620**
Bf	Borgaraflokkurinn (Citizens' Party)	1987	1	**15621**
Tf	þjodvarnarflokkurinn (National Preservation Party)	1953	1	**15710**
F	Framsóknarflokkurinn (Progressive Party)	1946–1995	16	**15810**
Kv	Samtök um Kvennalista (Women's Alliance)	1983–1995	4	**15951**
Total number of cases		75		

11. Irish Parties Covered

	Parties	Elections		MDS-ID
		first-last	no	
Greens	Ecology Party/Green Party/Comhaontas Glas	1989–1997	3	**53110**
WP	Pairti na nOiri (Workers' Party)	1981–1989	5	**53220**
DLP	Democratic Left Party	1992+1997	2	**53221**
LP	Páirti Lucht Oibre (Labour Party)	1948–1997	16	**53320**
PD	Progressive Democrats	1987–1997	4	**53420**
	Fine Gael (Familiy of the Irish)	1948–1997	16	**53520**
	Fianna Fáil (Soldiers of Destiny)	1948–1997	16	**53620**

CnP Clann na Poblachta (Republican Party)	1948–1965	6	**53714**
CnTClann na Talmhan (Party of the Land)	1948–1961	5	**53810**

Total number of cases   73

12. Israeli Parties Covered

Parties	Elections		MDS-ID
	first-last	no	
MAKI Miflaga Kommunistit Isrealit (Communist Party of Israel)	1949–1969	7	**72220**
MOKED (Focus)	1973	1	**72221**
PLPHareshima Ha'mitkademet le-Shalom (Progressive List for Peace)	1984+1988	2	**72222**
SHELLI Shalom le'Israel-Shivion le'Israel (Peace in Israel-Equality in Israel)	1977–1981	2	**72223**
RAKAH Reshima Kommunistit Hadasha (New Communist Party)	1965–1973	3	**72224**
HADASH Hazit Democratit le Shalom ve-Shivayon (Democratic Front for Peace and Equality) in 1996: Hadash/Balad (Democratic National Party)	1977–1996	6	**72225**
RATZ Hatnuah Lezhiot Ha'ezrach (Citizens' Rights Movement)	1973–1988	5	**72310**
MAPAM Mifleget Ha'poalim Hameuchedet (United Workers' Party)	1949–1965, 1988	7	**72311**
AMT Ma'arach (Alignment)	1969–1984	5	**72320**
RAFI Reshimat Poalei Israel (Israel Workers' List)	1965	1	**72322**
Mifleget Ha'avoda Ha'Israelit (Israeli Labour Party)	1965,1988, 1992+1996	4	**72323**
MAPAI Mifleget Poalei Eretz Israel (Workers' Party of the Land of Israel)	1949–1961	5	**72324**
Achdut Ha'avoda Poalei Zion (Unity of Labour/Workers for Zion)	1955–1961	3	**72325**
MERETZ merger between MAPAM and RATZ	1992+1996	2	**72326**
H'Miflaga H'Liberalit H'Atzmaut (Progressive and Independent Liberal Party)	1965–1981	5	**72410**
Miflaga Haliberalit (Liberal Party)	1961	1	**72411**
DASH Hatnuah Hademokratit Le-shinui (Democratic Movement for Change)	1977	1	**72412**
Shinui (Change)	1981+1984	2	**72413**

	Yachad (Together)	1984	1	**72414**
	Zionim Klalim (General Zionists')	1949–1959	4	**72420**
	Ometz (Courage)	1984	1	**72425**
	Ha'Derech Ha'shlishit (The Third Way)	1996	1	**72427**
	Yisrael Ba-Aliya (Israel for Immigration)	1996	1	**72428**
MAFDAL	Miflaga Datit Leumit (National Religious Party)	1955–1996	12	**72530**
	Agudat Israel/Poalei Agudat Israel (Association of Israel/Association of Israel Workers)	1949–1988	12	**72531**
TAMI	Tenua le'Masoret Israel (Movement for Israel's Tradition)	1981+1984	2	**72532**
SHAS	Shomrei Torah Sephardim (Sephardi Torah Guardians)	1984–1996	4	**72533**
	Morasha (Heritage)	1984	1	**72534**
	Yahadut HaTorah (United Torah Judaism, merger between Degel Hatorah and Agudat Israel)	1992+1996	2	**72535**
	Hamerkaz Hahofshi (Free Centre)	1969	1	**72610**
	Reshima Mamlachtit (State List)	1969	1	**72611**
Tehiya	Tenuat Hetehiya (Renaissance Movement)	1981–1992	4	**72612**
Tsomet	HaTenua LeHithadashot Zionit Vevilti Miflagtaim (Crossroads—non-aligned movement for Zionist Renewal)	1984–1992	3	**72613**
	Degel Hatorah (Torah Flag)	1988	1	**72614**
	Moledet (Homeland) merger with Tehiya in 1996	1988–1996	3	**72615**
	Herut (Freedom Party)	1949–1961	5	**72620**
GAHAL	Gahal-Gush-Herut Liberalim (Freedom-Liberal Block)	1965+1969	2	**72621**
	Likud (Union)	1973–1996	7	**72622**
	Shlomzion-Tenua Lehagshama Zionist (Realization of Zionism Movement)	1977	1	**72623**
	HaReshima Ha'aravit HaMeuchedet (United Arab List)	1988–1996	3	**72901**

Total number of cases   134

13. Italian Parties Covered

Parties		Elections		MDS-ID
		first-last	no	
FdV	Federazione dei Liste Verdi (Green Federation)	1987–1996	4	**32110**
PdUP	Manifesto/Partito di Unità Proletaria per il Comunismo (Manifesto/Party of Proletarian Unity for Communism)	1976–1983	3	**32210**
DP	Democrazia Proletaria (Proletarian Democracy)	1983+1987	2	**32211**
RC	Rifondazione Comunista (Newly Founded Communists)	1992–1996	3	**32212**
PCI	Partito Comunista Italiano (Communist Party)	1946–1996	14	**32220**
PDS	**renamed**: Partito Democratico della Sinistra (Democratic Party of the Left)	in 1990		
PR	Partito Radicale (Radical Party) **renamed:**	1976–1996	7	**32310**
	Lista Panella	in 1992		
	Lista Panella-Riformatori	in 1994		
	Lista Sgarbi-Panella	in 1996		
PSI	Partito Socialista Italiano (Socialist Party)	1946–1994	12	**32320**
RI	Rinnovamento Italiano (Italian Renewal)	1996	1	**32321**
PSU	United Socialist Party	1968	1	**32322**
PSLI	Partito Socialista dei Lavoratori Italiani (Socialist Party of Italian Workers)	1948–1992	10	**32330**
PSDI	**renamed**: Partito Socialista Democratico Italiano (Italian Democratic Socialist Party)	in 1972		
PRI	Partito Repubblicano Italiano (Republican Party)	1946–1992	12	**32410**
PLI	Partito Liberale Italiano (Liberal Party)	1946–1992	12	**32420**
DC	Democrazia Cristiana (Christian Democrats)	1946–1996	14	**32520**
PPI	**renamed**: Partido Populare Italiano (Italian Popular Party)	in 1994		

CCD	Centro Cristiano Democratico (Christian Democratic Centre)	1996	1	**32521**
PI	Patto per l'Italia (Pact for Italy)	1994	1	**32528**
AD	Alleanza Democratica (Democratic Alliance)	1994+1996	2	**32529**
FI	Forza Italia (Go Italy)	1994+1996	2	**32610**
MSI	Movimento Sociale Italiano (Italian Social Movement)	1948–1996	13	**32710**
MSI-DN	**renamed**: Movimento Sociale Italiano-Destra Nazionale (Italian Social Movement-Right National)	in 1972		
AN	**renamed**: Alleanza Nazionale (National Alliance)	in 1994		
LN	La Lega Nord (Northern League)	1992–1996	3	**32720**
LR	La Rete/Movimento per la Democrazia (The Network/Movement for Democracy)	1992+1994	2	**32951**

Total number of cases 119

14. Japanese Parties Covered

	Parties	Elections		MDS-ID
		first-last	no	
JCP	Nihon Kyosan-to (Japan Communist Party)	1960–1996	13	**71220**
JSP	Nihon Shakai-to (Japan Socialist Party)	1960–1996	13	**71320**
DSP	Minshu-Shakai-to (Democratic Socialist Party)	1960–1993	12	**71321**
SDF	Shaminren (Social Democratic Federation)	1979–1990	4	**71322**
CGP	Komei-to (Clean Government Party)	1967–1993	10	**71530**
LDP	Jiyu-Minshu-to (Liberal Democratic Party)	1960–1996	13	**71620**
NLC	Shin Jiyu Club (New Liberal Club)	1976–1986	5	**71621**
JRP	Shinsei-to (Japan Renewal Party)	1993	1	**71622**
NFP(New Frontier Party)	Sinshin	1996	1	**71623**

DPJ	Minshu (Democratic Party of Japan)	1996	1	**71624**
NP	Sakigake (New Party)	1993+1996	2	**71951**
JNP	Nihon Shin-to (Japan New Party)	1993	1	**71952**

Total number of cases   76

15. Luxembourgian Parties Covered

Parties		Elections		MDS-ID
		first-last	no	
GLEI	Greng Lëscht Ekologesch Initiativ (Green Left Ecological Initiative)	1989	1	**23111**
GAP	Di Grëng Alternativ (Green Alternative)	1984+1989	2	**23112**
GLEI-GAP		1994	1	**23113**
	Greng Lëscht Ekologesch Initiativ-Di Grëng Alternativ (Green Left Ecological Initiative-Green Alternative)			
PCL/KPL	Parti Communiste Luxembourgeois/ Kommunistesch Partei vu Lëtzeburg (Communist Party)	1945–1989	11	**23220**
POSL/LSAP				
	Parti Ouvrier Socialiste Luxembourgeois/Letzeburger Sozialistesch Arbeiterpartei (Socialist Workers' Party)	1945–1994	12	**23320**
	Groupement Patriotique et Démocratique (Patriotic and Democratic Group) **renamed:** Groupement Démocratique (Democratic Group)	1945–1994 in 1954	12	**23420**
PD/DP	**renamed:** Parti Démocratique/ Demokratesch Partei (Democratic Party)	in 1959		
PCS/CSV	Parti Chrétien Social/Chrëschtlech Sozial Vollekspartei (Christian Social People's Party)	1945–1994	12	**23520**
ADR	Aktiounskomitee fir Demokratie a Rentegerechtegkeet (Action Committee for Democracy and Pension Justice)	1989+1994	2	**23951**

Total number of cases   53

16. Dutch Parties Covered

Parties		Elections		MDS-ID
		first-last	no	
GL	Groen Links (Green Left)	1989–1998	3	**22110**
PPR	Politieke Partij Radicalen (Radical Political Party)	1971–1986	6	**22310**
PvdA	Partij van de Arbeid (Labour Party)	1946–1998	16	**22320**
D'66	Democraten'66 (Democrats'66)	1967–1998	10	**22330**
VVD	Volkspartij voor Vrijheid en Democratie (People's Party for Freedom and Democracy)	1946–1998	16	**22420**
CDA	Christen-Democratisch Appel (Christian Democratic Appeal)	1977–1998	7	**22521**
KVP	Katholieke Volkspartij (Catholic People's Party)	1946–1972	9	**22522**
ARP	Anti-Revolutionaire Partij (Anti-Revolutionary Party)	1946–1972	9	**22523**
DS'70	Democratische Socialisten'70 (Democratic Socialists'70)	1971–1977	3	**22524**
CHU	Christelijk-Historische Unie (Christian Historical Union)	1946–1972	9	**22525**
Total number of cases			88	

17. New Zealand Parties Covered

Parties		Elections		MDS-ID
		first-last	no	
LP	Labour Party	1946–1996	18	**64320**
	Alliance	1993+1996	2	**64321**
NP	National Party	1946–1996	18	**64620**
NZFP	New Zealand First Party	1993+1996	2	**64621**
	Social Credit/Democratic Party	1954–1990	13	**64951**
Total number of cases			53	

18. Norwegian Parties Covered

Parties		Elections		MDS-ID
		first-last	no	
NKP	Norges Kommunistiske Parti (Norwegian Communist Party)	1945–1957	4	**12220**
	Sosialistisk Folkeparti (Socialist People's Party)	1961–1997	10	**12221**
SV	renamed: Sosialistisk Venstreparti (Socialist Left Party)	in 1975		
DNA	Det Norske Arbeiderparti (Norwegian Labour Party)	1945–1997	14	**12320**
	Det Nye Folkepartiet (New People's Party);	1973	1	**12410**
DLF	renamed: Det Liberále Folkeparti (Liberal People's Party)	in 1980		
V	Venstre (Liberal Party)	1945–1997	14	**12420**
KrF	Kristelig Folkeparti (Christian People's Party)	1945–1997	14	**12520**
H	Høyre (Conservative Party)	1945–1997	14	**12620**
	Bondepartiet (Farmers' Party)	1945–1997	14	**12810**
SP	renamed: Senterpartiet (Centre Party)	in 1959		
	Anders Langes Parti (Anders Lange's Party);	1973–1997	7	**12951**
FrP	renamed: Fremskrittspartiet (Progress Party)	in 1977		
Total number of cases			92	

19. Portuguese Parties Covered

Parties		Elections		MDS-ID
		first-last	no	
PEV	Partido Ecologista 'Os Verdes' (Greens)	1983–1987	3	**35110**
UDP	União Democrática Popular (Popular Democratic Union)	1975–1987	7	**35210**
PCP	Partido Comunista Português (Portuguese Communist Party)	1975–1987	7	**35220**
CDU	Coligação Democrático Unitária (Unified Democratic Coalition)	1991+1995	2	**35229**

MDP	Movimento Democrático Português (Democratic Movement)	1975–1985	5	**35310**
PSP	Partido Socialista Portuguêsa (Portuguese Socialist Party)	1975–1995	9	**35311**
PRD	Partido Renovador Democrático (Democratic Renewal Party)	1985+1987	2	**35312**
PPD	Partido Popular Democrático (Popular Democratic Party)	1975–1995	9	**35313**
PSD	**renamed:** Partido Social Democráta (Social Democratic Party)			
CDS	Partido do Centro Democrático Social (Centre Social Democrats)	1975–1995	9	**35314**
PP	**renamed:** Partido Popular (Popular Party)	in 1995		
ID	Intervençao Democrática (Democratic Intervention)	1987	1	**35315**
ASDI	Associacao Social Democrata Independente (Independent Social Democrats)	1980	1	**35316**
UEDS	Uniao de Esquerda para a Democracia (Union of the Socialist and Democratic Left)	1980	1	**35317**
PPM	Partido Popular Monárquico (Popular Monarchist Party)	1976–1983	4	**35710**
PSN	Partido de Solidariedade Nacional (National Solidarity Party)	1991	1	**35951**
Total number of cases			61	

20. Spanish Parties Covered

Parties		Elections		MDS-ID
		first-last	no	
PCE/PSUC	Partido Communista de España (Communist Party)	1977–1996	7	**33220**
IU	**since** 1989: Izquierda Unida (United Left)			
PSOE	Partido Socialista Obrero Español (Spanish Socialist Workers' Party)	1977–1996	7	**33320**
UCD	Unión de Centro Democrático (Union of the Democratic Centre/Centrist Bloc)	1977–1982	3	**33430**
PDP	Partido Demócrata Popular (Popular Democratic Party)	1982+1986	2	**33438**
PL	Partido Liberal (Liberal Party)	1986	1	**33439**
CDS	Centró Democrático y Social (Centre Democrats)	1982–1993	4	**33512**

AP	Alianza Popular (Popular Alliance)	1977–1996	7	**33610**
PP	**renamed**: Partido Popular (Popular Party)	in 1989		
CiU	Convergència i Unió (Convergence and Union)	1979–1996	6	**33611**
EE	Euzkadiko Ezkerra (Basque Left)	1977–1989	5	**33901**
PNV/EAJ	Partido Nacionalita Vasco /Euskadi Alberti Jetzale (Basque Nationalist Party)	1977–1996	7	**33902**
EA	Eusko Alkartasuna (Basque Solidarity)	1989+1993	2	**33903**
PAR	Partido Argonés Regionalista (Aragonese Regionalist Party)	1977–1993	5	**33904**
ERC	Esquerra Republicana de Catalunya (Catalan Republican Left)	1977–1993	6	**33905**
PA	Partidu Andalucista (Andalusian Party)	1977+1979, 1989	3	**33906**

Total number of cases	65

21. Swedish Parties Covered

	Parties	Elections		MDS-ID
		first-last	no	
	Miljöpartiet de Gröna (Green Ecology Party)	1988–1998	4	**11110**
	Sveriges Kommunistiska Parti (Communist Party of Sweden)	1948–1998	17	**11220**
VK	**renamed**: Vänsterpartiet Kommunisterna (Left Communists Party)	in 1967		
Vp	**renamed**: Vänsterpartiet (Left Party)	in 1990		
SdaP	Socialdemokratistiska Arbetarepartiet (Social Democratic Labour Party)	1948–1998	17	**11320**
FP	Folkpartiet (People's Party)	1948–1998	17	**11420**
FP	**renamed**: Folkpartiet Liberalerna (Liberal People's Party)	in 1990		
KdS	Kristdemokratiska Samhällspartiet (Christian Democratic Community Party)	1985–1998	4	**11520**
	Hogerpartiet (Right Party)	1948–1998	17	**11620**
MSP	**renamed**: Moderata Samlingspartiet (Moderate Coalition Party)	in 1969		
	Bondeforbundet (Agrarian Party)	1948–1998	17	**11810**
CP	**renamed**: Centerpartiet (Centre Party)	in 1957		

NyD	Ny Demokrati (New Democracy)	1991	1	**11951**

Total number of cases   94

22. Swiss Parties Covered

Parties		Elections		MDS-ID
		first-last	no	
	Grüne (Greens)	1979–1995	5	**43110**
	renamed: GPS/PES Föderation der Grünen	in 1983		
	Parteien der Schweiz/Fédération Suisse			
	des Partis Écologistes (Federation of			
	Green Parties)			
	renamed: Grüne Partei der Schweiz/			
	Parti Écologiste	in 1987		
	Suisse (Green Party of Switzerland)			
SPS/PSS	Sozialdemokratische Partei der Schweiz/	1947–1995	13	**43320**
	Parti Socialiste Suisse			
	(Social Democratic Party)			
LdU/ADI	Landesring der Unabhängigen/	1947–1995	13	**43321**
	Alliance des Indépendants			
	(Independents' Alliance)			
FDP/PRD	Freisinnig-Demokratische Partei der Schweiz/	1947–1995	13	**43420**
	Parti Radical-Démocratique Suisse			
	(Radical Democratic Party)			
	Schweizerische Konservative Volkspartei/	1947–1995	13	**43520**
	Parti Populaire Conservateur Suisse			
	(Conservative People's Party)			
	renamed: Konservativ-Christlich Soziale	in 1957		
	Partei/Parti Conservateur Chretien Social			
	(Conservative Christian Social Party)			
CVP/PDC	**renamed**: Christlich Demokratische	in 1971		
	Volkspartei der Schweiz			
	/Parti Démocrate-Chrétien Suisse			
	(Christian Democratic People's Party)			
EVP/PEP	Evangelische Volkspartei der Schweiz/	1971–1995	7	**43530**
	Parti Populaire Evangelique Suisse			
	(Protestant Peoples' Party)			
	Nationale Aktion gegen die Überfremdung	1971–1995	7	**43710**
	von Volk und Heimat/Action Nationale			
	contre l'Emprise et la Surpopulation			
	Etrangère (National Action against Foreign			
	Domination);			

NA/AN	**renamed**: Nationale Aktion für Volk und Heimat/Action Nationale pour le Peuple et la Patrie (National Action for People and Fatherland)	in 1979	
SD	**renamed**: Schweizer Demokraten/ Démocrates Suisses (Swiss Democrats)	in 1991	
BGB	Schweizerische Bauern-, Gewerbe- und Bürgerpartei/Parti Suisse des Paysans, Artisans et Bourgeois (Farmers', Traders' and Citizens' Party)	1947–1995 13	**43810**
SVP/UDC	**renamed**: Schweizerische Volkspartei/ Union Démocratique du Centre (Swiss People's Party)	in 1971	
	Schweizer Auto Partei/Parti Automobiliste Suisse (Swiss Motorists' Party)	1987–1995 3	**43951**
FPS	**renamed**: Freiheitspartei der Schweiz (Freedom Party of Switzerland)		

Total number of cases   87

23. Turkish Parties Covered

Parties		Elections		MDS-ID
		first-last	no	
CHP	Cumhuriyet Halk Partisi (Republican People's Party)	1950–1977, 1995	9	**74321**
HP	Halkçi Parti (Populist Party)	1983	1	**74322**
SHP	Sosyal Demokrat Halçi Parti (Social Democratic Populist Party)	1987+1991	2	**74323**
DSP	Demokratik Sol Parti (Democratic Left Party)	1991+1995	2	**74324**
DP	Demokrat Parti (Democratic Party)	1950–1957	3	**74621**
AP	Adalet Partisi (Justice Party)	1961–1977	5	**74622**
ANAP	Anavatan Partisi (Motherland Party)	1983–1995	4	**74623**
DYP	Dogru Yol Partisi (True Path Party)	1987–1995	3	**74624**
MP	Millet Partisi (Nation Party)	1965+1969	2	**74625**
MDP	Milliyetçi Demokrasi Partisi (Nationalist Democratic Party)	1983	1	**74711**

MHP	Milliyetçi Hareket Partisi (National Action Party)	1961–1977	5	**74712**
MSP	Milli Selamet Partisi (National Salvation Party)	1973+1977	2	**74714**
RP	Refah Partisi (Welfare Party)	1987–1995	3	**74715**

Total number of cases   42

24. British Parties Covered

	Parties	**Elections**		**MDS-ID**
		first-last	no	
	Labour Party	1945–1997	15	**51320**
SDP	Social Democratic Party	1983+1987	2	**51330**
	Liberal Party	1945–1987	13	**51420**
LDP	Liberal Democratic Party	1992+1997	2	**51421**
	Conservative Party	1945–1997	15	**51620**

Total number of cases   47

25. US-American Parties Covered

Parties	**Elections**		**MDS-ID**
	first-last	no	
Democratic Party	1948–1996	13	**61320**
Republican Party	1948–1996	13	**61620**

Total number of cases   26

Appendix II

Manifesto Coding Instructions

1. Introduction

The object of analysing election programmes is to measure policy positions of parties across countries within a common framework. Election programmes are taken as indicators of the parties' policy emphases and policy positions at a certain point in time. Therefore, election programmes are subjected to quantitative content analysis. A classification scheme was designed to allow for the coding of all the content of election programmes for the post World-War-II period in a variety of countries.

A first version of the classification scheme was developed by David Robertson (1976: 73–5) for analyzing modes of party competition in Britain. In 1979, the 'Manifesto Research Group' (MRG) was constituted as a research group of the European Consortium for Political Research (ECPR) by scholars interested in a comparative content-analytic approach on policy positions of parties. During their work, the classification scheme was extended and revised to fit additional countries.

Since 1989 the Social Science Research Centre Berlin (WZB) provides resources for updating and expanding the MRG appendix paper is an introduction to the application of the coding scheme for coders who do not have the background knowledge of the MRG-members. Moreover, it provides investigators in countries not covered by the MRG/CMP with all the relevant information, definitions, and sources to apply the coding scheme to their respective countries.

2. Selection of Programmes

Programmatic statements are central features of parties. In party programmes, the political ideas and goals of parties are put on record. Although only few voters actually read party programmes, they are spread commonly through the mass media.

Among the different kinds of programme which are issued in many countries, the basis for this research are *election programmes*. The advantages of taking election programmes as a source for identifying political goals of parties are manifold:

1. Election programmes cover a wide range of political positions and themes and, therefore, can be seen as a 'set of key central statements of party positions' (Budge, Robertson and Hearl (eds.) 1987: 18).

2. Election programmes are authoritative statements of party policies because the programmes are usually ratified in party conventions.
3. Election programmes are representative statements for the whole party, not just statements of one faction or group within the party or of individual party members.
4. Election programmes are published before every election. Thus, changes of policy positions of parties over time can be studied.

According to the special significance of election programmes, the documents to be collected are the platforms of parties which are published for the election of representatives in the national assembly of a respective country. The sources of these programmes may be the parties themselves, associated research and training institutes or publications in newspapers, magazines, or books.

In some countries parties do not distribute election programmes. In this case, the description of election programmes given above serves as an 'ideal type' of document to be sought. The only documents available may be newspaper summaries of the parties' election pledges or reports of party representatives' speeches about policy positions and goals for the upcoming legislature. In any case the 'ideal type' of document which summarises authoritative statements of the party's policy positions for electioneering should be obtained as far as possible.

3. Selection of Parties

The collection should cover all the significant parties which are represented in the national assembly. The significance of parties is defined as the coalition (governmental) or blackmail potential of a party in a given party system (Sartori 1976: 121–5). Coalition potential is defined as 1. the actual or former membership in a government or 2. the possibility (feasibilty) of becoming a government party. Blackmail potential is defined as the party's impact on 'the tactics of party competition particularly when it alters the direction of the competition—by determining a switch from centripetal to centrifugal competition either leftward, rightward, or in both directions—of the governing-oriented parties.' (Sartori 1976: 123) These criteria for selection need consideration whether small parties, especially new ones like the Green Parties, affect party competition despite their small size.

4. The Coding Procedure

The election programmes are analysed by methods of content analysis which is 'a research technique for the objective, systematic, and quantitative description of the manifest content of communication' (Berelson 1971: 18). The method can be applied to a wide range of different materials and research questions. The purpose of this section is to describe the specific form of content analysis to undertaken in Manifesto research.

The specific kind of internal, quantitative analysis is derived from the ideas, policies, issues, and concerns parties stress in their platforms. The methods of coding are designed to be comparable over a wide range of countries irrespective of cultural and socio-economic differences. Therefore, a classification scheme with invariant general categories is used to cover the total content of election programmes by identifying the statements of preference expressed in the programmes. This classification scheme contains 56 different categories grouped into seven major policy domains: Each of the 56 categories sums up related issues in a way that changes over time can be measured across parties and cross-culturally. Thus, the coding procedure comprises a quantification (how many statements do parties make?) and a classification (what kind of statements do parties make?) of election programmes.

4.1. Quantification: The Coding Unit

The coding unit in a given programme is the *'quasi-sentence'*, defined as an argument. An argument is the verbal expression of one political idea or issue. In its simplest form, a sentence is the basic unit of meaning. Therefore, punctuation can be used as a guideline for identifying arguments. The starting point of coding is the sentence, but what we are aiming for is an argument. In its shortest form, a sentence contains a subject, a verb and an attribute or an adjective.

> Examples: 'We will cut taxes.'
> 'We will reduce our military forces.'

Obviously, these two sentences contain two different arguments which are easy to identify and to distinguish. But unfortunately, languages are more complex, and it is a question of style how the same political ideas might be expressed.

> Example: 'We will cut taxes and reduce our military forces.'

In this case, the two statements are combined in one sentence, but for our purposes are still treated as two different arguments. Long sentences are decomposed into 'quasi-sentences' if the sense changes within the sentence. In most cases, one sentence which covers two (or more) arguments can be easily transformed into two (or more) quasi-sentences by repeating substantives and/or verbs. Thus, a 'quasi-sentence' is a set of words containing, one and only one, political idea. It stops either at the end of an argument or at a full stop (period).

In many cases, arguments are combined and related into one sentence.

> Example: 'Because we want freedom, we need strong military forces.'

These are *two* quasi-sentences, because there are two political goals, i.e. freedom and strength of military forces, which can be transformed into two quasi-sentences:

Examples: 'We want freedom.'
                   'We need strong military forces.'

Thus, long sentences may combine two or more arguments which are often contained by commas, semicolons or colons. A list of arguments, sometimes marked with hyphens or dots, is treated as if separated with full stops.

Example: 'In international policy we shall take new initiatives.
We will:
                   - promote peace;
                   - ban chemical weapons;
                   - refuse to deploy Cruise missiles;
                   - begin discussions for the removal of nuclear bases;
                   - increase aid to developing countries;
                   - take action to protect the status of refugees."

This text contains seven quasi-sentences. Three of the arguments (1. ban chemical weapons; 2. refuse to deploy cruise missiles; 3. begin discussions for the removal of nuclear bases) express the same general idea, i.e. disarmament, but different issues in this policy field. Because distinct policies are mentioned for disarmament, three different quasi-sentences are identified. This list of policies may be given in the following way for which the same number of quasi-sentences is coded as for the list given above:

'In international policy we shall take new initiatives. We will promote peace, ban chemical weapons, refuse to deploy Cruise missiles, begin discussions for the removal of nuclear bases, increase aid to developing countries, and take action to protect the status of refugees.'

Thus, if different issues—however short—are dealt with in the same sentence they constitute different quasi-sentences even if they apply to the same policy field. On the other hand, the same argument may be very long and may occupy a lot of space, but still be only one quasi-sentence.

Detailed instructions, examples and coding exercises can be found in the CD-ROM.

Appendix III

Description of Manifesto Data Set

Units	Parliamentary parties at national elections
Number of countries	25
Number of parties	288
Number of elections	364
Time period covered	all elections between 1945 to 1998 except for the following countries:

Greece:	1974–1996
Japan:	1960–1996
Portugal:	1975–1995
Spain:	1977–1996
Turkey:	1950–1995

Number of cases	1991; including 73 cases of parties not represented in parliament (Absseat = 0) and 189 cases of estimated programmatic data (Progtype = 3)
Number of variables	3 identification variables 5 electoral data variables 59 programmatic data variables 4 programmatic dimensions
Data sources	Publicly available election statistics and content analyzed election programs or its nearest equivalents; see Appendix 4.

Identification Variables:

Country   Two digit code:

11	Sweden
12	Norway
13	Denmark
14	Finland
15	Iceland
21	Belgium
22	Netherlands
23	Luxembourg
31	France
32	Italy
33	Spain
34	Greece
35	Portugal
41	Germany
42	Austria
43	Switzerland
51	Great Britain

53	Ireland
61	United States
62	Canada
63	Australia
64	New Zealand
71	Japan
72	Israel
74	Turkey

Edate   Day, month and year of national election (DD.MM.YY)

Party   The party identification code consist of five digits. The first two digits repeat the country code. The third and fourth digit reflect a tentative grouping of political parties and alliances into the following party families:

100	ECO	Ecology Parties
200	COM	(Former) Communist Parties
300	SOC	Social Democratic Parties
400	LIB	Liberal Parties
500	CHR	Christian Democratic/religious Parties
600	CON	Conservative Parties
700	NAT	National Parties
800	AGR	Agrarian Parties
901	SIN	Special Interest Parties
950	ETH	Ethnic and Regional Parties
990	OTH	Electoral Alliances

If more than one political party of a specific party family is represented in a particular country, this fact is reflected in the fifth digit of the party code.

Electoral data variables:

Pervote   Per centage of votes gained by each party

Voteest   **0   original figure from data source**

Election statistics often assign votes to electoral coalitions as a whole and do not distinguish between component members. Votes for parties in electoral coalitions have been estimated on the basis of the distribution of seats between them:

1   estimated

Presvote   Per centage of votes in presidential elections; for USA only, 99,99 for all other countries.

Absseat   Absolute number of seats held by each party.

Totseats   Total number of seats in parliament.

Programmatic data variables:

Progtype   **1   Program of a single party**

As a rule, each party issues one program for each election.

2   Program of two or more parties

In a number of countries, parties compete as 'programmatic coalitions' by issuing joint programs. In these cases, the joint program was assigned to each of the parties of the programmatic coalition. Joint programs were introduced only if no single party program was available.

3   Estimate

For calculating median voter or median party figures, missing election programs have been estimated on the basis of available programs whenever a party obtained seats in parliament. Estimates were derived either by computing averages between two adjacent programs or by duplicating programmatic data. For three elections (Norway 1997, Denmark 1998, Spain 1996) estimates from preceding programs have been introduced because content analyses of election programs were not finished at publication date. For these cases, we will provide updates through Oxford University Press.

4   Platform of main party from 'programmatic coalition'

Some electoral coalitions did not issue joint programs. In these cases, the program of the main coalition party is used to measure positions of the electoral coalition as a whole.

Data Entries per101–per706   Per centages of fifty-six categories grouped into seven major policy areas. Because of the different length of documents, the number of (quasi-) sentences in each category is standardized taking the total number of (quasi-) sentences in the respective documents as a base. In the data set each of these categories is a variable that represents the per centage.

Domain 1: External Relations

per101   *Foreign Special Relationships: Positive*

Favourable mentions of particular countries with which the manifesto country has a special relationship. For example, in the British case: former colonies; in the German case: East Germany; in the Swedish case: the rest of Scandinavia; the need for co-operation with and/or aid to such countries.

per102   *Foreign Special Relationships: Negative*

Negative mentions of particular countries with which the manifesto country has a special relationship; otherwise as 101, but negative.

per103   *Anti-Imperialism*

Negative references to exerting strong influence (political, military or commercial) over other states; negative references to controlling other countries as if they were part of an empire; favourable mentions of decolonization; favourable references to greater self-government and independence for colonies; negative references to the imperial behaviour of the manifesto and/or other countries.

per104   *Military: Positive*

Need to maintain or increase military expenditure; modernising armed forces and improvement in military strength; rearmament and self-defence; need to keep military treaty obligations; need to secure adequate manpower in the military.

per105   *Military: Negative*

Favourable mentions of decreasing military expenditures; disarmament; "evils of war"; promises to reduce conscription, otherwise as 104, but negative.

per106   *Peace*

Peace as a general goal; declarations of belief in peace and peaceful means of solving crises; desirability of countries joining in negotiations with hostile countries.

per107   *Internationalism: Positive*

Need for international co-operation; co-operation with specific countries other than those coded in 101; need for aid to developing countries; need for world planning of resources; need for international courts; support for any international goal or world state; support for

UN.

per108   ***European Community: Positive***

Favourable mentions of European Community/European Union in general; desirability of expanding the European Community/European Union and/or of increasing its competence; desirability of the manifesto country joining or remaining a member.

per109   ***Internationalism: Negative***

Favourable mentions of national independence and sovereignty as opposed to internationalism; otherwise as 107, but negative.

per110   ***European Community: Negative***

Hostile mentions of the European Community/European Union; opposition to specific European policies which are preferred by European authorities; otherwise as 108, but negative.

Domain 2: Freedom and Democracy

per201   ***Freedom and Human Rights***

Favourable mentions of importance of personal freedom and civil rights; freedom from bureaucratic control; freedom of speech; freedom from coercion in the political and economic spheres; individualism in the manifesto country and in other countries.

per202   ***Democracy***

Favourable mentions of democracy as a method or goal in national and other organisations; involvement of all citizens in decision-making, as well as generalised support for the manifesto country's democracy.

per203   ***Constitutionalism: Positive***

Support for specific aspects of the constitution; use of constitutionalism as an argument for policy as well as general approval of the constitutional way of doing things.

per204   ***Constitutionalism: Negative***

Opposition to the constitution in general or to specific aspects; otherwise as 203, but negative.

Domain 3: Political System

per301   ***Decentralisation***

Support for federalism or devolution; more regional autonomy for policy or economy; support for keeping up local and regional customs and symbols; favourable mentions of special consideration for local areas; deference to local expertise.

per302   ***Centralisation***

Opposition to political decision-making at lower political levels; support for more centralisation in political and administrative procedures; otherwise as 301, but negative.

per303   ***Governmental and Administrative Efficiency***

Need for efficiency and economy in government and administration; cutting down civil service; improving governmental procedures; general appeal to make the process of government and administration cheaper and more effective.

per304   ***Political Corruption***

Need to eliminate corruption and associated abuse in political and public life.

per305   ***Political Authority***

Favourable mentions of strong government, including government stability; manifesto party's competence to govern and/or other parties' lack of such competence.

Domain 4: Economy

per401   ***Free Enterprise***

Favourable mentions of free enterprise capitalism; superiority of individual enterprise over state and control systems; favourable mentions of private property rights, personal enterprise and initiative; need for unhampered individual enterprises.

per402   ***Incentives***

Need for wage and tax policies to induce enterprise; encouragement to start enterprises; need for financial and other incentives such as subsidies.

per403   ***Market Regulation***

Need for regulations designed to make private enterprises work better; actions against monopolies and trusts, and in defence of consumer and small business; encouraging economic competition; social market economy.

per404   ***Economic Planning***

Favourable mentions of long-standing economic planning of a consultative or indicative nature, need for government to create such a plan.

per405   ***Corporatism***

Favourable mentions of the need for the collaboration of employers and trade union organisations in overall economic planning and direction through the medium of tripartite bodies of government, employers, and trade unions. This category was not used for Austria up to 1979, for New Zealand up to 1981, nor for Sweden up to 1988.

per406   ***Protectionism: Positive***

Favourable mentions of extension or maintenance of tariffs to protect internal markets; other domestic economic protectionism such as quota restrictions.

per407   ***Protectionism: Negative***

Support for the concept of free trade; otherwise as 406, but negative.

per408   ***Economic Goals***

Statements of intent to pursue any economic goals not covered by other categories in domain 4. This category is created to catch an overall interest of parties in economics and, therefore, covers a variety of economic goals.

per409   ***Keynesian Demand Management***

Demand-oriented economic policy; economic policy devoted to the reduction of depressions and/or to increase private demand through increasing public demand and/or through increasing social expenditures.

per410   ***Productivity***

Need to encourage or facilitate greater production; need to take measures to aid this; appeal for greater production and importance of productivity to the economy; increasing foreign trade; the paradigm of growth.

per411   ***Technology and Infrastructure***

Importance of modernisation of industry and methods of transport and communication; importance of science and technological developments in industry; need for training and research. This does not imply education in general (see category 506).

per412   ***Controlled Economy***

General need for direct government control of economy; control over prices, wages, rents, etc; state intervention into the economic system.

per413   ***Nationalisation***

Favourable mentions of government ownership, partial or complete, including government ownership of land.

per414   ***Economic Orthodoxy***

Need for traditional economic orthodoxy, e.g. reduction of budget deficits, retrenchment in crisis, thrift and savings; support for traditional economic institutions such as stock market and banking system; support for strong currency.

per415   ***Marxist Analysis***

Positive references (typically but not solely by communist parties) to the specific use of Marxist-Leninist terminology and analysis of situations which are otherwise uncodable. This category was not used for Austria 1945–79, for Australia, Japan and the United States up to 1980; for Belgium, Ireland, The Netherlands and New Zealand up to 1981; for Italy and Britain up to 1983; for Denmark, Luxembourg and

Israel up to 1984; for Canada, France and Sweden up to 1988.

per416   *Anti-Growth Economy*

Favourable mentions of anti-growth politics and steady state economy; ecologism; "Green politics"; sustainable development. This category was not used for Austria 1945–79, for Australia, Japan and the United States up to 1980; for Belgium, Ireland, The Netherlands and New Zealand up to 1981; for Italy and Britain up to 1983; for Denmark, Luxembourg and Israel up to 1984; for Canada, France and Sweden up to 1988; nor for Norway up to 1989. Test codings, however, have shown that parties before the beginning of the 1990s hardly ever advocated anti-growth policies.

Domain 5: Welfare and Quality of Life

per501   *Environmental Protection*

Preservation of countryside, forests, etc.; general preservation of natural resources against selfish interests; proper use of national parks; soil banks, etc; environmental improvement.

per502   *Culture*

Need to provide cultural and leisure facilities including arts and sport; need to spend money on museums, art galleries etc.; need to encourage worthwhile leisure activities and cultural mass media.

per503   *Social Justice*

Concept of equality; need for fair treatment of all people; special protection for underprivileged; need for fair distribution of resources; removal of class barriers; end of discrimination such as racial or sexual discrimination, etc.

per504   *Welfare State Expansion*

Favourable mentions of need to introduce, maintain or expand any social service or social security scheme; support for social services such as health service or social housing. This category excludes education.

per505   *Welfare State Limitation*

Limiting expenditure on social services or social security; otherwise as 504, but negative.

per506   *Education Expansion*

Need to expand and/or improve educational provision at all levels. This excludes technical training which is coded under 411.

per507   *Education Limitation*

Limiting expenditure on education; otherwise as 506, but negative.

Domain 6: Fabric of Society

per601   *National Way of Life: Positive*

Appeals to patriotism and/or nationalism; suspension of some freedoms in order to protect the state against subversion; support for established national ideas.

per602   *National Way of Life: Negative*

Against patriotism and/or nationalism; opposition to the existing national state; otherwise as 601, but negative.

per603   *Traditional Morality: Positive*

Favourable mentions of traditional moral values; prohibition, censorship and suppression of immorality and unseemly behaviour; maintenance and stability of family; religion.

per604   *Traditional Morality: Negative*

Opposition to traditional moral values; support for divorce, abortion etc.; otherwise as 603, but negative.

per605   *Law and Order*

Enforcement of all laws; actions against crime; support and resources for police; tougher attitudes in courts.

per606   *Social Harmony*

Appeal for national effort and solidarity; need for society to see itself as united; appeal for public spiritedness; decrying anti-social attitudes in times of crisis; support for the public interest.

per607   *Multiculturalism: Positive*

Cultural diversity, communalism, cultural plurality and pillarization; preservation of autonomy of religious, linguistic heritages within the country including special educational provisions.

per608   *Multiculturalism: Negative*

Enforcement or encouragement of cultural integration; otherwise as 607, but negative.

Domain 7: Social Groups

per701   *Labour Groups: Positive*

Favourable references to labour groups, working class, unemployed; support for trade unions; good treatment of manual and other employees.

per702   *Labour Groups: Negative*

Abuse of power of trade unions; otherwise as 701, but negative.

per703   *Agriculture and Farmers*

Support for agriculture and farmers; any policy aimed specifically at benefiting these.

per704   *Middle Class and Professional Groups*

Favourable references to middle class, professional groups, such as physicians or lawyers; old and new middle class.

per705   **Underprivileged Minority Groups**

Favourable references to underprivileged minorities who are defined neither in economic nor in demographic terms, e.g. the handicapped, disabled, homosexuals, immigrants, refugees etc.

per706   **Non-economic Demographic Groups**

Favourable mentions of, or need for, assistance to women, old people, young people, linguistic groups, etc; special interest demographicgroups of all kinds.

Peruncod   Per centage of uncoded (quasi-) sentences
            Missing information:
            11 Sweden 1948–1982= 99,99
            12 Norway 1945–1989= 99,99

Total   Total number of quasi-sentences
            Missing information: 12 Norway in 1989 = 9999

            Programmatic dimensions used in this volume:

Rile   Left-Right position of party as given in Michael Laver and Ian Budge (eds.) 1992, Party Policy and Government Coalitions, London: Macmillan.
            (per104+per201+per203+per305+per401+per402+per407+per414+ per505+per601+per603+per605+per606)–(per103+per105+per106+ per107+per403+per404+per406+per412+per413+per504+per506+ per701+per202).

Planeco   Planned Economy: per403+per404+per412.

Markeco   Market Economy: per401+per414.

Welfare   Welfare: per503+per504.

Intpeace   International Peace: per102+per105+per106.

Appendix IV

Missing Party Documents

The following list of missing election programs relates to all parties represented in the 25 parliaments 1945–98 (except parties subsumed under 'other parties' in election statistics) for which no programmatic data are available. It shows that our Manifesto Data Set includes all parties that are judged to be relevant in national contexts because, as a rule, missing parties are short-lived and occupy very few seats, only. If you have any platform from the following list of missing cases (or for missing Government Declaration estimates given in Appendix VI) we would be very glad if you could send a copy to one of the authors.

Countries	Parties	Election Years	Number of Seats
Australia	Lang Labor Party	46	1
	Country-Liberal Party	96	1
Austria	Communist Party	45,49,53,56	4,5,4,3
Belgium	Communist Party	46,49,50,54,58,61,65, 68,71,74,77,78,81	23,12,7,4,2,5,6,5,5, 4,2,4,2
	Democratic Union	46	1
	Dissident Catholic Lists	54,61	1,1
	Walloon Front	65	1
	Walloon Workers' Party	65	1
	Democratic Union for the Respect of Labour	78,81,85	1,3,1
	Banana	91	3
	National Front	91,95	1,2
Canada	Communist Party	45	1
	Canadian Popular Block	45	2
	Rally for Québec	65,68	9,14
Denmark	Schleswig Party	53,57,60,73,75,77	1,1,1,1,1,1
	Danish People's Party	98	13
Finland	Liberal League	62	1
	Constitutional Party of Finland	75,83	1,1
	Union for Democracy	75	1
	Ecological Party	95	1
France	*Independent Republicans	62,67,68,73	18,41,64,54
	Unified Socialist Party	62,67,73	2,3,2
	Left Radical Movement	73,78,81,86,88,93	11,10,14,13,9,6
Germany	-		
Greece	Pan-Agrarian Democratic Front	74,77	1,1
	Communist Party-Interior	74,77,85	2,1,1
	New Liberal Party	77	2
	Independent Muslim List	89–6,89–11,90	1,1,2
	Democratic Renewal	89–6,90	1,1
	Ecological Alternatives	89–11,90	1,1
	Left Coalition	90	4

Iceland	Association for Equality and Justice	87	1
Ireland	National Labour	48	5
	Ourselves	57	4
	Communists	57	1
	National Progressive Democrats	61	2
	National H-Block Committee	81	2
	Socialist Labour Party	81	1
	DSP Democratic Socialist Party	87,89	1,1
	Ourselves III	97	1
	Socialist Party	97	1
Israel	Progressive Party	49,51,55,59	5,4,5,6
	Minority Lists	49,51,55,59,61,65,69, 73,77	2,5,5,4,5,4,4,3,1
	Union of Israel Workers	49,51,55,59,61,65,69, 73,77,88	3,2,2,2,2,2,2,2,1,1
	Spiritual Centre	49,51	4,2
	Workers' Mizrachi Party	49,51	6,8
	Sephardi Party	49,51	4,2
	Yemenite Association	49,51	1,1
	Womens' International Zionists	49	1
	Fighters for Freedom	49	1
	This World/New Force	65,69	1,2
	Peace and Development	77	1
	Movement for State Renewal	81	2
	Thus (Kach)	84	1
	Centre Party	88	2
Italy	Sardinian Action Party	46,48,83,87	2,1,1,2
	Action Party	46	7
	Common Man Front	46	30
	Monarchist Party	46,48,53,58,63,68	16,14,40,11,8,6
	Union of Federalist Movements	46	4
	South Tyrol People's Party	48,53,58,63,68,72,76, 79,83,87,92,94	3,3,3,3,3,3,3,4,3,3, 3,3
	Community	58	1
	Popular Monarchist Party	58	14
	Aosta Valley List	58,63,79,83,87,92,94	1,1,1,1,1,1,1
	Socialist P. of Proletarian Unity	68	23
	Continuous Struggle	76	1
	Workers' Vanguard	76	2
	Trieste List	79	1
	Venetian League	83,92	1,1
	Lombard League	87	1
	Pensioners	92	1
	Southern Action League	94	1
Japan	United Democratic Socialists	93	4
	DRP Democratic Reform Party	96	1
Luxembourg	Independents of the East	45	1
	National Solidarity Party	64	2
	Social Democratic Party	74,79	5,2
	Forcibly Enlisted	79	1
	Independent Socialists	79	1
Netherlands	Communist Party	46,48,52,56,59,63,67, 71,72,77,81,82	10,8,6,7,3,4,5,6,7,2 ,3,3
	Political Reformed Party	46,48,52,56,59,63,67, 71,72,77,81,82,86,89, 94,98	2,2,2,3,3,3,3,3,3,3, 3,3,3,3,2,3
	Catholic National Party	48,52	1,2

	Pacifist Socialist Party	59,63,67,71,72,77,81, 82,86	2,4,4,2,2,1,3,3,1
	Reformed Political Union	63,67,71,72,77,81,82, 86,89,94,98	1,1,2,2,1,1,1,1,2,2, 2
	People's Party of the Right	63,67,71,72,77	3,7,1,3,1
	Middle Class Party	71	2
	Roman Catholic Party	72	1
	Reformed Political Federation	81,82,86,89,94,98	2,2,1,1,3,3
	Centre Party	82	1
	Evangelical People's Party	82	1
	Centre Democrats	89,94	1,3
	AOV Elderly People	94	6
	Socialist Party	94,98	2,5
	Union 55+	94	1
New Zealand	NLP New Labour Party	90	1
	Act New Zealand	96	8
	United New Zealand	96	1
Norway	Future for Finmark	89	1
	Red Electoral Alliance	93	1
	Coastal Party	97	1
Portugal	Reformists	79	5
Spain	Popular Socialist Party	77	5
	Catalan Centre Party	77	1
	Democratic Union of Catalonia	77	1
	Convergence of Catalonia	77	11
	National Union	79	1
	United People	79,82,86,89,93,96	3,2,5,4,2,2
	Canary People's Union	79	1
	Navarre People's Union	79	1
	Valencian Union	86,89,93	1,2,1
	Galician Coalition	86	1
	Canarian Coalition	86,89,93,96	1,1,4,4
	BNG Galician Nationalist Party	96	2
Sweden	Citizens' Coalition	64,68	3,4
	Middle Class Party	64,68	2,3
Switzerland	Democrats	47,51,55,59,63,67	5,4,4,4,4,3
	Liberal Party of Switzerland	47,51,55,59,63,67,71, 75,79,83,87,91,95	7,5,5,5,6,6,6,6,8,8, 9,10,7
	Swiss Labour Party	47,51,55,59,63,67,71, 75,79,83,87,91,95	7,5,4,3,4,5,5,4,3,1, 1,2,3
	Free Market Party	47	1
	Protestant People's Party	47,51,55,59,63,67	1,1,1,2,2,3
	Republican Movement	71,75,79	7,3,1
	Swiss Democrats	67	1
	Vigilance Party	75,79,83 ·	1,1,1
	United Socialist Party	75,79,83,87,91	1,1,1,1,1
	Progressive Organisations	79,83,87	3,3,3
	Free List	83	1
	Feminist Green Alternative	87,91,95	1,1,2
	League of the Tessins	91,95	2,1
	Federal Democratic Union	91,95	1,1
	Christian Social Party	91,95	1,1
Turkey	Peasant's Party	54	5
	Republican Nationalist Party	57	4
	Freedom Party	57	4
	New Turkey Party	61,65,69	65,19,6

	Turkish Labour Party	65,69	14,2
	Republican Reliance Party	69,73,77	15,13,3
	Turkish Union Party	69,73	8,1
	Democratic Party	73,77	45,1
United	ILP Independent Labour Party	45	3
Kingdom			
	United Ireland	45,50,51,55,66,70, 74–6,79,83,87	2,2,3,2,1,3,1,1,1,1
	Communist Party	45	2
	National Liberal Party	45	11
	SNP Scottish Nationalist Party	70,74–2,74–10,79,83, 87,92,97	1,7,11,2,2,3,3,6
	Party of Wales	74–2,74–10,79,83,87, 92,97	2,3,2,2,3,4,4
	Ulster Unionists and Loyalists	74–2,74–10,79,83,87, 97	1,1,1,1,3,10
	Alliance P. of Northern Ireland	74–2,74–10,79,83,87	11,10,10,15,13
	Social Democratic and Labour P.	92,97	4,3
	Ulster Unionist Party	92	9
	Democratic Unionist Party	92,97	3,2
	Ulster Popular Unionist Party	92	1
	Sinn Fein	97	2
	UKUP Unionist Party	97	1
USA	-		

* Contest elections as independent candidates without an election program

Appendix V

Mean Percentage for Parties on Four Policy Stands

Mean values for four scales in 18 countries for time periods 1945–1998 and 1972–1998*

Country	Party	Time period	Planned economy	Market economy	Welfare	International peace
AUSTRALIA	ALP	1946–1998	4.59	1.67	10.54	1.92
	ALP	1972–1998	3.22	1.99	12.39	1.06
	LPA	1946–1998	0.90	16.27	5.23	0.58
	LPA	1972–1998	0.74	16.31	5.52	0.74
	DLP	1955–1977	2.92	5.87	5.34	0.75
	NPA	1946–1998	0.73	17.38	2.35	0.24
	NPA	1972–1998	1.28	15.69	3.10	0.19
AUSTRIA	Greens	1986–1995	0.66	1.18	10.33	1.55
	SPO	1949–1995	5.18	2.52	14.85	3.36
	SPO	1972–1995	2.35	2.32	16.18	1.70
	FPO	1949–1995	3.13	7.53	9.18	1.75
	FPO	1972–1995	1.25	8.95	9.35	0.67
	OVP	1949–1995	1.29	13.02	9.17	0.87
	OVP	1972–1995	1.66	15.10	8.21	0.73
	LF	1994–1995	1.80	21.57	13.69	0.00

Country	Party	Time period	Planned economy	Market economy	Welfare	International peace
BELGIUM	PSB/BSP	1946–1977	6.60	0.65	14.66	3.28
	SP (Flemish)	1978–1995	5.70	1.77	15.59	2.60
	PS (Walloon)	1978–1995	3.52	2.35	10.62	2.09
	PLP	1946–1968	0.89	16.52	4.92	1.77
	PVV (Flemish)	1968–1991	1.26	11.87	5.21	1.11
	PRL (Walloon)	1971–1995	3.80	7.68	4.36	0.11
	PSC/CVP	1946–1965	3.30	4.15	11.47	0.78
	CVP (Flemish)	1968–1995	2.34	2.86	6.92	1.07
	PSC (Walloon)	1968–1995	2.56	2.97	6.98	1.00
	RW	1971–1981	6.12	1.38	6.04	0.56
	FDF	1968–1991	2.33	1.42	5.11	0.58
	FDF	1974–1991	2.97	1.90	5.95	0.46
	VU	1961–1995	2.65	2.52	5.50	1.23
	VU	1974–1995	1.92	3.25	6.56	1.33
	VB	1991–1995	1.35	2.81	8.51	0.43
CANADA	NDP	1945–1997	10.35	0.66	19.73	3.17
	NDP	1972–1997	9.07	0.33	19.73	3.17
	LP	1945–1997	3.14	4.69	12.60	1.53
	LP	1972–1997	3.29	4.05	12.48	1.62
	PCP	1945–1997	2.09	5.87	8.77	1.55
	PCP	1972–1997	2.50	8.58	8.17	1.40
	SOCRED	1945–1968	4.09	8.59	12.19	1.72

Country	Party	Time period	Planned economy	Market economy	Welfare	International peace
FRANCE 5TH REPUBLIC	Greens	1993–1997	3.08	0.77	18.38	3.62
	PCF	1958–1997	9.15	0.11	14.70	6.63
	PCF	1973–1997	10.22	0.06	15.88	4.48
	PS	1958–1997	7.33	0.71	13.54	6.90
	PS	1973–1997	7.20	0.80	14.19	3.73
	MRP/CENTRE	1958–1968	1.30	3.55	9.23	1.05
	GAULLIST/RPR	1958–1997	3.84	6.19	10.15	1.78
	GAULLIST/RPR	1973–1997	2.54	8.84	11.62	0.88
	UDF	1993–1997	0.00	10.91	8.38	0.82
	FN	1986 & 1997	0.67	5.96	0.37	0.15
GERMANY	Greens	1983–1998	1.96	0.71	10.49	10.12
	PDS	1990–1998	1.63	0.21	16.69	5.06
	SPD	1949–1998	4.41	2.47	15.21	4.06
	SPD	1972–1998	2.78	1.77	15.18	4.83
	FDP	1949–1998	3.15	7.65	6.41	4.23
	FDP	1972–1998	3.14	6.71	6.35	3.75
	CDU/CSU	1949–1998	4.08	7.83	10.07	3.09
	CDU/CSU	1972–1998	2.78	6.84	9.60	2.69
GREAT BRITAIN	Conservative	1945–1997	3.42	6.62	7.42	1.99
	Conservative	1974–1997	2.44	8.22	8.31	0.94
	Labour	1945–1997	8.06	1.35	12.69	4.31

Country	Party	Time period	Planned economy	Market economy	Welfare	International peace
GREAT BRITAIN (cont)	Labour	1974–1997	7.70	1.52	12.57	3.89
	Liberal Democrat	1945–1997	5.42	3.85	8.90	3.39
	Liberal Democrat	1974–1997	6.79	2.23	11.82	1.66
GREECE	KKE	1974–1996	1.84	0.10	6.94	1.87
	PASOK	1974–1996	3.74	0.82	14.18	1.63
	EDIK	1974–1977	1.51	0.52	9.97	3.80
	New Democracy	1974–1996	1.66	5.96	3.73	2.21
IRELAND	Greens	1992–1997	2.01	0.32	12.08	3.19
	Workers' Party	1982–1989	0.19	0.00	27.50	1.18
	Democratic Left	1992–1997	5.14	1.18	32.71	1.92
	Irish Labour Party	1948–1997	9.07	1.89	22.08	1.19
	Irish Labour Party	1973–1997	7.32	2.87	26.30	1.54
	Fine Gael	1948–1997	5.97	10.33	12.06	2.29
	Fine Gael	1973–1997	6.96	7.77	13.45	1.76
	Fianna Fail	1949–1997	3.02	2.75	8.84	2.86
	Fianna Fail	1973–1997	3.90	1.64	9.38	4.03
	Progressive Democrat	1987–1987	5.24	8.86	10.99	0.49
ISRAEL	MAKI	1949–1969	0.89	0.00	7.86	16.58
	RAKAH	1965–1973	0.00	0.00	0.00	43.25
	MAPAM	1949–1965	5.62	0.24	7.83	12.62
	SHELLI	1977–1981	2.83	0.00	7.06	0.13

Country	Party	Time period	Planned economy	Market economy	Welfare	International peace
GREAT BRITAIN (cont)	Labour	1974–1997	7.70	1.52	12.57	3.89
	Liberal Democrat	1945–1997	5.42	3.85	8.90	3.39
	Liberal Democrat	1974–1997	6.79	2.23	11.82	1.66
GREECE	KKE	1974–1996	1.84	0.10	6.94	1.87
	PASOK	1974–1996	3.74	0.82	14.18	1.63
	EDIK	1974–1977	1.51	0.52	9.97	3.80
	New Democracy	1974–1996	1.66	5.96	3.73	2.21
IRELAND	Greens	1992–1997	2.01	0.32	12.08	3.19
	Workers' Party	1982–1989	0.19	0.00	27.50	1.18
	Democratic Left	1992–1997	5.14	1.18	32.71	1.92
	Irish Labour Party	1948–1997	9.07	1.89	22.08	1.19
	Irish Labour Party	1973–1997	7.32	2.87	26.30	1.54
	Fine Gael	1948–1997	5.97	10.33	12.06	2.29
	Fine Gael	1973–1997	6.96	7.77	13.45	1.76
	Fianna Fail	1949–1997	3.02	2.75	8.84	2.86
	Fianna Fail	1973–1997	3.90	1.64	9.38	4.03
	Progressive Democrat	1987–1987	5.24	8.86	10.99	0.49
ISRAEL	MAKI	1949–1969	0.89	0.00	7.86	16.58
	RAKAH	1965–1973	0.00	0.00	0.00	43.25
	MAPAM	1949–1965	5.62	0.24	7.83	12.62
	SHELLI	1977–1981	2.83	0.00	7.06	0.13

Country	Party	Time period	Planned economy	Market economy	Welfare	International peace
	HADASH/BALAD	1977–1996	2.38	0.60	10.01	25.81
	RATZ	1973–1988	3.08	0.59	8.88	6.43
	MERETZ	1992–1996	0.00	1.56	12.65	12.70
	Labour	1949–1996	3.30	1.87	8.99	7.40
	Labour	1973–1996	3.60	2.60	8.79	8.97
	Achdut Ha'Avodah	1959–1961	2.50	0.00	7.70	5.00
	Progressive	1965–1981	1.31	3.65	13.85	11.64
	Progressive	1973–1981	1.13	2.61	13.89	12.62
	General Zionist	1959–1969	1.92	5.87	3.60	3.04
	DASH/Shinui	1977–1984	0.65	3.02	6.29	5.29
	TAMI	1981–1984	2.08	0.00	20.47	0.00
	NRP	1955–1996	1.92	1.70	2.60	2.33
	NRP	1973–1996	2.87	2.13	2.97	3.31
	SHAS	1984–1996	0.00	1.59	0.00	16.80
	Agudat Israel/UTJ	1959–1996	1.51	2.24	3.65	5.16
	Agudat Israel/UTJ	1973–1996	2.15	3.2	3.53	6.14
	Likud	1949–1996	1.88	5.29	6.50	6.58
	Likud	1973–1996	0.40	5.56	8.37	7.93
	Tehiya	1981–1992	0.86	5.67	4.51	4.55
	Tsomet	1988–1992	0.00	12.42	14.55	6.67
	Moledet	1988–1996	0.00	3.26	1.04	0.00
ITALY	Greens	1987–1996	6.72	0.00	4.04	2.28
	Rifond. Comunista	1992–1996	8.71	1.50	11.42	3.46

Country	Party	Time period	Planned economy	Market economy	Welfare	International peace
ITALY (cont)	PCI/PDS	1945–1996	4.27	2.74	7.29	4.26
	PCI/PDS	1972–1996	4.47	4.72	8.24	1.33
	PSI	1946–1992	3.26	1.52	7.62	3.34
	PSI	1972–1992	3.18	2.16	8.10	2.51
	PSDI	1948–1996	3.59	3.16	7.65	1.44
	PSDI	1972–1996	3.10	3.99	7.27	0.37
	PRI	1946–1992	2.61	4.59	4.05	0.98
	PRI	1972–1992	1.51	5.78	3.85	0.57
	PLI	1946–1992	2.55	9.99	5.60	0.96
	PLI	1972–1992	2.11	6.86	7.53	0.51
	Christian Democrat	1946–1996	2.48	3.50	5.66	1.16
	Christian Democrat	1972–1996	3.04	4.50	4.20	0.31
	Democratic Alliance	1994–1996	3.75	5.11	7.59	0.00
	Forza Italia	1994–1996	0.20	9.70	1.67	0.00
	AN/MSI	1948–1996	2.00	2.43	3.31	0.25
	AN/MSI	1972–1996	2.03	2.34	3.87	0.03
	Lega Nord	1994–1996	4.98	3.07	2.62	1.16
JAPAN	JCP	1960–1993	6.67	3.86	12.63	19.79
	JCP	1972–1993	6.04	5.58	13.00	17.92
	JSP	1960–1993	6.04	1.87	15.19	16.52
	JSP	1972–1993	5.24	2.81	16.04	16.39
	DSP	1960–1993	6.27	1.95	9.13	6.18
	DSP	1972–1993	5.09	2.93	12.00	4.01

Country	Party	Time period	Planned economy	Market economy	Welfare	International peace
	LDP	1960–1993	5.69	5.01	12.17	3.76
	LDP	1972–1993	4.92	5.46	12.92	2.33
	CGP	1967–1993	7.36	2.43	15.68	13.88
	CGP	1972–1993	5.88	2.75	15.38	13.38
	SDF	1986–1990	1.69	1.69	5.99	11.10
	NLC	1983–1986	0.00	8.45	7.60	11.41
	NP	1993–1996	1.16	1.19	8.14	2.38
NETHERLANDS	Greens	1988–1998	2.61	0.22	14.02	3.55
	PvdA	1946–1998	5.46	1.89	15.99	4.54
	PvdA	1972–1998	5.54	2.01	16.07	4.67
	D'66	1967–1998	4.66	2.47	12.57	3.15
	D'66	1972–1998	4.99	2.50	11.99	3.10
	VVD	1946–1998	2.38	13.87	8.86	0.66
	VVD	1972–1998	1.90	11.47	7.01	0.81
	CDA	1977–1998	3.74	3.40	9.66	2.19
	KVP	1946–1972	2.72	7.99	15.69	1.46
	ARP	1946–1972	4.00	7.04	12.11	1.26
	CHU	1946–1972	2.29	5.18	11.64	1.81
NEW ZEALAND	Labour	1946–1996	8.38	2.19	15.51	1.29
	Labour	1972–1996	5.76	2.22	15.99	1.20
	NP	1946–1996	2.57	6.09	9.91	0.40
	NP	1972–1996	2.19	5.25	11.44	0.33

Country	Party	Time period	Planned economy	Market economy	Welfare	International peace
NEW ZEALAND (cont)	SOCRED	1954–1990	15.57	10.23	11.98	1.15
	SOCRED	1972–1990	6.88	3.73	10.29	1.39
NORWAY	Socialist Left	1945–1993	6.22	0.75	15.36	6.91
	Socialist Left	1973–1993	5.53	0.17	20.41	3.78
	Social Democrat	1945–1993	8.08	0.51	14.25	1.85
	Social Democrat	1973–1993	5.91	0.79	15.09	2.40
	Liberal	1945–1993	4.25	2.25	13.96	1.47
	Liberal	1973–1993	4.60	1.08	14.49	1.81
	Christian Peoples'	1945–1993	2.11	2.39	12.74	1.40
	Christian Peoples'	1973–1993	3.30	1.27	13.22	1.76
	Hoyre	1945–1993	3.15	12.11	9.52	0.33
	Hoyre	1973–1993	4.12	9.27	10.37	0.43
	Centre Party	1945–1993	2.15	3.90	10.60	0.75
	Centre Party	1973–1993	3.01	1.57	11.85	1.02
SPAIN	PCE	1977–1993	4.84	0.13	11.10	2.30
	PSOE	1977–1993	3.20	1.27	15.12	1.09
	UCD	1977–1982	3.82	4.60	14.55	1.35
	CDS	1982–1993	8.05	2.33	13.36	1.16
	AP/PP	1979–1993	2.91	8.19	12.56	0.15
	CiU	1982–1993	3.19	6.54	9.59	0.72
	PNV	1977–1993	1.67	3.02	11.16	0.85
	Basque Solidarity	1989–1993	2.28	2.98	8.60	7.08

Country	Party	Time period	Planned economy	Market economy	Welfare	International peace
	Catalan Republican	1977–1993	3.89	1.82	10.07	2.77
SWEDEN	Greens	1988–1998	5.22	4.11	13.80	3.45
	VK	1948–1998	11.51	1.27	18.49	8.31
	VK	1973–1998	11.58	0.76	19.83	4.78
	SSA	1948–1998	3.35	5.81	25.01	3.13
	SSA	1973–1998	1.36	8.93	21.28	3.32
	FL	1948–1998	2.05	10.12	18.42	2.23
	FL	1973–1998	1.64	11.21	15.39	1.54
	MS	1948–1998	0.18	27.50	6.86	0.98
	MS	1973–1998	0.21	21.26	7.97	1.46
	CP	1948–1998	2.69	8.01	16.60	1.59
	CP	1973–1998	2.64	6.35	16.70	1.52
USA	Democrat	1948–1996	4.03	1.59	8.58	5.61
	Democrat	1948–1997	2.61	1.60	9.73	6.60
	Republican	1948–1998	1.03	8.21	3.38	2.89
	Republican	1948–1999	1.11	7.64	3.20	2.89

Notes:
*The four policy indicators—Planned Economy, Market Economy, Welfare and International Peace—are included in the data set for party policy estimates and electoral data (Appendix V in the CD-ROM).Their composition is as follows.

Planned Economy	Market Economy	Welfare	International Peace
403 Regulation of Capitalism	401 Enterprise	503 Social Justice	102 Special Foreign Relations –ve
404 Economic Planning	414 Economic Orthodoxy	504 Social Services +ve	105 Military –ve
412 Controlled Economy			106 Peace

These indicators represent specific policy areas which give rise to particular concerns on the part of the public, parties and governments. They are also central components of Left-Right ideological discriminators.

The three general indicators concern the economy, welfare and peace issues. The economic element is divided into two separate components—planned economy and market economy, reflecting the two major trends in economic theory.

Internal consistency can also be assessed in terms of measuring the degree to which parties change position over the period concerned by comparing time points separated by ten year intervals, notably the four decades from 1950–90. The reliability of these measures is also assessed and results are noted below. For a thorough discussion of the technical procedures used see David Heise 1969, "Separating Reliability and Stability in Test-Retest Correlation", *American Sociological Review*, 33: 93–101, which also forms the basis of much of the analysis discussed in Chapter 6 of this volume.

Estimates of Stability and Reliability of Party Positions for Ten Year Intervals, 1950–1990

Indicator	Stability	Reliability
Left-Right	.88	.80
Planned economy	.55	.96
Market economy	.68	.73
Welfare	.90	.53
International peace	.51	.98

A comparison of mean values for the two time periods concerned provides us with a general measure of how far parties have shifted their position in terms of both emphasis and ideological direction. This may be seen pictorially by reference to Figure 2.1 in Chapter 2 for the Left-Right scale, and the general movement along the other four indicators can be noted by reference to the mean values provided.

It must be stated that the time periods 1945–98 and 1972–98 are for general guidance only as each country obviously holds elections at different times. Thus the overall time span normally includes all party positions for all elections included in the data set, so that in the case of Great Britain, for example, the overall time period is 1945 to 1997. The shorter, recent period starts with the first election after 1971. Thus for Great Britain the time span is 1974 to 1997.

There are inevitably a few cases which cannot fit into this overall pattern. In the case of France, only the Fifth Republic is included here, so that the general starting point is 1958. With regard to Belgium, the party system fragmented into linguistic wings at different points in time, generally between 1968 and 1974. Thus the particular point at which each party changed is taken as the break point. The same is true for some of the minor parties in Israel, and of course the second main religious party, SHAS, only entered the electoral arena in 1984 and is only included in the more recent period.

Spain, Portugal and Greece only emerged from varying periods of dictatorship in the 1970s, so that the first elections held under the newly constituted arrangements are taken as the starting point. Obviously this means that no comparison with earlier experience is possible.

Appendix VI

Description of Government Declaration Data

Units	Government declarations
Number of countries	11
Number of cases	174
Time period covered	1945 until middle/end of the 1980s except
	Belgium: 1945–1981
	Luxembourg: 1945–1979
	France: 1959–1983
	Italy: 1948–1982
	Germany: 1949–1998
	Ireland: 1981–1982
Number of variables	3 identification variables
	58 programmatic data variables
Data sources	Michael Laver and Ian Budge (eds.) 1992: Party Policy and Government Coalitions, Houndmills, Basingstoke, Hampshire: The MacMillan Press. Parts of the data prepared for this book were destroyed during transmission.

Identification Variables:

Country	Two digit code:
	11 Sweden
	12 Norway
	13 Denmark
	21 Belgium
	22 Netherlands
	23 Luxembourg
	31 France
	32 Italy
	41 Germany
	51 Great Britain
	53 Ireland
	72 Israel
govID	Identification number of government as given in Jaap Woldendorp, Hans Keman and Ian Budge 2000, Party Government in 48 Democracies (1945–1998), Kluwer Academic Publishers: Dordrecht, Boston and London.
inauddat	Day, month and year of inauguration (DD.MM.YYYY) of government as given Jaap Woldendorp, Hans Keman and Ian Budge 2000, Party Government in 48 Democracies (1945–1998), Kluwer Academic Publishers: Dordrecht, Boston and London.

Programmatic data variables:	
Data Entries **per101–** **per706**	Per centages of fifty-six categories grouped into seven major policy areas.—as Appendix III

Cases included in the 'Government Declarations' data set. The following chart provides for identification of the government declarations included in the data set by identification number, date of inauguration and name of Prime Minister, according to the study compiled by Woldendorp, Keman and Budge (2000) and cited in full above. As stated in the original study for which this data was compiled (Laver and Budge (eds.) 1992—cited in full above) not every government formed in the countries covered was necessarily included. Sometimes governments did not publish declarations and simply pledged to continue the declared programme of their immediate predecessor. In addition, we have identified a number of minor inaccuracies in some of the cases and these are also omitted from the data set.

Country	ID No.	Government Start date	Prime Minister
SWEDEN			
	0	31.05.45	Hansson
	1	11.10.46	Erlander 1
	2	28.10.48	Erlander 2
	3	30.09.51	Erlander 3
	4	21.09.52	Erlander 4
	5	26.09.56	Erlander 5
	6	30.10.57	Erlander 6
	7	02.06.58	Erlander 7
	8	01.10.60	Erlander 8
	9	04.10.64	Erlander 9
	10	29.09.68	Erlander 10
	11	15.10.69	Palme 1
	12	29.09.70	Palme 2
	13	31.10.73	Palme 3
	14	04.10.76	Fälldin 1
	15	13.10.78	Ullsten
	16	12.10.79	Fälldin 2
	17	22.05.81	Fälldin 3
	18	08.10.82	Palme 4

19	04.10.86	Palme 5
20	01.03.86	Carlsson 1
21	04.10.88	Carlsson 2

NORWAY

1	01.11.45	Gerhardson 2
4	12.10.53	Torp 2
5	21.01.55	Gerhardson 4
7	11.09.61	Gerhardson 6
10	11.10.65	Borten 1
13	18.10.72	Korvald
14	16.10.73	Bratteli 2
15	12.01.76	Nordli 1
21	09.05.86	Brundtland

DENMARK

2	13.11.47	Hedtoft 1
4	27.10.50	Eriksen 1
6	30.09.53	Hedtoft 3
7	01.02.55	Hansen 1
8	28.05.57	Hansen 2
10	18.11.60	Kampmann 2
12	26.09.64	Krag 2
13	28.11.66	Krag 3
14	01.02.68	Baunsgaard
17	19.12.73	Hartling
18	13.02.75	Jørgensen 2
19	25.02.77	Jørgensen 3
20	30.08.78	Jørgensen 5
23	10.09.82	Schlüter 1
24	24.01.84	Schlüter 2

BELGIUM

3	11.03.46	Spaak 1
4	01.04.46	Van Acker 3
5	02.08.46	Huysmans
8	17.08.49	Eyskens 1
9	30.06.50	Duvieusart
10	18.08.50	Pholien
11	15.01.52	Van Houte
12	22.04.54	Van Acker 4
13	26.06.58	Eyskens 2
14	07.11.58	Eyskens 3
16	25.04.61	Lefevre

	17	28.07.65	Harmel
	18	20.03.66	Vanden Boeynants 1
	19	18.06.68	Eyskens 4
	20	21.01.72	Eyskens 5
	21	26.01.73	Leburton
	22	25.04.74	Tindemans 1
	23	12.06.74	Tindemans 2
	26	20.10.78	Vanden Boeynants 1
	27	03.04.79	Martens 1
	29	18.05.80	Martens 3
	30	22.10.80	Martens 4
	31	06.04.81	Mark Eyskens
NETHERLANDS			
	1	03.07.46	Beel 1
	3	15.03.51	Drees 2
	12	06.07.71	Biesheuval 1
	14	11.05.73	Del Uyl
	18	04.11.82	Lubbers 1
	19	14.07.86	Lubbers 2
	20	07.11.89	Lubbers 3
LUXEMBOURG			
	1	20.11.45	Nat. Unity (Dupong)
	2	01.03.47	Dupong 1
	3	14.07.48	Dupong 2
	4	03.07.51	Dupong 3
	6	29.06.54	Bech 2
	9	18.07.64	Werner 2
	10	04.01.67	Werner 3
	11	31.01.69	Werner 4
	13	15.07.79	Werner 5
FRANCE			
5th REPUBLIC	29	08.01.59	Debré
	30	15.04.62	Pompidou 1
	32	06.12.62	Pompidou 3
	33	09.01.66	Pompidou 4
	34	08.04.67	Pompidou 5
	36	12.07.68	Couve de Murville
	38	07.07.72	Messmer 1
	39	05.04.73	Messmer 2
	41	28.05.74	Chirac 1
	42	17.08.76	Barre 1

	43	30.03.77	Barre 2
	44	04.04.78	Barre 3
	46	23.06.81	Mauroy 2
	47	22.03.83	Mauroy 3
ITALY			
	5	23.05.48	De Gasperi 5
	6	27.01.50	De Gasperi 6
	7	26.07.51	De Gasperi 7
	8	17.07.53	De Gasperi 8
	9	17.08.53	Pella
	10	19.01.54	Fanfani
	11	11.02.54	Scelba
	12	06.07.55	Segni 1
	13	20.05.57	Zoli
	14	10.07.58	Fanfani 2
	15	16.02.59	Segni 2
	16	25.03.60	Tambroni
	17	26.07.60	Fanfani 3
	18	21.02.62	Fanfani 4
	19	21.06.63	Leone 1
	20	05.12.63	Moro 1
	21	22.07.64	Moro 2
	22	23.02.66	Moro 3
	23	25.06.68	Leone 2
	24	12.12.68	Rumor 1
	25	05.08.69	Rumor 2
	26	27.03.70	Rumor 3
	27	06.08.70	Colombo
	29	18.02.72	Andreotti 1
	30	26.06.72	Andreotti 2
	31	08.09.73	Rumor 4
	32	14.03.74	Rumor 5
	33	23.11.74	Moro 4
	34	13.02.76	Moro 5
	35	29.07.76	Andreotti 3
	36	13.03.78	Andreotti 4
	37	21.03.79	Andreotti 5
	38	05.08.79	Cossiga 1
	39	04.04.80	Cossiga 2
	40	19.10.80	Forlani 1
	41	28.06.81	Spadolini 1
	42	23.08.82	Spadolini 2

	43	11.12.82	Fanfani 5
GERMANY			
	1	15.09.49	Adenauer 1
	2	09.10.53	Adenauer 2a
	5	22.10.57	Adenauer 2d
	7	14.11.61	Adenauer 4a
	10	16.10.63	Erhard 1
	11	26.10.65	Erhard 2
	13	01.12.66	Kiesinger
	14	22.10.69	Brandt 1
	16	15.12.72	Brandt 3
	17	16.05.74	Schmidt 1
	18	15.12.76	Schmidt 2
	19	04.11.80	Schmidt 3
	21	04.10.82	Kohl 1
	22	30.03.83	Kohl 2
	23	11.03.87	Kohl 3
	25	17.01.91	Kohl 5
	26	17.11.94	Kohl 6
	27	27.09.98	Schröder
IRELAND			
	13	30.06.81	Fitzgerald 1
	15	14.12.82	Fitzgerald 2
ISRAEL			
	1	10.03.49	Ben Gurion 1
	2	30.10.50	Ben Gurion 2
	4	07.10.51	Ben Gurion 3
	5	23.12.52	Ben Gurion 4
	6	07.01.54	Sharrett
	7	02.11.55	Ben Gurion 5
	12	16.12.59	Ben Gurion 7
	14	02.11.61	Ben Gurion 8
	17	10.01.66	Eshkol 3
	19	17.03.69	Meir 1
	20	15.12.69	Meir 2
	23	03.06.74	Rabin 1
	25	21.12.76	Rabin 3
	26	19.06.77	Begin 1
	27	24.10.77	Begin 2
	28	05.08.81	Begin 3
	31	13.09.84	National Unity (Peres)

Bibliography of Manifesto-based Research

Adams, James and Merrill, Samuel (1998), 'Spatial Competition with Biased Voters', Department of Political Science, University of California at Santa Barbara.

Baron, David (1991), 'A Strategic Bargaining Theory of Government Formation in Parliamentary Systems', *American Political Science Review*, 85: 137–64.

Bartolini, S. and Mair, Peter (1990), *Identity, Competition and Electoral Availability: The Stabilisation of European Electorates 1885–1985*. Cambridge: Cambridge University Press.

Budge, Ian, Robertson, David and Hearl, Derek J. (eds.) (1987), *Ideology, Strategy and Party Change: Spatial Analyses of Post-War Election Programmes in 19 Democracies*. Cambridge: Cambridge University Press.

—— Crewe, Ivor, McKay, David and Newton, Kenneth (1998, 2000), *The New British Politics*. London: Pearson.

—— and Farlie, Dennis J. (1977), *Voting and Party Competition*. London & New York: Wiley.

—— (1994), 'A New Spatial Theory of Party Competition: Uncertainty, Ideology and Policy Equilibria Viewed Comparatively and Spatially', *British Journal of Political Sciences*, 24: 443–67.

—— and Hofferbert, Richard (1990), 'Mandates and Policy Outcomes: US Party Platforms and Federal Expenditure', *American Political Science Review*, 84: 111–31.

—— and Laver, Michael (1993), 'The Policy Basis of Government Coalitions: A Comparative Investigation', *British Journal of Political Sciences*, 23: 499–519.

—— *et al* (1997), *The Politics of the New Europe: Atlantic to Urals*. London: Longman.

—— and Laver, Michael (1986), 'Policy, Ideology and Party Distance: Analysis of Election Programmes in 19 Democracies', *Legislative Studies Quarterly*, 11: 607–15.

—— Tanenbaum, Eric and Bara, Judith (1999), *Monitoring Democratic Five-Year Plans: Multiple Coding of British Manifestos and US Platforms*, Swindon: ESRC Report R00022289.

Dalton, Russell J. and Wattenberg, Martin P. (eds.) (2000), *Parties without Partisans: Political Change in Advanced Industrial Democracies*. Oxford: Oxford University Press.

Evans, Geoffrey and Norris, Pippa (eds.) (1999), *Critical Elections: British Parties and Voters in Long-Term Perspective*. London: Sage.

Gabel, Mathew and Huber, John (2000), 'Putting Parties in Their Place', *American Journal of Political Sciences*, 44: 94–103.

Gallagher, Michael, Laver, Michael and Mair, Peter (1992), *Representative Government in Western Europe.* New York: McGraw Hill.

Gibbons, Matthew (2000), Election Programmes in New Zealand Politics, Ph.D. Thesis, University of Waikato, New Zealand.

Hofferbert, Richard and Budge, Ian (1992), 'The Party Mandate and the Westminster Model: Election Programmes and Government Spending in Britain 1948–1985', *British Journal of Political Sciences,* 22: 151–82.

—— and Klingemann, Hans-Dieter (1990), 'The Policy Impact of Party Programmes and Government Declarations in the Federal Republic of Germany', *European Journal of Political Research,* 18: 277–304.

Imbeau, Louis M and McKinley, Robert (1996), *Comparing Government Activity.* London: Macmillan.

Janda, Kenneth, Harmel, Robert and Goff, Patricia (1995), 'Changes in Party Identity: Evidence From Party Manifestos', *Party Politics,* 1: 171–96.

Keman, Hans (ed.) (1997), *The Politics of Problem-Solving in Post-War Democracies.* Basingstoke: Macmillan.

Kim, Hee Min and Fording, Richard C. (1988), 'Voter Ideology in Western Democracies 1946–1989', *European Journal of Political Research,* 33: 73–97.

King, Gary, Laver, Michael, Hofferbert, Richard, Budge, Ian, and McDonald, Michael (1993), 'Party Platforms, Mandates and Government Spending', *American Political Science Review,* 87: 744–58.

Klingemann, H.D. and Fuchs, Dieter (eds.) (1995), *Citizens and the State.* Oxford: Open University Press.

—— Hofferbert, Richard I., Budge, Ian *et al* (1994), *Parties, Policies and Democracy.* Boulder Co: Westview.

Krouwel, Andre (1998), *The Catch-All Party in Western Europe: A Study in Arrested Development.* Amsterdam: CT Press.

Kirchner, Emil (ed.) (1988), *Liberal Parties in Western Democracies.* Cambridge: Cambridge University Press.

Lane, Jan-Erik and Ersson, Svante (1991), *Politics and Society in Western Europe,* 2nd ed. London: Sage.

Laver, Michael and Budge, Ian (eds.) (1992), *Party Policy and Government Coalitions.* London: Macmillan.

—— (ed.) (2001), *Estimating the Policy Positions of Political Actors.* London: Sage.

—— and Garry, John (2001), 'Estimating Policy Positions from Party Manifestos', *American Journal of Political Sciences,* forthcoming.

Mair, Peter (1986), 'Locating Irish Political Parties on a Left-Right Dimension: An Empirical Enquiry', *Political Studies,* 44: 456–65.

—— (1987), *The Changing Irish Party System: Organization, Ideology and Electoral Competition.* London: Pinter.

McDonald, Michael, Budge, Ian and Hofferbert, Richard (1999), 'Party Mandate Theory and Time Series Analysis', *Electoral Studies,* 18: 587–96.

Pennings, Paul (1998), 'Party Responsiveness and Socio-Economic Problem-Solving in Western Democracies', *Party Politics,* 4: 393–404.

—— and Lane, J.E. (eds.) (1998), *Comparing Party System Change.* London: Routledge.

Pétry, François (1988), 'The Policy Impact of Canadian Party Programs', *Canadian Public Policy*, 14: 376–89.

—— (1995), 'The Party Agenda Model: Election Programmes and Government Spending in Canada', *Canadian Journal of Political Sciences*, 28: 51–84.

—— (1991), 'Fragile Mandate: Party Programmes and Public Expenditures in the French Fifth Republic', *European Journal of Political Research*, 20: 149–71.

Riker, William (ed.) (1993), *Agenda Formation*. Ann Arbor: University of Michigan Press.

Robertson, David (1976), *A Theory of Party Competition*. London and New York: Wiley.

Saglie, Jo (1998), 'A Struggle for the Agenda? Norwegian parties and the European Issues 1989–1995', *Party Politics*, 4: 262–84.

Strom, Kaare and Liepart, Jorn (1989), 'Ideology, Strategy and Party Competition in Post-War Norway', *European Journal of Political Research*, 17: 263–88.

Schofield, Norman (1993), 'Political Competition and Multiparty Coalition Governments', *European Journal of Political Research*, 23: 1–33.

Thome, Helmut (1999), 'Party Mandate Theory and Time-Series Analysis: A Methodological Comment', *Electoral Studies*, 18: 569–85.

Thomson, Robert (1999), *The Party Mandate: Election Pledges and Government Actions in the Netherlands*. Amsterdam: CT Press.

Webb, Paul (2000), *The Modern British Party System*. London: Sage.

General Bibliography

Achen, Christopher H. (1975), 'Mass Political Attitudes and the Survey Response', *American Political Science Review*, 69: 1218–31.

Adams, James (1998), 'A Theory of spatial competition with biased voters', Paper, Department of Political Science, University of California, Santa Barbara.

—— (2001), 'A Theory of Spatial Competition with Biased Voters', *British Journal of Political Science*, 31: 210–23.

—— and Merrill, Samuel (1998), 'Spatial Competition with Biased Voters', Department of Political Science, University of California at Santa Barbara.

Alexa, Melina (1997), *Computer-assisted Text Analysis Methodology in the Social Sciences*. Mannheim: ZUMA Arbeitsbericht Nr 97/07.

Bara, Judith (1998), 'Multiple Coding of British and American Parties' Manifestos and Platforms', Paper presented to Annual Users' Meeting of TMR-LSF, Cologne, ZA EUROLAB.

—— (2001), 'Tracking Estimates of Public Opinion and Party Policy Intentions in Britain and the USA' in Laver, Michael (ed.) *Estimating the Policy Positions of Political Actors*. London: Routledge.

Baron, David (1991), 'A Strategic Bargaining Theory of Government Formation in Parliamentary Systems', *American Political Science Review*, 85: 137–64.

Barry, Brian (1965), *Political Argument*. London: Routledge and Kegan Paul.

—— (1975), *Sociologists, Economists and Democracy*. London: Collier-Macmillan.

Bartolini, S. and Mair, Peter (1990), *Identity, Competition and Electoral Availability: The Stabilisation of European Electorates 1885–1985*. Cambridge: Cambridge University Press.

Bell, Daniel (1962), *The End of Ideology*. New York: Random House.

Berelson, Bernard (1952), *Content Analysis in Communications Research*. Glencoe, Ill: The Free Press.

—— (1954), 'Content Analysis' in Lindzey, Gordon (ed.) *Handbook of Social Psychology, Volume I*. Reading, MA: Addison-Wesley.

—— (1971), *Content Analysis in Communications Research*. New York: Hafner.

—— Lazarsfeld, Paul and Gaudet, Hazel (1944), *The Peoples' Choice*. New York: Columbia University Press.

Black, Duncan (1958), *The Theory of Committees and Elections*. Cambridge: Cambridge University Press.

Blais, Andre, Blake, Donald and Dion, Stephane (1993), 'Do Parties Make a Difference?: Parties and the Size of Government in Liberal Democracies', *American Journal of Political Science*, 37.

Bohrnstedt, George W. and Knoke, David (c1985), *Statistics for Social Data Analysis.* Itasca, Ill: F. E. Peacock.

Borg, Olavi (1966), 'Basic Dimensions of Finnish Party Ideologies: A Factor Analytical View', *Scandinavian Political Studies* 1: 94–117.

Browne, Eric C., Gleiber, D.W. and Mashoba, C. (1984), 'Evaluating Conflicting Interest Theory: Western European Cabinet Coalitions, 1945–1980', *British Journal of Political Science*, 4: 1–32.

Budge, Ian, Robertson, David and Hearl, Derek J. (eds.) (1987), *Ideology, Strategy and Party Change: Spatial Analyses of Post-War Election Programmes in 19 Democracies.* Cambridge: Cambridge University Press.

—— Crewe, Ivor, McKay, David and Newton, Kenneth (1998, 2000), *The New British Politics.* London: Pearson.

—— and Farlie, Dennis J. (1977), *Voting and Party Competition.* London & New York: Wiley.

—— —— (1978), 'The Potentiality of Dimensional Analyses for Explaining Voting and Party Competition', *European Journal of Political Research*, 6: 203–31.

—— and Robertson, David (1987), 'Do Parties Differ and How?' Comparative Discriminant and Factor Analyses' in Budge, Ian, Ribertson David and Hearl, Derek J. (eds.) *Ideology, Strategy and Party Change: Spatial Analyses of Post-War Election Programmes in 19 Democracies.* Cambridge: Cambridge University Press.

—— (1994), 'A New Spatial Theory of Party Competition: Uncertainty, Ideology and Policy Equilibria Viewed Comparatively and Spatially', *British Journal of Political Science*, 24: 443–67.

—— Tanenbaum, Eric and Bara, Judith (1999), *Monitoring Democratic Five-Year Plans: Multiple Coding of British Manifestos and US Platforms*, Swindon: ESRC Report R00022289.

—— (2000), 'Expert Judgements of Party Policy Positions: Uses and Limitations in Political Research', *European Journal of Political Research*, 37: 103–13.

—— (2001), 'Validating Party Policy Placements', *British Journal of Political Science*, 31: 210–23.

—— and Hofferbert, Richard I. (1990), 'Mandates and Policy Outcomes: US Party Platforms and Federal Expenditure', *American Political Science Review*, 84: 111–31.

—— —— (1992), 'The Party Mandate and the Westminster Model: Party Programmes and Government Spending in Britain, 1948–1985', *British Journal of Political Science*, 22.

—— —— (1992), 'Party Platforms, Mandates and Government Spending', *American Political Science Review*, 87: 744–50.

—— and Laver, Michael (1993), 'The Policy Basis of Government Coalitions: A Comparative Investigation', *British Journal of Political Sciences*, 23: 499–519.

—— et al (1997), *The Politics of the New Europe: Atlantic to Urals.* London: Longman.

—— and Laver, Michael (1986), 'Policy, Ideology and Party Distance: Analysis of Election Programmes in 19 Democracies', *Legislative Studies Quarterly*, 11: 607–15.

Burt, Ian (1997), 'Party Policy: Decision Rule of Chance? A Note on Budge's New Spatial Theory of Party Competition', *British Journal of Political Science*, 27: 647–58.

Calvert, Randall (1986), *Models of Imperfect Information in Politics*, Boston, Mass: Harwood Academic Publishers.

Castles, F. and Mair, P. (1984), 'Left-Right Political Scales: Some Expert Judgements', *European Journal of Political Research*, 12: 73–88.

Chafee, S.H. and Hochheimer, J.L. (1985), 'The Beginnings of Political Communication Research in the United States' in Gurevitch, M. and Levy, M.R. (eds.) *Mass Communications Yearbook 5*. Beverley Hills, CA: Sage.

Coughlin, Peter J. (1992), *Probabilistic Voting Theory*. Cambridge: Cambridge University Press.

Cusack, Thomas R. and Garrett, Geoffrey (1993), 'The Expansion of the Public Economy Revisited: The Politics of Government Spending, 1960–1988', Wissenschaftszentrum Berlin: Photocopy.

Dalton, Russell J. and Wattenberg, Martin P. (eds.) (2000), *'Parties without Partisans: Political Change in Advanced Industrial Democracies'*, Oxford: Oxford University Press.

Dodd, L.C. (1976), *Coalitions in Parliamentary Government*. Princeton, NJ: Princeton University Press.

Downs, Anthony (1957), *An Economic Theory of Democracy*. New York: Harper.

Easton, David (1965), *A Systems Analysis of Political Life*. New York: John Wiley and Sons.

Evans, Geoffrey and Norris, Pippa (eds.) (1999), *Critical Elections: British Parties and Voters in Long-Term Perspective*. London: Sage.

—— Heath, Anthony and Payne, Clive (1999), 'Class: Labour as a Catch All Party' in Evans, Geoffrey and Norris, Pippa (eds.) *Critical Elections: British Parties and Voters in Long-Term Perspective*. London: Sage.

Fairclough, Norman (2000), *New Labour, New Language?* London: Routledge.

Franklin, Mark (1985), *The Decline of Class Voting in Britain: Changes in the Bias of Electoral Choice, 1964–1983*. Oxford: The Clarendon Press.

Fuchs, Dieter and Klingemann, Hans-Dieter (1990), 'The Left-Right Schema' in Jennings, M. Kent *et al* (eds) *Continuities in Political Action*. Berlin: Walter de Gruyter.

Fukuyama, Francis (1991), *The End of History and the Last Man*. New York: The Free Press.

Gabel, Mathew and Huber, John (2000), 'Putting Parties in Their Place', *American Journal of Political Sciences*, 44: 94–103.

Gallagher, Michael, Laver, Michael and Mair, Peter (1992), *Representative Government in Western Europe*. New York: McGraw Hill.

Gibbons, Matthew (2000), Election Programmes in New Zealand Politics, Ph.D. Thesis, University of Waikato, New Zealand.

Ginsberg, Benjamin (1976), 'Elections and Public Policy', *American Political Science Review*, 70: 41–9.

Grofman, Bernard (1982), 'A Dynamic Model of Proto-Coalition Formation in Ideological Space', *Behavioural Science*, 27: 22–90.

Gross, Donald A. and Sigelman, Lee (1984), 'Comparing Party Systems: A Multidimensional Approach', *Comparative Politics*, 463–79.

Guildford, J.P. and Hoepfner, R. (1969), 'Comparison of Varimax Rotation with Rotations to Theoretical Targets', *Educational and Psychological Measurement*, 29: 3–23.

Harmel, Robert, Janda, Kenneth and Tan, A. (1995), 'Substance vs Packaging: An Empirical Analysis of Parties' Issue Profiles', Paper presented to Annual Meeting of American Political Science Association, Chicago.

Hearl, Derek (1988), 'Ambivalence Revisited: An Analysis of Liberal Party Manifestos since 1945' in Kirchner, Emil (ed) *Liberal Parties in Western Democracies*. Cambridge: Cambridge University Press.

Heise, David, R. (1969), 'Separating Reliability and Stability in Test-Retest Correlation', *American Sociological Review*, 33: 93–101.

Hofferbert, Richard I. and Budge, Ian (1992), 'The Party Mandate and the Westminster Model: Election Programmes and Government Spending in Britain 1948–1985', *British Journal of Political Sciences*, 22: 151–82.

—— —— and McDonald, Michael D. (1993), 'Party Platforms, Mandates and Government Spending', *American Political Science Review*, 87: 747–50.

—— and Klingemann, Hans-Dieter (1990), 'The Policy Impact of Party Programmes and Government Declarations in the Federal Republic of Germany', *European Journal of Political Research*, 18: 277–304.

Huber, John and Inglehart, Ronald (1995), 'Expert Interpretations of Party Space and Party Locations in 42 Societies', *Party Politics*, 1: 73–111.

Imbeau, Louis M. and McKinley, Robert (1996), *Comparing Government Activity*. London: Macmillan.

Inglehart, Ronald (1977), *The Silent Revolution*. Princeton, NJ: Princeton University Press.

—— (1990), *Culture Shift in Advanced Industrial Society*. Princeton, NJ: Princeton University Press.

—— (1997), *Modernization and Post-Modernization: Cultural, Economic and Political Change in 43 Societies*. Princeton, NJ: Princeton University Press.

—— and Klingemann, Hans-Dieter (1976), 'Party Identification, Ideological Preference and the Left-Right Dimension among Western Mass Publics' in Budge, Ian, Crewe, Ivor and Farlie, Dennis (eds) *Party Identification and Beyond: Representations of Voting and Party Competition*. London: John Wiley and Sons.

Iyengar, Shanto (1993), 'Agenda Setting and Beyond: Television News and the Strength of Political Issues' in Riker, William (ed.) *Agenda Formation*. Ann Arbor: University of Michigan Press.

Jacoby, William G. (1995), 'The Structure of Ideological Thinking in the American Electorate', *American Journal of Political Science*, 39: 314–35

Janda, Kenneth (1980), *Political Parties: A Cross-National Survey*. New York: The Free Press.

—— Harmel, Robert, Edens, Christine and Goff, Patricia (1995), 'Changes in Party Identity: Evidence From Party Manifestos', *Party Politics* 1: 171–96.

Kalogeropoulou, Efthalia (1989), 'Election Promises and Government Performance in Greece', *European Journal of Political Research*, 17: 289–311.

Keman, Hans (ed.) (1997), *The Politics of Problem-Solving in Post-War Democracies.* Basingstoke: Macmillan.

Kim, Hee Min and Fording, Richard C. (1998), 'Voter Ideology in Western Democracies 1946–1989', *European Journal of Political Research*, 33: 73–97.

—— —— (2000a), 'Government Partisanship in Western Democracies, 1945–1989', Florida State University and the University of Kentucky: Unpublished Manuscript.

—— —— (2000b), 'Does Tactical Voting Matter? The Political Impact of Tactical Voting in Recent Canadian Elections', Paper Presented at the Annual Meeting of the American Political Science Association.

—— —— (2001), 'Does Tactical Voting Matter? The Political Impact of Tactical Voting in Recent British Elections', Comparative Political Studies, forthcoming.

King, Gary, and Laver, Michael (1993), 'Party Platforms, Mandates and Government Spending', *American Political Science Review*, 87: 744–58.

—— —— (1999), 'Many Publications But Still No Evidence', *Electoral Studies*, 18: 597–8.

Kirchheimer, Otto (1966), 'The Transformation of Western European Party Systems' in Lapalombara, Joseph and Weiner, Myron (eds.) *Political Parties and Political Development.* Princeton, NJ: Princeton University Press.

Kirchner, Emil (ed.) (1988), *Liberal Parties in Western Democracies.* Cambridge: Cambridge University Press.

Kitschelt, Herbert (1994), *The Transformation of European Social Democracy.* Cambridge: Cambridge University Press.

Kleinnijenhuis, Jan and Pennings, Paul (1999), 'Measurement of Party Positions on the Basis of Party Programs, Media Coverage and Voter Perceptions', Paper Presented to European Consortium for Political Research Joint Sessions of Workshops, Mannheim.

—— and Rietberg, E.M. (1995), 'Parties, Media, The Public and The Economy', *European Journal for Political Research*, 28: 95–118.

Klingemann, Hans-Dieter (1983), *Computerunterstutzte Inhaltsanalyse in der Eemprischen Sozialforschung.* Frankfurt: Campus Verlag.

—— (1995), 'Party Positions and Voter Orientations' in Klingemann, H.D. and Fuchs, Dieter (eds.) *Citizens and the State.* Oxford: Oxford University Press.

—— and Fuchs, Dieter (eds.) (1995), *Citizens and the State.* Oxford: Oxford University Press.

—— Hofferbert, Richard I., Budge, Ian *et al* (1994), *Parties, Policies and Democracy.* Boulder, Co: Westview.

Krouwel, Andre (1998), *The Catch-All Party in Western Europe: A Study in Arrested Development.* Amsterdam: CT Press.

Knutsen, Oddbjorn (1988), 'The Impact of Structural and Ideological Party Cleavages in Western European Democracies: A Comparative Empirical Analysis', *British Journal of Political Science*, 18: 323–52.

Krippendorf, Klaus (1980), *Content Analysis: An Introduction to Its Methodology.* Beverley Hills CA: Sage.rouwel, Andre (1998), *The Catch-All Party in Western Europe: A Study in Arrested Development.* Amsterdam: CT Press.

Lancaster, Thomas D. and Lewis-Beck, Michael (1986), 'The Spanish Vote: Tradition, Economics, Ideology', *Journal of Politics*, 48: 648–74.

Lane, Jan-Erik and Ersson, Svante (1991), *Politics and Society in Western* Europe, 2nd edition. London: Sage.

Langford, Tom (1991), 'Left-Right Orientation and Political Attitudes: A Reappraisal and Class Comparison', *Canadian Journal of Political Science*, 24: 475–99.

Laponce, Jean (1981), *Left and Right: The Topography of Political Perceptions*. Toronto: University of Toronto Press.

Lasswell, Harold and Kaplan, Abraham (1952), *Power and Society: A Framework for Political Inquiry*. New Haven: Yale University Press.

—— Leites, Nathan *et al* (1965), *Language of Politics: Studies in Quantitative Semantics*, 2nd edition. New York: George W. Steven.

—— Lerner, Daniel and Pool, Ithiel de Sola (1952), *The Comparative Study of Symbols*. Stanford, CA: Stanford University Press.

Laver, Michael and Budge, Ian (eds.) (1992), *Party Policy and Government Coalitions*. London: Macmillan/ New York: St. Martins.

—— (ed.) (2001), *Estimating the Policy Positions of Political Actors*. London: Routledge.

—— and Garry, John (1998), 'Estimating Policy Positions from Party Manifestos', Paper presented at European Consortium for Political Research Joint Sessions of Workshops, Warwick.

—— —— (1999), 'Estimating Policy Positions from Party Manifestos', Paper presented at European Consortium for Political Research Joint Sessions of Workshops, Mannheim.

—— —— (2001), 'Estimating Policy Positions from Party Manifestos', American Journal of Political Sciences, forthcoming.

—— and Hunt, W. Ben (1992), *Policy and Party Competition*. New York and London: Routledge.

—— and Schofield, Norman (1990), *Multiparty Government: The Politics of Coalition in Europe*. Oxford and New York: Oxford University Press.

Levitan, Teresa E. and Miller, Warren (1979), 'Ideological Interpretations of Presidential Elections', *American Political Science Review*, 73: 751–71.

Lewis-Beck, Michael (1988), *Economics and Elections*. Ann Arbor: University of Michigan Press.

Lijphart, Arend (1984), *Democracies: Patterns of Majoritarian and Consensus Government in 21 Countries*. New Haven: Yale University Press.

Lipset, Seymour Martin and Rokkan, Stein (1967), 'Cleavage Structures, Party Systems and Voter Alignments: An Introduction' in Lipset, Seymour Martin and Rokkan, Stein (eds.) *Party Systems and Voter Alignments*. New York: The Free Press.

Luebbert, Gregory (1986), *Comparative Democracy: Policy-making and Government Coalitions in Europe and Israel*. New York: Columbia University Press.

McAllister, Ian and Moore, Rhonda (1991), 'The Issues that Divided the Parties, 1946–1990' in McAllister, Ian and Moore, Rhonda (eds.) *Party Strategy and Change: Australian Electoral Speeches Since 1946*. Melbourne: Longman Cheshire.

McDonald, Michael D. and Mendes, Silvia M. (1999) 'The Policy Space of Party Manifestos', Paper presented at European Consortium for Political Research Joint Sessions of Workshops, Mannheim.

—— Budge, Ian and Hofferbert, Richard (1999), 'Party Mandate Theory and Time Series Analysis', *Electoral Studies*, 18: 587–96.

McKelvey, R. (1976), 'General Conditions for Global Intransitivities in Formal Voting Models', *Econometrica*, 47: 1085–111.

—— and Ordeshook, P. (1985a), 'Elections with Limited Information: A Fulfilled Expectation Model Using Contemporaneous Poll and Endorsement Data as Information Sources', *Journal of Economic Theory*, 35: 55–85.

—— —— (1985b), 'Sequential Elections with Limited Information', *American Journal of Political Science*, 29: 480–512.

—— —— (1990), 'A Decade of Experimental Research on Spatial Models of Elections and Committees' in Enelow, James M. and Hinich, Melvin J. (eds.) *Advances in the Spatial Theory of Voting*. Cambridge: Cambridge University Press.

Madge, John (1953), *The Tools of Social Science*. London: Longman.

Mair, Peter (1986), 'Locating Irish Political Parties on a Left-Right Dimension: An Empirical Enquiry', *Political Studies*, 44: 456–65.

—— (1987), *The Changing Irish Party System: Organization, Ideology and Electoral Competition*. London: Pinter.

Mastropaolo, Alfio and Slater, Martin (1987), 'Italy 1946–1979: Ideological Distances and Party Movements' in Budge, Ian, Robertson, David and Hearl, Derek J. (eds.) *Ideology, Strategy and Party Change: Spatial Analyses of Post-War Election Programmes in 19 Democracies*. Cambridge: Cambridge University Press.

—— —— (1992), 'Party Policy and Coalition Bargaining in Italy 1948–1987' in Laver, Michael and Budge, Ian (eds.) *Party Policy and Government Coalitions*. London: Macmillan/ New York: St. Martins.

Miller, S. (1977), 'News Coverage of Congress: The Search for the Ultimate Spokesman', *Journalism Quarterly*, 54: 459–65.

Morgan, M.J. (1976), 'The Modelling of Government Coalition Formation: A Policy-Based Approach with Interval Measurement', Unpublished PhD. Thesis, University of Michigan.

Muller, Wolfgang C. and Strom, Kaare (eds.) (2000), *Coalition Governments in Western Europe*. Oxford: Oxford University Press.

Nagel, Jack (1998), 'Social Choice in a Pluralitarian Democracy: The Politics of Market Liberalization in New Zealand', *British Journal of Political Science*, 28: 223–67.

Namenwirth, J. Zvi and Brewer, T.L. (1966), 'Elite Editorial Comment on the European and Atlantic Communities in 4 Countries' in Stone, P.J., Dunphy, D.C., Smith, M.S. and Ogilvie, D.M. (eds.) *The General Inquirer: A Computer Approach to Content Analysis*. Cambridge, Mass: MIT Press.

—— (1969), 'Some Long and Short-Term Trends in One American Political Value: A Computer Analysis of Concern with Wealth in 62 Party Platforms' in Gerbner, George (ed.) *The Analysis of Communication Conflict*. New York: John Wiley.

—— and Lasswell, Harold (1970), *The Changing Language of American Values: A Computer Study of Selected Party Platforms*. Beverley Hills, CA: Sage.

Nie, Norman H., Verba, Sidney and Petrocik, John R. (1976), *The Changing American Voter*. Cambridge Mass: Harvard University Press.

North, R.C., Holsti, O.R., Zaninovitch, M.G. and Zinnes, D.A. (1963), *Content Analysis: A Handbook with Applications for the Study of International Crisis*. Evanston, Ill: Northwestern University Press.

Ordeshook, Peter (1986), *Game Theory and Political Theory: An Introduction*. Cambridge: Cambridge University Press.

Page, Benjamin (1978*)*, *Choices and Echoes in Presidential Elections: Rational Man and Elected Democracy*. Chicago: Chicago University Press.

Pennings, Paul (1998), 'Party Responsiveness and Socio-Economic Problem-Solving in Western Democracies', *Party Politics*, 4: 393–404.

—— and Lane, J.E. (eds.) (1998), *Comparing Party System Change*. London: Routledge.

Percheron, Annick and Jennings, M. Kent (1981), 'Political Continuities in French Families' *Comparative Politics*, 13: 421–36.

Pétry, François (1988), 'The Policy Impact of Canadian Party Programs', *Canadian Public Policy*, 14: 376–89.

—— (1995), 'The Party Agenda Model: Election Programmes and Government Spending in Canada', *Canadian Journal of Political Sciences*, 28: 51–84.

—— (1991), 'Fragile Mandate: Party Programmes and Public Expenditures in the French Fifth Republic', *European Journal of Political Research*, 20: 149–71.

Pool, Ithiel de Sola (1951), *Symbols of Internationalism*. Stanford CA: Stanford University Press.

Pomper, Gerald (1980), *Party Renewal in America*. New York: Praeger.

Rallings, Colin (1987), 'The Influence of Election Programmes: Britain and Canada 1945–1979' in Budge, Ian, Robertson, David and Hearl, Derek J. (eds.) *Ideology, Strategy and Party Change: Spatial Analyses of Post-War Election Programmes in 19 Democracies*. Cambridge: Cambridge University Press.

Ranney, Austin (ed.) (1962), *Essays in the Behavioural Study of Politics*. Urbana, Ill: University of Illinois Press.

Riffe, Daniel, Lacy, Stephen and Fico, Frederick G. (1998), *Analyzing Media Messages: Using Quantitative Content Analysis in Research*. Mahwah, NJ: Lawrence Earlbaum.

Riker, William (1962), *The Theory of Political Coalitions*. New Haven: Yale University Press.

—— (ed.) (1993), *Agenda Formation*. Ann Arbor: University of Michigan Press.

Roberts, Carl W. (ed.) (1997), *Text Analysis for the Social Sciences*. Mahwah, NJ: Lawrence Earlbaum.

Robertson, David (1976), *A Theory of Party Competition*. London and New York: Wiley.

—— (1987), 'Britain, Australia, New Zealand and the United States 1946–1981: An Initial Comparative Analysis' in Budge, Ian, Robertson, David and Hearl, Derek J. (eds.) *Ideology, Strategy and Party Change: Spatial Analyses of Post-War Election Programmes in 19 Democracies*. Cambridge: Cambridge University Press.

Rose, Richard (1964), 'Parties, Factions and Tendencies in Britain', *Political Studies*, 12: 33–46.

—— (1969), 'The Variability of Party Government', *Political Studies* 17: 413–45.

—— (1974), *The Problem of Party Government*. London: Macmillan.

Saglie, Jo (1998), 'A Struggle for the Agenda? Norwegian parties and the European Issues 1989–1995', *Party Politics*, 4: 262–84.

Sartori, Giovanni (1976), *Parties and Party Systems: A Framework for Analysis*. Cambridge: Cambridge University Press.

Sanders, David and Price, Simon (1991), *Economic Competence, Rational Expectations and Government Popularity in Post-War Britain.* Colchester: ESRC Research Centre in Micro-Social Change.

Saward, M. (1998), *The Terms of Democracy.* Cambridge: Polity.

Schofield, Norman (1993), 'Political Competition and Multiparty Coalition Governments', *European Journal of Political Research,* 23: 1–33.

—— and Laver, M. (1985), 'Bargaining Theory and Portfolio Payoffs in European Coalition Governments, 1945–1983', *British Journal of Political Science,* 15: 143–64.

Sedelow, Walter A. and Sedelow, Sally Y. (1978), 'Formalised Historiography: The Structure of Scientific and Literary Texts Part 1' *Journal of the History of Behavioural Sciences,* 14: 247–63.

Sened, I. (1995), 'Equilibria in Weighted Voting Games with Side Payments', *Journal of Theoretical Politics,* 7: 283–300.

—— (1996), 'A Model of Coalition Formation: Theory and Evidence', *Journal of Politics,* 58: 350–72.

Stimson, James A., McKuen, Michael S. and Erikson, Robert S. (1995), 'Dynamic Representation', *American Political Science Review,* 89: 543–65.

Stokes, Donald E. (1966), 'Spatial Models of Party Competition' in Campbell, Angus, Converse, Philip E., Miller, Warren E. and Stokes, Donald E. (eds.) *Elections and the Political Order.* New York: Wiley.

Stone, P.J., Dunphy, D.C., Smith, M.S. and Ogilvie, D.M. (eds.) (1966), *The General Inquirer: A Computer Approach to Content Analysis.* Cambridge, Mass: MIT Press.

Strom, Kaare and Liepart, Jorn (1989), 'Ideology, Strategy and Party Competition in Post-War Norway', *European Journal of Political Research,* 17: 263–88.

Sullivan, John L. and O'Connor, Robert E. (1972), 'Electoral Choice and the Popular Control of Public Policy: The Case of the 1966 House Elections', *American Political Science Review,* 66: 1256–68.

Thomas, John C. (1975), *The Decline of Ideology in Western Political Parties: A Study of Changing Policy Orientations.* London: Sage.

Thome, Helmut (1999), 'Party Mandate Theory and Time-Series Analysis: A Methodological Comment', *Electoral Studies,* 18: 569–85.

Thomson, Robert (1999), *The Party Mandate: Election Pledges and Government Actions in the Netherlands.* Amsterdam: CT Press.

Van der Brug, Wouter (1999), 'Party Platforms and Voters' Perceptions', Paper presented at European Consortium for Political Research Joint Sessions of Workshops, Mannheim.

Volkens, Andrea (1992), *Content Analysis of Party Programmes in Comparative Perspective: Handbook and Coding Instructions.* Berlin: Wissenschaftszentrum.

—— (1994), *Comparative Manifestos Project: Data-Set CMP94.* Berlin: Wissenschaftszentrum.

—— (2000), *Die PDS im Parteiensystem.* Berlin: Bundesstiftung Rosa Luxemburg/Dietz Verlag.

Von Beyme, Klaus (1985), *Political Parties in Western Democracies.* Aldershot: Gower.

Ware, Alan (1996), *Political Parties and Party Systems.* Oxford: Oxford University Press.

Warwick, Paul V. (1992), 'Ideological Diversity and Government Survival in Western European Parliamentary Democracies', *Comparative Political Studies*, 25: 332–61.

—— (2000), 'Policy Horizons in West European Parliamentary Systems', *European Journal of Political Research*, 38: 37–61.

Webb, Paul (2000), *The Modern British Party System*. London: Sage.

Weber, Robert P. (1990), *Basic Content Analysis*, 2nd edition. Newbury Park, CA: Sage.

Wilde Kelly, Ann and Sine, A.M. (1990), 'Language as Research Data: Application of Computer Content Analysis in Nursing Research', *Advances in Nursing Science*, 12: 32–40.

Woldendorp, Jaap, Keman, Hans and Budge, Ian (1993), 'Party Government in 20 Democracies', *European Journal of Political Research*, 24: 1107 (Special Edition: *Political Data 1945–1990*).

—— —— —— (1998), 'Party Government in 48 Democracies: An Update, 1993–1995', *European Journal of Political Research*, 33: 125–64.

—— —— —— (2000), 'Party Government in 20 Democracies, 1945–1998'. Dordrecht, Boston and London: Kluwer Academic Publishers.

Zuell, Cornelia, Harkness, Janet and Hoffmeyer-Zlotnik, Jurgen H.P. (eds.) (1996), *Text Analysis and Computers*. Mannheim: ZUMA.

Bibliography of Electoral Data Sources

Banks, Arthur S. (ed.) (diverse), *Political Handbook of the World*. Binghampton: CSA Publications/New York: Mc Graw-Hill.

Bille, Lars (1995), 'Denmark', *European Journal of Political Research*, 28: 313–21.

Carty, R.K. (1994), 'Canada', *European Journal of Political Research*, 26: 255–68.

—— (1998), 'Canada', *European Journal of Political Research*, 34: 363–71.

Del Castillo, Paul and Lourdes López Nielo (1994), 'Spain', *European Journal of Political Research*, 26: 423–9.

Deruette, Serge and Loeb-Mayer, Nicole (1992), 'Belgium', *European Journal of Political Research*, 22: 363–72.

—— (1996), 'Belgium', *European Journal of Political Research*, 30: 287–98.

Diskin, Abraham (1993), 'Israel', *European Journal of Political Research*, 24: 467–74.

Hardarson, Ólafur Th. (1992), 'Iceland', *European Journal of Political Research*, 22: 429–35.

—— (1996), 'Iceland', *European Journal of Political Research*, 30: 367–76.

Heidar, Knut (1994), 'Norway', *European Journal of Political Research*, 26: 389–95.

Hirsch, Mario (1995), 'Luxembourg', *European Journal of Political Research*, 28: 415–20.

Ignazi, Piero (1993), 'Italy', *European Journal of Political Research*, 24: 475–83.

—— (1995), 'Italy', *European Journal of Political Research*, 28: 393–405.

—— (1996), 'Italy', *Electoral Studies*, 15: 595.

Irwin, Galen A. (1998), 'The Dutch Parliamentary Election of 1998', *Electoral Studies*, 18: 271–300

Jerusalem Post, 31 May 1996, pages 1–5 on breakdown of results for Elections to 14th Knesset, 1996.

Katz, Richard S. (1992), 'United States', *European Journal of Political Research*, 24: 563–72.

—— (1994), 'United States', *European Journal of Political Research*, 28: 505–11.

Keesing's *Record of World Events* (diverse).

Ladner, Andreas (1992), 'Switzerland', *European Journal of Political Research*, 22: 527–36.

—— (1996), 'Switzerland', *European Journal of Political Research*, 30: 469–78.

Michael Laver/Ian Budge (eds.) (1992), *Party Policy and Government Coalitions*. Houndmills, Basingstoke, Hampshire: Macmillan Press.

Lucardie, Paul and Voerman, Gerrit (1995), 'The Netherlands', *European Journal of Political Research*, 28: 427–36.

266   *Mapping Policy Preferences*

Mackerras, Malcolm and Mcallister, Ian (1994), 'Australia', *European Journal of Political Research*, 26: 231–9.
Mackie, Thomas T. (1993), 'United Kingdom', *European Journal of Political Research*, 24: 555–62.
—— Richard, Rose (1991), *The International Almanac of Electoral History*. Houndsmill, Basingstoke, Hampshire, London: Macmillan, 3rd edition.
Mackie, Thomas T. (1991), 'General Elections in Western Nations during 1989', *European Journal of Political Research*, 19: 157–62.
—— (1992), 'General Elections in Western Nations during 1990', *European Journal of Political Research*, 21: 317–32.
Marsh, Michael (1993), 'Ireland', *European Journal of Political Research*, 24: 455–66.
—— (1998), 'Ireland', *European Journal of Political Research*, 34: 429–39.
Mavrogordatos, George Th. (1994), *European Journal of Political Research*, 26: 313–318.
Miller, Alan William (1997), *Atlas of United States Presidential Elections 1932–1996*. Richmond, Virginia: Klipsan Press.
Müller, Wolfgang C. (1996), 'Austria', *European Journal of Political Research*, 30: 275–85.
—— (1995), 'Austria', *European Journal of Political Research*, 28: 277–89.
Narud, Hanne Marthe (1998), 'Norway', *European Journal of Political Research*, 34: 485–92.
Poguntke, Thomas (1995), 'Germany', *European Journal of Political Research*, 28: 341–52.
Shiratori, Rei (1994), 'Japan', *European Journal of Political Research*, 26: 355–60.
Sorene, James (1999), *Elections in Israel: Background Information*. Embassy of Israel, UK, 3rd Edition.
State Institute of Statistics (1992), *20.10.1991 Results of General Election of Representatives, Results by Districts*, 1522: XII–XIII.
State Institute of Statistics (1996), *Statistical Yearbook of Turkey 1995*, 1845: 208.
—— (1996), *24.12.1995 General Election of Representatives, Results by Districts*, 1874: 2–3.
—— (1996), *Statistical Indicators 1923–1995*, 1883: 93.
State of Israel (1990), *Statistical Abstract of Israel 1990*, 41, 550ff.
Stock, Maria (1992), 'Portugal', *European Journal of Political Research*, 22: 505–11.
—— and José Maria Magone (1995), 'Portugal', *European Journal of Political Research*, No: 445–52.
Sundberg, Jan (1992), 'Finland', *European Journal of Political Research*, 22: 391–9.
—— (1996), 'Finland', *European Journal of Political Research*, 30: 321–30.
Tagesspiegel 15.10.1998 'Die PDS gewinnt, die FDP verliert'.
Vowles, Jack (1994), 'New Zealand', *European Journal of Political Research*, 26: 375–87.
—— (1998), 'New Zealand', *European Journal of Political Research*, 34: 475–83.
Webb, Paul. 'United Kingdom', *European Journal of Political Research* 34: 539–49.
Widfeldt, Anders and Jon Pierre (1992), 'Sweden', *European Journal of Political Research*, 22: 519–26.
—— —— (1995), 'Sweden', *European Journal of Political Research*, 28: 477–85.

Woldendorp, Jaap, Keman, Hans and Budge, Ian (1998), Party Government in 20 Democracies: an update (1990–1995), *European Journal of Political Research*, 33: 25–164.

———— ———— ———— (2000), 'Party Government in 20 Democracies, 1945–1998'. Dordrecht, Boston and London: Kluwer Academic Publishers.

www.agora.stm.it/elections/election.htm

www.fec.gov

www.ipu.org

Ysmal, Colette (1998), 'France', *European Journal of Political Research*, 34: 393–401.

Index